ORIENTING VIRTUE

ORIENTING VIRTUE

*Civic Identity and Orientalism
in Britain's Global Eighteenth Century*

BETHANY WILLIAMSON

UNIVERSITY OF VIRGINIA PRESS
Charlottesville and London

University of Virginia Press
© 2022 by the Rector and Visitors of the University of Virginia
All rights reserved
Printed in the United States of America on acid-free paper

First published 2022

9 8 7 6 5 4 3 2 1

Library of Congress Cataloging-in-Publication Data

Names: Williamson, Bethany, author.
Title: Orienting virtue : civic identity and orientalism in Britain's global eighteenth century / Bethany Williamson.
Description: Charlottesville : University of Virginia Press, 2022. | Includes bibliographical references and index.
Identifiers: LCCN 2022023747 (print) | LCCN 2022023748 (ebook) | ISBN 9780813947600 (hardcover ; acid-free paper) | ISBN 9780813947617 (paperback ; acid-free paper) | ISBN 9780813947624 (ebook)
Subjects: LCSH: English literature—18th century—History and criticism. | Virtue in literature. | National characteristics, English, in literature. | Orientalism in literature. | LCGFT: Literary criticism.
Classification: LCC PR448.V57 W55 2022 (print) | LCC PR448.V57 (ebook) | DDC 820.9/005—dc23/eng/20220726
LC record available at https://lccn.loc.gov/2022023747
LC ebook record available at https://lccn.loc.gov/2022023748

Cover art: *The Grand Vizier Giving Audience to the British Ambassador*, Francis Smith, ca. 1760. (Yale Center for British Art, Paul Mellon Collection)

For my family

No people can be great who have ceased to be virtuous.
—Samuel Johnson, "An Introduction to the Political State of Great Britain" (1756)

CONTENTS

Acknowledgments | xi

Introduction: Defining English Virtue in the Global
    Eighteenth Century   1

1 | "Our Lusts Gave Us Liberty": Mercantile Might
    and English Republicanism in Neville's *Isle of Pines*   37

2 | "Striking Sail" in Satire: Heroic Virtue and the
    Mughal Machiavelli in Dryden's *Aureng-Zebe*   66

3 | Recovering the "True Spirit of Liberty":
    Gulliver's Travels in Sparta and Japan   102

4 | "Happy to Be Enslaved": Feminist Orientalism
    and the Constraints of Romance in Pix's *Ibrahim*,
    Kindersley's *Letters*, and Lennox's *Female Quixote*   134

5 | Rasselas's "Conscious Virtue": Cosmopolitan Civics
    in Johnson and Ellis Cornelia Knight   168

Afterword: A Kantian Legacy of Cosmopolitan
    Virtue Signaling   195

Notes | 201
Bibliography | 225
Index | 245

ACKNOWLEDGMENTS

It is a pleasure and a privilege to acknowledge some of the many debts I have accumulated in the course of completing this book.

My deepest thanks go to my dissertation advisors and academic mentors, especially Rajani Sudan, who changed the arc of my intellectual journey by showing me the scintillating side of the eighteenth century, and Bob Markley, whose generous, incisive feedback has sharpened my thinking and this project in numerous ways. Tim Rosendale and Dennis Foster helped me ask better questions about language and desire. Don Deardorff and Peggy Wilfong unlocked for me, so many years ago, the delightful work of literary analysis.

The English Department at Southern Methodist University provided generous research support and an exceptionally hospitable scholarly community throughout my initial work on this project. My thanks go to all of the Taos workshop crew, but especially to Steven Weisenburger and Tom DiPiero, along with Kristina Booker, Chris Goldsmith, Julianne Sandberg, and Charles Wuest, for their insights and feedback on early drafts. Other intellectual communities supported and shaped this book in meaningful ways, including the SMU Dedman College Interdisciplinary Institute's "Global Early Modern Studies" fellows seminar; a National Endowment for the Humanities Summer Institute at Indiana University, organized by Kaya Şahin and Julia Schleck, on "Beyond East and West: Exchanges and Interactions across the Early Modern World"; and the Chawton House Library, where I spent an unforgettably glorious May working in the archives. I'm grateful to The Huntington Library for their generous reader access, and to the many eighteenth-centuryists I've learned from, while presenting portions of this material at conferences for the American and Western Societies for Eighteenth-Century Studies.

I am fortunate now to work with smart, kind colleagues and wonderful students at Biola University. My particular thanks go to the English Department and the School of Humanities and Social Sciences for supporting a publishing subvention, and to Chris Davidson, Melissa Schubert, and Shelley Garcia for their help to secure it; to Maria Su Wang, for reading early drafts on Dryden; to the library staff who facilitated my *many* ILL requests; to the university for funding conference travels and a spring 2016 course release; and to my students, who never fail to remind me why the ideas in this book still matter.

Angie Hogan has been a superb editor—insightful and encouraging, from our first conversation at ASECS—and I'm grateful to Angie and the entire team at the University of Virginia Press for shepherding this book to completion with such competence and care (during a global pandemic, no less!). Special thanks go to Wren Morgan Myers for their editorial expertise; to Cecilia Sorochin for the creative cover design; and to copyeditor Emily Shelton for her detail-oriented eye. My sincere thanks go, too, to the press's two anonymous readers for taking time to engage with my ideas and provide generous and helpful feedback on the manuscript.

I gratefully acknowledge that material from chapter 1 is reprinted here, revised and with permission, from an article which first appeared in *Eighteenth-Century Fiction* 27, no. 1 (2014).

Finally, I could not have completed this project without the life-giving encouragement of my dear friends and the unwavering love, support, and good cheer of my Gilmour and Williamson families. This book is dedicated to my family—especially to my parents, who gave me the gifts of education, and to Jeremy, my best friend and favorite critic. Thank you for being my people and reminding me who and whose I am.

ORIENTING VIRTUE

INTRODUCTION
Defining English Virtue in the
Global Eighteenth Century

'Tis well that virtue gives nobility,
How shall we else the want of birth and blood supply?
—Daniel Defoe, *The True-Born Englishman* (1701)

Bare Vertue can't make Nations live
In Splendour; they, that would revive
A Golden Age, must be as free,
For Acorns, as for Honesty.
—Bernard Mandeville, *The Fable of the Bees* (1714)

WHAT DOES IT MEAN TO be a "virtuous" citizen? While virtue claims are ubiquitous in the literature of England's long eighteenth century—referring variously to the chastity of a woman, the heroism of a ruler, or the qualities that make a nation great—virtue's definition is more often assumed than explained. *Orienting Virtue* contends that the problem of defining *national* virtue hinges on the difficulty of articulating an absolute concept of moral value in the context of dynamic global networks. In literary representations of civic identity, virtue claims offer an epistemological framework, letting writers with diverse politico-economic aims imagine a future in which England's moral and material worth remains intact despite evidence of weakness or corruption. Writers across genres, including Henry Neville, John Dryden, Jonathan Swift, Charlotte Lennox, Jemima Kindersley, and Samuel Johnson, deploy or interrogate such virtue claims to *orient* their readers both chronologically and geographically, as they express dissatisfaction about England's present political climate while stressing an always-potential moment of greatness vis-à-vis other nations. Together, these claims underscore how Enlightenment England's story of distinctive political virtue is predicated not on innate moral strength but rather on unstable assumptions about cultural differences between East and West.

My goal in *Orienting Virtue* is not to trace every meaning or inflection of virtue during this period, but to consider how virtue comes to stand, metonymically, for an English narrative of past, present, and future greatness that is predicated on virtuous difference from other nations' peoples and pasts. The primary method of my study is a close reading of literary texts, informed by deconstructive attention to the discursive power of "virtue." These readings are shaped, too, by the assumptions of postcolonial scholarship, which examines how "many of the attributes of modern European societies" that literary texts encode "derive from the political-economic, social, and cultural developments that also shaped the colonial and commercial expansion of European power across the globe."[1]

In his paean to the city of London, John Dryden illustrates such virtue discourse at work, showing how assumptions of national virtue are both differential—defined as the negation of vices attributed to others—and undergirded by a belief in England's unique, divinely ordained purpose. Amid descriptions of Anglo-Dutch battles, a devasting plague, and the Great Fire of 1666, Dryden extols the city's distinctive "virtues" as evidence of an essential and divinely preserved national "Virtue." He dedicates *Annus Mirabilis* not to a person but to London itself—a "City, which has set a pattern to all others of true Loyalty, invincible Courage, and unshaken Constancy."[2] "Other cities have been prais'd for the same Virtues," he admits, "but I am much deceiv'd if any have so dearly purchas'd their Reputation." He goes on to assure his readers, "Heaven never made so much Piety and Virtue, to leave it miserable. I have heard indeed of some virtuous persons who have ended unfortunately, but never of any virtuous nation:

Providence is engaged too deeply, when the Cause becomes so general." Dryden situates the disaster, disease, and political unrest of London's "annus mirabilis" within this narrative of unshaken virtue, noting that the city's "afflictions are not more the effects of God's displeasure...than occasions for the manifesting of your Christian and Civil virtues." He goes on to predict the imminent rise of England's capital to global glory and boundless prosperity vis-à-vis foreign caches of wealth. Like Arabia's mythical "Phoenix in her ashes,"[3] he enthuses, the "famed emporium" of London will rise from its fiery crucible:

Now, like a Maiden Queen, she will behold,
From her high turrets, hourly suitors come:
The East with incense, and the West with gold,
Will stand, like suppliants, to receive her doom.[4]

Throughout his poem, Dryden represents virtue as both a cause and an effect, both a capacity and an action. He suggests in the dedication that while London "dearly purchas'd" its "reputation" by maintaining "true Loyalty [and] invincible Courage" in the face of trials and travails, thereby proving England itself to be a "virtuous nation," "Heaven" was at the same time "engaged ... deeply" in "ma[king]" and preserving that virtue. "Virtue," as Dryden uses the term, indicates both an English capacity for virtuous progress and the tangible proof of that progress in the form of national prosperity; in other words, virtue requires a complex synthesis of human effort and divine agency.

Dryden's vision of a modern, prosperous post-1666 London is based on a fantasy of East and West Indian plenitude and passivity, indicating that England's capacity to achieve the virtue Dryden attributes to it is contingent upon global resources and relationships. As Suvir Kaul has argued, Dryden's poetic "construction of a united, puissant nation represents not only the defeat of rival European powers but the mercantile and (at least potentially) imperial subordination of other regions of the globe."[5] Indeed, the virtue Dryden praises is not entirely English, insofar as it stems from "the spicy shore[s]" of the East Indies and the precious metal mines of the West (*Annus*, 70). To complete its transformation from ashes to glory, London must take its rival Amsterdam's place in discovering, monopolizing, and exploiting "eastern quarries," "hot Ceylon spicy forests," and, eventually, India's "riches of the rising sun" (32, 35). If, as Dryden suggests, the new London will be "all divine with gold," boasting the increasing wealth that indicates providential blessing, such wealth requires that an elusively "constant trade-wind will securely blow" (70). As with the transformation of London itself, gold morphs from something base into something blessed when it is reworked to grace the façade of such a "virtuous" city (69).

Dryden's depiction of national virtue as both divinely inherited and humanly merited illustrates how Britain's patriotic virtue discourse is rooted in an unstable fantasy of English exceptionalism. Even before the 1707 Act of Union, claims to 'English' and 'British' identity were mutually constitutive. On one hand, Krishan Kumar explains in *The Making of English National Identity*, "'England' is a highly emotive word [that] has served, in a way never attained by 'Britain' . . . to focus ideas and ideals" for writers who used it nostalgically to evoke "the font of freedom and the standard of civilization, a place of virtue as well as of beauty."[6] As Linda Colley maps out in *Britons: Forging the Nation, 1707–1837*, the rising tide of patriotic "Britishness" in the eighteenth century signified, by contrast, a Protestant political identity defined largely against Catholic France. And yet, Kumar notes, "Britishness, whether among Scots, Welsh, Anglo-Irish or North American colonists, always contained a core of Englishness," and British ideals "were as likely to be couched in the terms of English political discourse."[7] What has been less often examined is how this concept of "virtue" Kumar highlights—with its connotations of national 'spirit' and 'character'—evokes not only nostalgia for England's storied past but also a sense of "the wider world within which 'England' and 'Englishness' find their meaning."[8] As Ian Baucom puts it, by "creating an empire whose commercial, political, demographic, and cultural economies depended on a continuous traffic between the English here and the imperial there, England rendered its spaces of belonging susceptible to a virtually infinite, and global, series of renegotiations."[9] Dryden demonstrates, however, that these "infinite" and inherently "global ... renegotiations" of England's character were at play long before its empire was solidified.

Meanwhile, as a brief examination of classical virtue discourse and its contested Enlightenment threads will show, Dryden's emphasis on the material basis of national virtue points to a destabilizing shift in virtue's meaning—particularly in its focus on telos—that had worked its way into British moral philosophy. Alasdair MacIntyre contends that the Enlightenment project of rooting morality in reason was the death knell of virtue ethics and, in a broader sense, of the notion of virtue as a stable signifier of moral worth. The Aristotelian tradition offered a teleological narrative of virtue rooted in assumptions about the "fundamental contrast between man-as-he-happens-to-be and man-as-he-could-be-if-he-realized-his-essential nature"; within this tradition, "ethics is the science which is to enable men to understand how they make the transition from the former state to the latter."[10] Aristotle's *Nicomachean Ethics* built on Platonic premises about the *political* stakes and aims of virtue. Insofar as virtue refers to "states of character," Aristotle argues, the state of virtue is one of "bring[ing] into good condition the thing of which it [virtue] is the excellence and makes the work of that thing be done well."[11] According to Aristotle's ethical theory, "enduring dispositions of character and intellect, are central to our lives" insofar as those "virtues, along with external goods, enable us to live flourishing or *eudaimon* lives in accordance with our nature as rational beings."[12] The Stoics added to Aristotle's emphasis on cardinal virtues (such as temperance and justice) "an inventory of social or cooperative virtues" that accounted for natural "impulses and dispositions of a more directly self-interested sort"; according to the Stoics, who focused on singular virtue over the lesser virtues of individual traits, "rational agency" is the "source of human freedom" that allows humans to act in accord with their own *and* others' well-being.[13] The Judeo-Christian and (while less influential in England) Islamic traditions of virtue built on Aristotle's model by aligning his theory with theistic beliefs in divine revelation and humans' need for supernatural help to achieve ideals of moral behavior. Christianity added to Aristotle's limited end of earthly *eudaimonia* an emphasis on eternity, reinforcing in spiritual terms the teleological idea of virtue as an ideal worth striving for. Central to all of these traditions was a clear emphasis on telos undergirding dual assumptions that virtue is "humanly possible" to achieve and yet involves a lifelong, "perpetual task" of pursuit.[14]

Eighteenth-century thinkers engaged the Aristotelian-Stoic-Christian notion of virtue in ways that, according to MacIntyre, radically altered virtue discourse by disavowing this teleological premise. The sentimentalism put forth by Scottish Enlightenment philosophers Francis Hutcheson, David Hume, and Adam Smith aimed to "put ethics on a more scientific footing" by "attack[ing] the theological rationalists" and emphasizing the empirical experience of one's own interests within one's circle of influence.[15] Recognizing, in Hutcheson's words, that "Wealth and Power [are] the great Engines of Virtue," they sought to understand how such "engines" could work in conjunction with the disinterested benevolence and "publick Love" of moral virtue.[16] Hutcheson was responding to Bernard Mandeville's satirical *Fable of the Bees,* in which the London-based economist and political philosopher cynically argues that moral virtue is contingent on the practice of various politico-economic vices, among them "Fraud, Luxury, and Pride."[17] To those who would characterize virtue either as a "pure effect of Religion" (86) or as "its own reward" (91), Mandeville responds that people "give the Name of VIRTUE to every Performance" that affirms their "Rational Ambition of being good" (86). In this sense, whatever "certain Pleasure" or "Satisfaction" one takes in one's virtuous behavior actually stems from the prideful act of "Contemplating [their] own Worth"—one's sense of virtue is synonymous with their tenuous grasp on and relation to the value of things and persons within an ever-shifting socioeconomic milieu (92). Virtue claims, according to Mandeville and the moral sense philosophers, albeit in different ways and with different aims, can and often do serve as a way to rationalize desire. By reframing the object of desire in terms of reason—specifically, an economic logic—that object becomes a good in itself. By the end of the eighteenth century, Immanuel Kant had absorbed the work of the moral sense philosophers, finding their ideas compelling but "imperfect," insofar as he did not believe subjective experience could adequately account for or compel moral obligation; for Kant, the freedom to act morally depends upon choices constrained by purely rational notions of moral duty.[18] Ultimately, according to MacIntyre, Enlightenment discourses of virtue ended up being incoherent and self-defeating on both theoretical and practical levels. It was not only that "in a world of secular rationality religion could no longer provide . . . a shared background and foundation for moral discourse and action."[19] Enlightenment thinkers were also keenly aware that postlapsarian "reason [could] supply . . . no genuine comprehension of man's true end"—and, more important, that without a recognition of end, reason could not lay the groundwork for "transitions from potentiality to act."[20] Eviscerated of its practical power in the present, Enlightenment virtue discourse was transfixed in a state of *potentiality,* drawing its meaning purely from past signification and future possibility.

Orienting Virtue examines how literary texts negotiate English political identity within this broader problem of moral philosophy, particularly as Hutcheson articulates it: How do "external goods" (per Aristotle) enable or hinder moral interactions with others? According to MacIntyre, the Enlightenment project of rooting virtue claims in contextualized individual reason undermined the teleological underpinnings of those claims. And yet, when writers like Dryden deploy virtue claims to mark their nation's moral worth, especially in comparison to other empires or emerging nation-states, we can see a residual assumption of Aristotelian telos reasserting itself.[21] Given that Dryden's impulse is hardly an isolated one, *Orienting Virtue* traces how virtue claims emerge in literature throughout the long eighteenth century at moments of perceived political and moral crisis. When Dryden voices England's claim to a divinely ordained virtuous future at a moment of immense loss, his virtue claim stands in for (the lack of) virtue itself, compensating for any absence of its ostensible or expected rewards. The virtue claim depends on deferral, harkening back to the classical assumption that virtue is always *in progress* and rooted in a particular end of earthly—political—flourishing. For English, and later British, writers, this claim is rooted in collective beliefs about originary English liberties and growing anxieties about maintaining those liberties while pursuing the external goods necessary to British eudaimonia.

I turn next to consider how these writers' project of reconciling civic virtue with commercial self-interest was shaped by England's tenuous position in a world dominated by China's economy and the legendary strengths of other Asian empires. Compelled by their global context, writers deploy tripartite virtue claims—in which moral worth is defined not solely as human excellence and/or chastity but also as a sign of God's favor, however long deferred—to reframe England's present weakness in terms of its past legacy and future ambitions.

RECONCILING COMMERCE AND VIRTUE IN THE GLOBAL EIGHTEENTH CENTURY

By the early part of the eighteenth century in England, the philosophical project to find a rational basis for moral virtue was well underway. Two centuries of religious, political, economic, scientific, social, and environmental upheaval had contributed to England's bloody Civil Wars and the Glorious Revolution of 1688. Enlightenment thinkers responded by positing reason, carefully cultivated and rightly used, as an antidote to flawed authorities and traditions. In his 1699 *An Inquiry concerning Virtue,* Anthony Ashley Cooper, the Third Earl of Shaftesbury, writes, "Virtue (which is Goodness or Soundness of Affection in a rational Creature) depends on a right knowledge of what is right and wrong"; neither "custom" nor "religion" can "alter [its] eternal measures and true nature."[22] In other words, he suggests, in a somewhat circular fashion, virtue proves a person to be reasonable, while reason proves one's "certain Interest or *Good*" to be virtuous. By linking virtue and reason, and by implying that morality and self-interest coincide in rational individuals for the common good of profit and improvement,[23] Shaftesbury articulates a defining cultural tension between aristocratic and progressive notions of virtue as an inherited quality versus an earned one.[24] The opening quotes by Defoe and Mandeville attest to this shift in representation, as "vertue" morphs from an aristocratic right to the product of mercantile labor, signified more by "supply" than "splendour."

At the crux of Shaftesbury's definition of virtue were contemporary debates about commerce. As J. G. A. Pocock has argued, insofar as a "right to things became a way to the practice of virtue" in the early eighteenth century, virtue came to signify the natural byproduct of a newly "commercial humanism," marked increasingly by "manners" and taste rather than the political quality of civic humanism.[25] At the same time, property, once a stable sign of propriety, became a means to it through consumption and exchange; land, once linked to lineage, was tapped for saleable resources. As a result, English men and women increasingly connected virtue—both in the sense of an abstract, ostensibly self-evident quality and in its specific arenas of political praxis—to an individual capacity for reason and to the material consequences of this capacity. Virtue became synonymous with evident economic affirmation of one's moral goodness. And yet virtue could not be so neatly redefined. Even as people questioned older and apparently irrational links between noble bloodlines and moral stature, they continued to explain virtue in terms of privilege, property, and civic responsibility, alongside those of work and wealth.

Joseph Addison's famous description of London's Royal Exchange illustrates this shift of virtue discourse in response to commercial forces. He describes in the *Spectator* no. 69 the "mutual Intercourse and Traffick among Mankind" (par. 4) that makes his fictional observer "fancy" himself not just an "Englishman" but also, like Diogenes the Cynic, a "Citizen of the World" (1). Waxing eloquent about the benefits of global commerce, a phenomenon that redistributes nature's "Blessings" among "the several Parts of the Globe," Mr. Spectator marvels at how commodities like "the Muff and the Fan come together from the different Ends of the Earth," at how "the Brocade Petticoat rises out of the Mines of *Peru,* and the Diamond Necklace out of the Bowels of *Indostan*" (4). His "own Country" is dependent on this world market, he notes, insofar as "its natural Prospect [is] without any of the Benefits and Advantages of Commerce":

INTRODUCTION | 9

Our Melons, our Peaches, our Figs, our Apricots, and Cherries, are Strangers among us, imported in different Ages, and naturalized in our *English* Gardens . . . they would all degenerate and fall away into the Trash of our own Country, if . . . left to the Mercy of our Sun and Soil. . . . Our Ships are laden with the Harvest of every Climate: Our Tables are stored with Spices, and Oils, and Wines: Our Rooms are filled with Pyramids of *China,* and adorned with the Workmanship of *Japan:* Our Morning's-Draught comes to us from the remotest Corners of the Earth: We repair our Bodies by the Drugs of *America,* and repose our selves under *Indian* Canopies . . . the Vineyards of *France* [are] our Gardens; the Spice-Islands our Hot-Beds; the *Persians* our Silk-Weavers, and the *Chinese* our Potters. (5)

Meanwhile, Mr. Spectator insists, "the green Fields of *Britain*" produce valuable resources despite their natural deficiencies (5). "Our *English* Merchant converts the Tin of his own Country into Gold and exchanges his Wooll for Rubies," he writes; as a result of this mercantile alchemy, even the grateful "*Mahometans* are cloathed in our *British* Manufacture, and the Inhabitants of the Frozen Zone warmed with the Fleeces of our Sheep" (6). Mr. Spectator concludes his observations by comparing his own view of the Exchange to one from an imagined past: "I have often fancied one of our old Kings standing in Person . . . and looking down upon [this] wealthy Concourse of People," he writes; "how would he be surprised . . . to see so many private Men, who in his Time would have been the Vassals of some powerful Baron, Negotiating like Princes" (7). Addison's analogy between today's merchant and yesterday's vassal foregrounds the shift in perceptions about the basis and definition of national virtue. By the early eighteenth century, the exemplar of virtue had shifted from individual nobleman to dutiful gentleman, the manner of virtue from chivalry to civility, the chief criterion of virtue from birth to merit, and the proof of virtue from land to things. The Royal Exchange, as Addison describes it, embodied this new virtue, insofar as it was characterized by cosmopolitan sensibility, urban sociability, assiduous industry, and commercial valuation. If, as Pocock argues, the neoclassical citizen saw virtue and commerce as antithetical, then the perpetual "encounters with things and persons" Mr. Spectator documents catalyzed a reinterpretation of commercial enterprise as a pathway—rather than a threat—to civic virtue.[26] Through such enterprise, England hoped to avoid the fate of ancient empires like that of Rome, whose instructive decline in civic virtue and ultimate fall, as historian Edward Gibbon famously delineated later in the century, "was the natural and inevitable effect of immoderate greatness" and "prosperity" itself.[27]

Notably, however, Mr. Spectator's optimistic belief that the Exchange might "revive" what Mandeville calls the "Splendour" of Europe's "Golden Age" is as full of "fancy" as are his ruminations on the past. In particular, the sheer prominence of Asian goods in a celebrated London market—a symbolically significant material imbalance—renders Addison's portrait as much a fantasy as Dryden's *Annus Mirabilis*. With the exceptions of French "vineyards" and "the drugs of America," the commodities he lists were grown or manufactured in China, Japan, India, Persia, and the Indian Ocean's Spice Islands. This proliferation of Eastern goods threatened English virtue in both symbolic and practical ways. Long after English writers and critics accepted their nation's commercial growth as inevitable and even beneficial, they continued to worry about what Lady Mary Wortley Montagu called trade's "epidemical" effects on society.[28] Whereas Mr. Spectator celebrates the Exchange as a literal "*Emporium* for the whole Earth" and a symbolic hub of cosmopolitan exchange, the satirist Edward Ward denounces it as "the merchants' seraglio."[29] With this image, which taps into European stereotypes about the decadence of Islamic empires, Ward reinvigorates a fear first articulated by classical theorists: unbridled trade erodes the republic and its citizens' liberty by cultivating a corrupting lust for the luxurious, the foreign, and the effeminate. Mingled with a fear of enervating luxury was a keen recognition that things retain traces of the spaces whence they come. While sugar and other Caribbean imports evoked the troubling moral implications of the triangular trade, seventeenth-century imports like coffee, tea, chocolate, and spices carried with them English fears of French or Islamic absolutism and tyranny, or anxieties about the long-lasting Dutch monopoly on East Asian trade. Even the foreign William of Orange's glorious but self-interested rescue of Protestant liberties was accompanied by Queen Mary's introduction of tulips, oranges, and chinoiserie to the English court.[30] In this regard, Addison's Whiggish enthusiasm for commerce was just one side of a vigorous debate about the cultural and political promise and perils of trade.

More practically, Asian imports were draining England's coffers of the very wealth that Addison and his fellow proponents of trade hoped—and fantasized—might shore up their claims to a newly commercial and cosmopolitan virtue. Addison situates Britain at the fulcrum of global trade, ideally located between the two "ends of the Earth" (Indostan and Peru) and poised both to facilitate and to benefit from the perpetual movement of goods from one to the other. In fact, however, his description of England's role at the center of a bustling global marketplace is largely a dream. "Our Morning's-Draught" of coffee "comes to" the London Exchange not "from the remotest Corners of the Earth" (or, as he implies, negligible peripheries) but from what early modern Londoners understood to be its economic hubs in the East. Despite England's growth in naval and manufacturing technologies, throughout the seventeenth and for much of the eighteenth centuries, Ottoman coffee, Arabian horses, Chinese porcelain, Indian calicos, and nutmeg, peppercorns, and other spices from Indian Ocean islands were just some of the many goods circulating among cities in Europe and the East with little regard for English supply and demand. As Nabil Matar and Gerald MacLean have argued in their study of early modern England's engagement with the geopolitical powers of the Ottoman Levant, its North African regencies, and the Mughal and Safavid empires of Southeast Asia, in regard to these commodities the English repeated a pattern of "importation, imitation, and invention, followed by domestication."[31]

Moreover, early modern Europe's economic expansion was driven by and dependent upon Far East Asia's well-established markets. As Kenneth Pomeranz has argued, the world before 1800 was "polycentric ... with no dominant center."[32] Far Eastern and Western European states alike sought to cultivate resources and develop innovative technologies; for much of early modernity—"a period in world history characterized by intense cultural, political, military, and economic contact," as Charles Parker notes—these ostensibly opposite regions were more similar than not in the successes they achieved.[33] Great Britain joined the global economy belatedly, only after it had gained access to America's vast tracts of land and precious metal mines and learned to exploit its own coal resources. Meanwhile, and until Europe's economic "divergence" from China, Japan, and India by the nineteenth century (a phenomenon whose causes are complex and, even in hindsight, subject to debate), East Asian markets were "better-functioning" and self-sufficient, with little need of or desire for European goods.[34] Daniel Defoe acknowledges this inequity at the start of his propagandistic novel, *A New Voyage round the World* (1725), in which he seeks to drum up interest in and support for exploring the Pacific and colonizing South America. Responding to objections from his fellow sea-faring merchants, Defoe's narrator admits, "We had nothing on board but *European* Goods, which were not fitted for the *East Indies,* where Money only was suitable to the Market we were to make."[35] He goes on to hint at London's eager participation in a triangular traffic of gold and silver that stretched from Spanish-controlled New World mines to Asia's vast markets for luxury commodities, to Europe's courts and tea tables, drawing and dressing rooms. In light of a seemingly unquenchable outflow of bullion in exchange for consumable, and often even superfluous, goods, Addison's "emporium" argument is double-edged, for it minimizes both England's tenuous supply-side role in the Exchange and the implications of Asia's dominance therein.

Addison's description of the Exchange highlights an important concern for seventeenth- and eighteenth-century writers: If England's national virtue depends on robust and reciprocal trade relationships with other nations, and if these relationships are contingent not only on the favor or relative weakness of rival European merchants but also on a vibrant and autonomous Asian supply chain, then what *is* (or what was, or what will be) English virtue? In other words, what essential quality or qualities allow England to distinguish itself as morally excellent and praiseworthy? At a moment when English men and women across the status spectrum felt keenly the effects of what Defoe calls in *The True-Born Englishman* "the want of birth and blood"—both literally, thanks to foreign monarchs, and figuratively, given England's belated entry onto the global stage—the claim to *be* virtuous was a claim to moral excellence or superiority that had to be cultivated and proven, rather than assumed.[36] In this sense, for Defoe, a tireless defender of England's trading priorities, along with Addison and their contemporaries, virtue is simultaneously a future ideal, the actions required to bring that ideal to fruition, and the originary, even transcendent, power driving that action. In other words, virtue is both a moral and a material quality: it exists prior to (and catalyzes) action while it is also an action (or a series of actions) that validates the superiority of its empowering source.

In order to define English virtue in a way that enables present action and future results, while losing none of its validating power, English writers during the seventeenth and eighteenth centuries worked to bring virtue back, both conceptually and physically, from a distant time—by evoking forebears from ancient England and classical Greece, Rome, and Sparta, as well as by expressing a residual generic and thematic fascination with romance—and from distant places, most consistently in Asia. In this sense, Mr. Spectator's rhetoric parallels the work of the Exchange itself: it collapses time and space, bringing together the virtues of "private Men" and "old Kings" just as it does nature's dispersed "Blessings." According to Mr. Spectator's "fanc[iful]" comparison of the past and present Exchange, regular Englishmen have become "like Princes" through "Intercourse and Traffick." In other words, he suggests, they have successfully translated the ostensibly self-evident virtues of England's aristocratic royalty into the measurable virtue of the modern merchant-man. And yet, as the economic historians cited earlier make clear, this translation was not yet successful or complete in an empirically provable sense. If we follow the logic of Addison's analogy, we might infer that the qualities of "Princes" are neatly transferred to the erstwhile "Vassals." And yet the very movement of transfer calls attention to difference as well as similarity; in the space of the simile, something gets lost. Modern virtue, as Addison describes it, is a product of "Traffick" not only across seas but also across "different ages." For example, the present moment—when "our ships *are* laden," and "our tables *are* stored," and "our rooms *are* filled"—is a product of the medieval silk industry, of Elizabethan tastes for southern European fruits, of the Anglo-Dutch spice wars of the early and mid-seventeenth century, and of more recent scientific endeavors to discover the requisite technologies and materials for imitating "the Workmanship of *Japan*" and of Chinese "Potters" (emphasis added). In other words, alongside his description of England's newly commercial virtue, Addison offers a theory of history that links this virtue to an idealized past. Virtue becomes synonymous with the efficacy both of products themselves (the "virtues of" this or that) and of the processes of production and exchange that allow (and, ostensibly, will continue to allow) England to claim these products as evidence of its worth. As English virtue gets redefined throughout the eighteenth century as an internal and self-regulating quality rather than an externally enforced standard of conduct, it carries with it rather than purges anxieties about whence it came.

A note on definition is in order here. For purposes of this study, I draw on *The Oxford English Dictionary*'s tripartite definition of "virtue." First, in its English medieval usage and following, virtue denotes a form of moral excellence, a quality that demonstrates one's "conformity of life and conduct with the principles of morality."[37] Stemming etymologically from the Latin *vir*, or man, virtue signifies human potential at its peak. A virtuous person is superior to—more fully human than—one who is not (or less) virtuous. Virtue denotes here a neo-Aristotelian trajectory of civic-minded identity, by which one understands one's value within a sociopolitical order and the community that order fosters. To return to Shaftesbury's argument, it is both an impetus for and a result of human reason, rightly used. But it is also a site for competing notions of what makes and marks a person of excellence: land or goods, lineage or improvement, restraint or consumption, Machiavellian *virtù* or personal morality, loyalty or resistance to monarchical rule.[38]

A second, and slightly later, definition of virtue is sexual chastity or virginity, "especially on the part of a woman" (*OED*). In contrast to the numerous modes of excellence (e.g., martial or political) available to men, English literature from medieval romance onward portrays chastity as a woman's sole source and signifier of virtue. But here, too, the shift from chivalric cultures to a social order shaped by volatile forces of commerce and credit inevitably altered virtue's moral and material meaning. As public and ostensibly masculine virtues of restraint, civic duty, and land-based liberty gave way to private and ostensibly feminine virtues of polite sociability and domestic refinement, there emerged what E. J. Clery has described as a "feminization debate" regarding the effects of this transformation.[39] On one hand were those who anxiously denounced the feminine along with effeminate qualities, locating in a mysterious figure of "Lady Credit" a lust for luxury and an "endemic changeability" that threatened to sever English virtue from its illustriously stable roots.[40] On the other hand, as Robert Markley has argued, there remained a strong tradition of masculinizing credit that can be seen in the work of Defoe, who "links [public] credit to the ancient, honorable, and masculinist institutions that comprise his vision of the 'Constitution' of the nation."[41] According to Defoe, the forces of credit and chastity, masculinity and femininity, are ineluctably linked. As he asserts in *The Complete English Tradesman* (1726), "The credit of a tradesman ... is the same thing in its nature as the virtue of a lady."[42] In context, Defoe is neither denigrating trade nor making an idle analogy. Credit is, for him, "the off-spring of universal probity"; it is both product and sign of "the Honour, the Justice, the Fair-Dealing, and the equal Conduct of Men, Bodies of Men, Nations, and People."[43] As this cultural shift and surrounding debates played out, Michael McKeon argues, the gradual dissociation of virtue from aristocratic honor "simultaneously encourages its relocation within ... women," who "come to embody the locus and refuge of honor as virtue."[44] As the chaste female body became the protector-guarantor of patrilinear honor, "chastity" evoked contradictory definitions of absolute purity (abstention or isolation from corrupting influences) and of the ability to face and withstand temptation (externally conforming to a new order without sacrificing one's essential purity). In this regard, the feminized virtue of chastity supplements—and at times stands in for—the masculinized virtue of excellence.

A third and final definition of virtue is "the power or operative influence inherent in a supernatural or divine being" (*OED*). In this sense, virtue signifies a quality of potency or efficacy that would be otherwise impossible for a natural, limited entity to achieve. Where the truly worthy human's actions or motives are insufficient or flawed, the supernatural agent steps in to ensure virtue's effects. For the English, there is a particularly Protestant logic at work here, too, insofar as these effects take material form. Andrew McRae has described how a shift in "moral economy" accompanied early modern England's move from a feudal-agrarian system to a mercantile one.[45] By the time of the Restoration, "the Elizabethan ideal" of "order, economic stability and social hierarchy" had been replaced by a Baconian push for improvement that was driven by an optimistic "conception of the capacity of humanity to repair some of the effects of the Fall."[46] Whereas productivity for the sake of subsistence required conformity to carefully enforced social codes, productivity with a goal of future profit demanded an "ethos of godly individualism" and a "restless ingenuity."[47] As Algernon Sidney put it in his *Discourses concerning Government* (1698), "God helps those who help themselves."[48] Despite vigorous debates regarding the most ethical or efficacious ways to recover golden age abundance and prelapsarian order, many seventeenth- and early eighteenth-century English people believed in the biblical imperative—grounded in their interpretation of Genesis's account of Adam and Eve's expulsion from Eden—that scarcity was sinful and prosperity a sign of virtue. And, indeed, despite the Enlightenment's oft-cited shift toward secular reason, there remains in writers' virtue claims a residual and often explicit Christian providentialism according to which virtue can only be *truly* efficacious when ordained, animated, and sustained by God.[49] For example, Gottfried Wilhelm von Leibniz, a proponent of rationalism who wrestled with the gap between virtue in theory and virtue in practice, observed that the Chinese excel in practical ethics (i.e., in experience and tradition) but not in theoretical truths (reason, logic, and the sciences that depend on this kind of thinking).[50] Naturally, he pointed to "cultural exchange" as the medium by which these nations, with their respective moral codes, could sharpen each other. But Leibniz could not get around one problem: according to the Protestant paradigm, "morality follows from knowledge of God and his use of reason," whereas the admittedly superior Chinese claim to moral excellence exists apart from, and thus cannot be empowered by, a supernatural agent.[51]

This belief in supernatural agency persisted despite the broader Enlightenment shift toward secular virtue discourse, to which not all writers acquiesced. Sir Richard Steele—Addison's Anglo-Irish cofounder of the *Spectator*—illuminates how Protestant beliefs about human and divine agency continued to shape the meaning of virtue in the context of European geopolitics. In his first publication, *The Christian Hero*, Steele questions, "Why is it that the Heathen struts, and the Christian sneaks in our Imagination?" before going on to explicate examples of admirable pagan virtue from the past, including Caesar, Cato, Cassius, and Brutus.[52] He concludes that each of these examples is incomplete, for "'twas in Providence to frustrate their Counsels, by turning that Virtue to their Ruin, which they had ensnared for their Protection" (30). Steele draws general principles from the lives of these tragic Romans, emphasizing that "Man . . . is at once an Engine and Engineer," with distinct but limited agency over the outcomes of his behavior (35). All of the social "contracts and policies" people use to "defen[d] against themselves" underscore the general "fallen condition" of humankind, Steele contends—namely, "a monstrous excrescence of the mind, which makes superfluity, riches, honour and distinction, but mere necessities of life" (40). This postlapsarian condition of *desire* "is incapable of being reliev'd" and only "increases with its acquisitions" (40). For Steele, the only "redemption" to this state of desirous depravity comes through Jesus Christ, who exemplifies "an Accident of Ambition" (47) that shatters human "slavery" to the "imaginary notions of freedom" promised by worldly wealth (41). Steele surmises that Christian virtue often "sneaks in our Imagination" precisely because it is countercultural, subordinating worldly fame and riches to eternal glory.

Even as Steele emphasizes the countercultural elements of Judeo-Christian virtue, he aligns with his secular contemporaries' politico-economic notions of virtue by recognizing that any promised *visible* rewards of virtue will likely be deferred. Despite his emphasis on the eternal rewards of salvation, he frames his discussion of virtuous political praxis in terms of the temporal concerns of European rulers and their citizenry. Steele recognizes that the state of humankind is one of "great desire" which "'tis never to be satisfy'd" (74). The answer to this state, he contends, cannot be "the Heathen Virtues" of Cato or Brutus, since these are "little else but Disguis'd or Artificial Passions" (74). Given that the human condition is one of insatiable desire, Steele contends that "our Good God... claims not an utter extirpation, but the *direction* only of our passions" (74). He goes on to argue that "[God] has provided also for this great desire, in giving it a scope as boundless as it self; and *since 'tis never to be satisfy'd, hath allow'd it an aim* which may supply it with eternal employment... what more glorious ambition can the mind of man have, than to consider it self actually imploy'd in the service of, and in a manner in conjunction with, the mind of the universe, which is for ever busie without toil, and working without weariness" (74, emphasis added). According to Steele, Christianity offers an understanding of virtue that "resolve[s] all our perplex'd notions of justice, generosity, patience and bravery, into that one easie and portable virtue, Piety" (75). This "portable virtue" informs an ethic of "charity or compassion," leading us to "exten[d] our Arms to embrace all mankind" (78). Steele goes on to note that any hero at the helm of a nation hoping for God's blessing *must* practice Christian virtue. "Without such Ties of *real and solid Honour,* there is no way of forming a Monarch, but after the *Machiavilian* Scheme," he writes, "by which a Prince must ever *seem* to have all Virtues, but really to be Master of none" except as "they serve his interests" (83, emphasis added). By contrast, the virtuous Christian prince, unswayed by "the luxury of a *Persian*" (83), recognizes "that there is a deep interest to ourselves" in obtaining earthly wealth yet holding that wealth lightly, deferring ultimate satisfaction for heaven while understanding that, on earth, "good intention is subject to be changed and interrupted... by accident [and] mistake" (79). In other words, the Christian hero is not swayed from their purpose by interrupting "accident[s]" but instead realizes that "there may be in the womb of Time great incidents" which bring about reversals of fortune—making "the catastrophe of a prosperous life as unfortunate, as the particular scenes of it were successful" (87). The virtuous hero rests not in immediate, visible results but in the "hope that there is an Almighty, by whose influence the terrible enemy" falls (87). In the end, Steele argues, the virtuous prince benefits their entire community and serves as a "universal good not to be engrossed by us only; for distant potentates implore his friendship, and injur'd empires court his assistance" in times of global turbulence. The Christian hero is, on the basis of his virtue, "the Hope and Stay of Europe" (87).

In sum, if this tripartite definition of excellence, purity, and divine efficacy shows how virtue discourse becomes a way of knowing and representing oneself in comparison or contrast to others, it also highlights the burden of proving one's virtue to a watching world. Framed in this way, virtue is both a natural and a supernatural quality, something bestowed and something earned. It is simultaneously a quality one must measure or prove through action *and* a quality that is essential and innate, a mark of having arrived or of having nothing left to prove. In Aristotelian terms, virtue is both an action (situated perfectly between the extremes of excess and lack) and a deferred disposition to act. These competing definitions pose a dilemma: If virtue is both an action and a quality that motivates or drives that action, it generally cannot be both at any given moment. For by what test can a woman both prove her purity and remain pure? Or, when the Englishman's acceptable proof of "conformity" to "the principles of morality" has shifted from the physical features and privileged status of nobility to the fluctuating value of his stock, how can he know whether and how the "principles" themselves have shifted?[53] In other words, how does one know oneself to *be* virtuous when one must prove one's virtue over and over again?

An example from Daniel Defoe's Preface to *Moll Flanders* illustrates how discourses of moral excellence, economic prosperity, and sexual purity coalesce in the concept of virtue. In the preface, Defoe's female narrator offers a conventional statement of intent and a preemptive apology for any objectionable material the reader may encounter. After every effort to make the heroine's "Story" "what you now see it to be," "to wrap it up so clean" and "put it into a Dress fit to be seen," the narrator states, "what is left 'tis hop'd will not offend the chastest Reader."[54] She goes on to claim that the primary "purposes" of the novel are "to recommend Vertue, and generous Principles, and to discourage and expose all sorts of Vice and Corruption of Manners" (3). At the same time, she notes, the novel is "chiefly recommended to those who know how to Read it"—that is, to readers who are "vertuous" already (2). Only *these* readers will be able to overlook "the amorous Chain of Story" and see what "will appear to have more real Beauty": specifically, the "repentance" of Moll and her lover, and "how unable they are to preserve the most solemn Resolutions of Vertue *without divine Assistance*" (3, emphasis added).

It is worth noting the narrator's use of metaphor here. She claims that the "original of [Moll's] Story" is riddled with "Debauchery and Vice," whereas "the Copy" is told in "modester Words" (1). Ostensibly, the "chastest Reader" (2) should see only the "Dress," or the cleaned-up copy of the original (1). But it is this same virtuous reader who, with "just Discernment," will learn from her "expos[ure]" to vice to see "real Beauty" rather than mere sensationalism (3). In other words, the chaste reader sees both the dress and what is beneath the dress; by peering beneath the dress, however, the chaste reader puts herself in danger of losing her chastity (or at least of giving the appearance of losing it, which is nearly the same thing). In this sense, vice both inoculates the reader and markets the story, whereas virtue—in any absolute sense—is never actually present. Even purportedly "real Beauty" is merely the appearance of it: all of Moll's repentance, reform, and concluding "resolve to spend the Remainder of our Years in sincere Penitence" cannot recover what she has lost (343). These same problems of defining and maintaining virtue reverberate elsewhere in the novel, when, for example, Moll misleads her newest lover to think her "a Woman of Fortune" and "a very modest sober Body" (138). Neither descriptor is true, of course, and Moll justifies the lie by differentiating between virtue as the copy or "dress" of truth and virtue as the essential but inevitably ephemeral quality of chastity: "How necessary it is for all women who expect anything in the world, to preserve the character of their virtue, even when perhaps they may have sacrificed *the Thing itself*," she says (138). Defoe's mingling of "manners" and chastity under the same rubric of virtue foregrounds the broader, national project to which his praise for trade attests: that of "preserv[ing] the character of ... virtue" regardless of whether "the thing itself" still exists, or ever did. For Moll, as for eighteenth-century England as a whole, the "character" of virtue (that is, its "distinctive mark, evidence, or token," as opposed to its essence, which Moll calls "the Thing itself") has become, or at least looks like, "Fortune," in its dual senses of supernatural design and economic plenitude. In this sense, virtue can only be known by the very proofs that negate it.[55]

COSMOPOLITANISM, ORIENTALISM, AND THE DEFERRAL OF ENGLISH VIRTUE

If virtue's definitional instability posed a problem for moralists like Defoe to solve, this reasoned play of "virtue" and "value" also functioned as a strategy for dealing with a second, and more troubling, dilemma: how to think about England's national character vis-à-vis the more prosperous—and thus, in some sense, more virtuous—empires of the East. Throughout the seventeenth century and for much of the eighteenth, the Chinese, Japanese, and Mughal Indian empires (and, to a lesser extent, the Ottomans) were more prosperous than England, both in terms of agricultural fertility and, as Addison hints, in the superior quality and quantity of their export goods. As Leibniz hinted, too, China's example consistently threatened the notions of human excellence, moral purity, and providential favor that were essential to Protestant England's virtuous self-definition. The cosmopolitan reciprocity Addison celebrates was a double-edged sword. If early English identity comprised a mixture of foreign people, things, and ideas—and, by extension, accompanying virtues from elsewhere—these virtues had to be disciplined, domesticated, and reclassified as innately English qualities that could then be exported to ostensibly blank spaces and uncivilized peoples of the world. Kasey Evans contends, for example, that, as early as the sixteenth century, the New World offered England a fertile soil for transforming "Aristotelian virtue to colonial vice."[56]

If the New World provided a testing ground for English virtues like temperance during Europe's long early modern moment of political and economic redefinition, powerful Eastern empires posed particular problems and provided potential solutions for English writers, politicians, and others who were contemplating the dubious morality of commerce and conquest. For it was often by evoking Eastern ideas, practices, and markets that English writers were able to envision the conceptual and physical sources of their own virtue. By calling attention to Eastern influence (and sometimes dominance) in the most important of English institutions—economic, scientific, military, political, religious, and generic—scholars have offered useful correctives to Edward Said's seminal argument in *Orientalism* about Western hegemony in the East. Some have gone so far as to dismiss his work as "anachronistic and reductive."[57] Yet the questions Said sparked regarding how and why the paradigm of orientalism emerged have remained fruitful ones for scholars of early modernity and contested narratives of "Enlightenment."[58] Whereas Islam itself was "a lasting trauma" for Western Christendom, Said argues, a more nebulous Orient had stood in the Western imaginary "since antiquity [as] a place of romance, exotic beings, haunting memories and landscapes, [and] remarkable experiences."[59] Qualifying Said's argument about how European writers developed orientalism as a discursive and institutional framework for varied fantasies (and, eventually, for imperial dominance), scholars have proposed that there existed earlier modes of orientalist thought. Building on Ros Ballaster's work about the influence of oriental fictions on the rise of the English novel, for example, Srinivas Aravamudan has offered a usefully capacious definition of a "transcultural, cosmopolitan, and Enlightenment-inflected orientalism [that] existed at least as an alternative strain before 'Saidian' Orientalism came about."[60] This "Enlightenment orientalism," as he calls it, was, in effect, "a Western style for translating, anatomizing, and desiring the Orient."[61] Meanwhile, focusing specifically on the impact of Chinese commodities on England's sense of virtuous identity, Chi-ming Yang has described "early modern Orientalism" as "a structure of ambivalence resulting from the desire for East Indies markets and the encounter with their superior moral and economic example."[62]

Orienting Virtue enters this conversation about early English orientalisms by considering how seventeenth- and eighteenth-century writers developed a discourse of virtue to negotiate their economic, cultural, and intellectual debts to Eastern philosophy, markets, and courts. According to scholars such as David Porter, Eugenia Zuroski, Robert Markley, and Yang, it was China, in particular, that offered a "hypothetical model of virtuous paganism for England's new mercantile empire."[63] Not only was China extraordinarily prosperous, but also, unlike "the 'primitive' cultures of sub-Saharan Africa and the Americas" or "the legendary fallen empires of Egypt, Mexico, and Peru," as Porter argues, "China was acknowledged the seat of a great and ancient civilization whose cultural achievements not only reached back four thousand years but also continued to rival those of Europe into the current age."[64] In its ancient language and Confucian principles, China offered English writers an alternative "model of continuity, stability, and authenticity" and a way to reframe their own relationship to the past and the future.[65] Building on Porter's argument, Zuroski identifies a "taste" for "Chinese things" as the litmus test for English identity. "Before England could conceive of projecting itself into the world, and onto other nations, in the fashion of an empire," she contends, "it had to imagine itself capable of taking the world into itself while remaining identifiably English."[66] Subsuming the problem of virtue into one of English subjectivity, Zuroski argues that a mid-eighteenth-century shift from "aristocratic cosmopolitanism" to "orientalist nationalism" parallels the shift from a Lockean model of identity—which "figures lack as a fertile space" for improvement, accomplished through an ordered accumulation of "things not English"—to an internal, domesticated, and "rational self-moderation."[67] In other words, England "comes into its own as a national power" in the same way (and at the same time) that orientalism emerges as a successful narrative strategy: first, it imports foreign objects, along with "older forms of English culture, specifically cosmopolitanism," and then it "purg[es]" from England's collective consciousness any trace of or tolerance for the oriental ideas that accompany these objects, including "residual traces of aristocratic power" and "sensual fantasy and desire."[68] The early modern clash between aristocratic and bourgeois values, in this regard, is one that the English resolve by looking outside of themselves, only to internalize what they find.[69] These scholars point to Britain's intensifying commercial priorities as the catalyst for a shift in attitude toward China later in the century, from one of "reverential awe" to one of "dismissive contempt."[70]

Orienting Virtue is indebted to these studies of how British identity evolved vis-à-vis China. However, by excavating aspects of English virtue discourse that remained consistent, and consistently unstable, throughout the period, despite shifts in global status and attitude, it builds on these studies in two ways. First, *Orienting Virtue* broadens the geographical scope of inquiry from a single representative Asian region—whether China, the Ottoman Levant, or Mughal India—to think more expansively about how English writers conflated empires and nations of "the East" to develop their rhetoric of national virtue. Yang's reminder in her introduction to a 2014 issue of *Eighteenth-Century Studies* not "to homogenize the Afro-Eurasian world from Egypt to China" is apt.[71] And yet, as I have argued, "virtue" cannot be reduced to the moral wisdom of Confucius, just as it cannot be reduced to medieval standards of female chastity or to Aristotelian absolutes. Thus, while Yang notes that China is a "cultural intermediary that links together a greater Orient" through "its strategic ties to other times, places, and civilizations of the East and the West," the focus on China as exemplary among Asia's "pagan empires" risks minimizing the intersecting relevance of such studies as Humberto Garcia's *Islam and the English Enlightenment, 1670–1840*, which posits an explicitly "Islamic republicanism" as crucial to Enlightenment England's political thought.[72] Moreover, despite their awareness of global differences in custom and character, and despite the nuances of their politico-economic relationships with specific empires in the East, English writers frequently joined their European counterparts in conflating Eastern places and peoples, drawing on what Suvir Kaul has called a "remarkable accretion of repeated tropes, metaphors, images, [and] modes of description."[73]

Arguing in 1694, for example, that "the Eastern Nations come nothing short of the Western in Wit and Judgment," Antoine Galland adds that "under the Name of Eastern People, I include not only the Arabians and Persians, but also the Turks and Tartars, and almost all the other Nations of Asia, to the Borders of China, both Mahometans and Pagans."[74] Of course, Europeans represented China, Japan, India, Arabia, the Ottoman Empire, and "the other Nations of Asia" in different ways at different times for specific, often calculated, reasons. Moreover, as Britain's global fortunes improved, English writers inevitably modified their rhetorical stance to accommodate shifting geopolitical interests. And yet, I argue, writers' virtue claims often depended, at least in part, on their strategic conflation of distinct regions and empires in "the East." If China and Japan were obvious moral-material foils to a less prosperous England at the turn of the eighteenth century, the Islamic empires possessed their own brands of heroic virtue that tested, and thereby helped to prove, England's own. Rather than think metonymically about China as the exemplar of Eastern virtue, then, I focus on showing how writers represent "the East" in deliberately nebulous ways in order to construct their definitional strategy of deferral.

Second, my project resists a linear historical chronology in which English men and women embrace cosmopolitan pluralism during the latter half of the seventeenth century and early decades of the eighteenth, only to disavow foreign things and ideas by the mid-to-late eighteenth century. I do not contest that significant shifts occurred across this period; as Pomeranz and other global historians have made clear, the growing pains of modernity and distribution of global resources affected East and West in different ways. And yet, rather than a neat shift in English attitudes, we see both cosmopolitan and orientalist sentiments coexisting throughout the period. By theorizing virtue in more nuanced ways, we can trace a slightly different narrative framework for English identity and, later, the British Empire. The "thing itself" of virtue, as Defoe calls it, is defined not only by shifting relations to trade and consumption but also by its ability to signify excellence, purity, and supernatural efficacy; the meaning of virtue depends, in this sense, on the self-consciously contradictory ways in which people define and attribute it. To the extent that virtue is and must remain both a material and an immaterial quality, some aspect of it remains constant (and is defined in consistently anxious ways) throughout early modernity. Wolfram Schmidgen has argued that Defoe, along with many of his contemporaries, saw the fact that "English culture... is irreducibly mixed and impure" as a productive "source of national superiority" rather than a threat to or a contaminant of it.[75] Given this embrace of mixture, Schmidgen contends, it is time to question the critical assumption "that the process of modernization is animated by an ordering impulse that disciplines the heterogeneity and multiplicity of traditional societies."[76] Indeed, as I argue here and in the following chapters, writers could not erase residual definitions and foreign sources of England's virtue claims. Some, like Mandeville, were aware that virtue claims could be used to justify dubious political and economic ends. As a result, we see some writers interrogating teleological narratives of modernity and the virtue claims that uphold them, instead considering England's place in global history in more circular (even, in a sense, revolutionary) terms. As Addison suggests in his comparison of merchants to princes, the meaning of virtue emerges out of a conscious movement *between* times *and* places rather than a simple translation from past to present or from there to here. Orienting virtue, in this sense, was never just a matter of reconciling commercial interest with aristocratic values; rather, it was an endless process of reiterating England's moral-political character in terms of different times *and* places.

In their praise for cosmopolitan observation and exchange, many of the writers I examine make clear that virtue is not a zero-sum game (if they are virtuous, we are not, and vice versa) but rather a form of self-knowledge that depends upon one's claims to moral excellence, to providential power, and, if not to "the thing itself" of absolute chastity, then at least to a level of "integrity" manifested in the "character of uncorrupted virtue."[77] As we learn from Defoe's Moll, however, "the character of [one's] virtue" may look very much like vice and may, in fact, cover up a lack of virtue "itself." In this regard, virtue "itself" proves difficult to translate, particularly between places like China and England. For even as it "enter[s] the market as an object of consumption," virtue also transcends the market, resisting evidence of early modern England's 'unvirtuous' economic, political, and even moral subservience to other nations.[78] To interrogate English virtue discourse, in this sense, is to take up Felicity Nussbaum's call to "pursu[e] a genealogy of the global in articulation with 'modernity' and 'postmodernity'"—thinking not only in terms of commercial relationships between nations but also of the network through which the possession of things took on moral significance.[79] English virtue was not forged or sustained by appropriating Confucian wisdom or the workmanship of Chinese potters, but rather through an ongoing struggle to parse how the English are *like* others (whether the kings of old, the Chinese, or the Mahometans) and *not like* them (because they are modern, they are Protestant, they are future global powers, they are *English*).

In short, English virtue claims are forged through the differential work of analogy. In his book *Analogical Thinking: Post-Enlightenment Understanding in Language, Collaboration, and Interpretation,* Ronald Schleifer describes analogy as a form for imitating and negotiating the complex relationship between language and experience. Analogical thinking, he contends, "reconceives both the local and the global—both empiricism and idealism, or matter and energy—in terms of the complexity of activity and historical events."[80] Whereas empirical analysis assumes a world of mechanistic matter that is "simple, essentially atemporal, and self-evidently self-same and unchanging," analogy assumes the coexistence—and constant shift—of similarity and difference; consequently, "the action of analogy, is to start over, again and again."[81] As John Locke argues in his *Essay concerning Human Understanding* (1690), analogy is a crucial mechanism for connecting new to old experiences and observed phenomena to those unobserved. The "rule of analogy," he writes, governs the pursuit of all kinds of knowledge, from the scientific to the moral: "Analogy in these matters is the only help we have," for "it is from that alone [that] we draw all our grounds of probability."[82] As Locke points out, the idea of "virtue" is "generally approved, not because innate, but because profitable"—because "God [has], by an inseparable connexion, joined virtue and public happiness together, and made the practice thereof necessary to the preservation of society, and visibly beneficial to all with whom the virtuous man has to do," we see that men act virtuously out of self-interest rather than out of a sense of moral good (1.3.6, 29). Locke moves from delineating a philosophical principle of rational, divinely endorsed self-interest to questioning its practical impact: "Where then are those innate principles of justice, piety, gratitude, equity, chastity?" (1.3.9, 31). Once again, we see the conflict between what Defoe calls "the character of virtue" and "the thing itself." Even as Locke troubles his readers' understanding of "virtue" as an absolute principle or ideal, arguing that virtue must be understood in practical and theoretical terms of profit, he unapologetically explains virtue's power in transcendent terms. Virtue and self-interest go together because "God" has decreed them "inseparable."

For Locke, as for many of his contemporaries, the definition of virtue is shaped by a theologically inflected notion of scarcity and prosperity. If virtue is both a cause and effect of one's link to supernatural agency, then there must be similarity between past and present, princes and merchants. And yet, according to the rules of analogy, there must be difference, too. With this in mind, if we think of eighteenth-century virtue as merely the visible evidence of commercial success, or as England's laudable but temporary "capacity for cosmopolitanism," then we minimize the anxieties Defoe, Addison, and others express regarding where *English* virtue comes from in terms of time and place.[83] Defining English virtue in and for the global eighteenth century is a matter of identifying, again and again, England's shifting position in relation to different historical trajectories, value systems, religious paradigms, and moral codes. And it is a matter of confronting contradictory notions of virtue as a form of restraint (in the forms Locke refers to, for example, "of justice, piety, gratitude, equity, chastity") or as a divinely endowed right to indulge by pursuing profit regardless of moral price. "It is not clear that as a whole early modern Londoners were particularly cosmopolitan in their outlook," Robert K. Batchelor argues, if by that term we mean the "broader ethical stance" espoused by Addison's fictional citizen of the world.[84] Instead, we see English writers and thinkers engaging with ever-shifting global forces, particularly "Asian urbanism, science, and maritime trade."[85] Through this engagement, they strive to maintain and articulate a sense of what makes them—as English men and women—both similar to and different from their own ancestors and their fellow global citizens. In the end, virtue claims do not indicate an achievement of moral standards; instead, they offer a framework for forging and reforging a civic-national identity within a global network of things, places, and ideas.

CHAPTER SUMMARY

In the readings of texts that follow, I do not suggest that writers' references to virtue throughout the long eighteenth century are uninflected by their specific political, historical, economic, religious, and social contexts, or that virtuous "liberty" refers to the same political commitments in 1666 as it does in 1726 or in 1790. Yet what is missing in chronological studies that foreground a decisive shift in English subjectivity—from a cosmopolitan virtue that embraces difference in the late seventeenth century to a domestic, self-regulating, and nationalist virtue by the late eighteenth—is an attention to what medievalist Geraldine Heng has called "global temporalities." Heng argues that "the study of the global past in deep time" considers modernity as not just a transnational but also a "transhistorical phenomenon," one that repeats itself, "each time with difference," across artificial periodic boundaries.[86] Such a perspective on the *longue durée* can help us understand how Enlightenment writers use a tripartite definition of virtue to negotiate complex global relationships. As I have argued, English virtue depends on a process of bringing things back from elsewhere, conceptually and physically, to reinvigorate the nation's moral and material sense of self and self-worth. Insofar as this process must be performed over and over again, "virtue" carries the burden of being complicit in its own undoing—again, to prove one's moral superiority is to succumb to the vice of pride; to prove one's chastity is, in essence, to be unchaste; to prove supernatural agency is to render the supernatural disappointingly natural. The idea of virtue is tasked with covering over so many contradictions that it ends up unable to refer to anything but itself. Writers respond to this dilemma of representing national virtue by working to translate tropes of heroism from East to West; to juxtapose ancient stories with glorious visions for the future; and to convincingly analogize "our old kings" to a modern Mr. Spectator, Citizen of the World.

The book's five chapters focus on moments of political or cultural dissatisfaction in England: the aftermath of the Civil Wars, the succession crisis leading up to the Glorious Revolution, the rise of Sir Robert Walpole's Whigs, the corrupting lethargy of mid-century luxury, and the eighteenth century's finale of revolutions. At each juncture, writers including Henry Neville, John Dryden, Jonathan Swift, Charlotte Lennox, and Samuel Johnson, among others, attempt to illustrate English virtue in action by turning to Eastern exemplars—highlighting the political pragmatism of the legendary Mughal ruler Aurangzeb, for instance, or exploring the possibilities of women's virtuous agency within the constrictions of a seraglio. When these arguments turn political—that is, when writers seek to make these examples useful for English readers—the displacement begins. Translated back home and into English contexts, others' virtues take on negative meaning; at home, virtue signifies deferred agency rather than positive moral-political identity. Across the eighteenth century, writers deploy these deferred virtue claims to point to a "middle way" between conserving ancient ideals and celebrating the realities of their globalizing society. The writers whose work I examine are self-conscious about the importance of history, aware of their contemporary global networks, and overtly concerned with England's virtuous character and reputation, in both moral and material senses. They make clear, in one way or another, that virtue is at once an essential performance and a paradoxical one; they recognize that, by definition, virtue works both as a process and as the negation of [need for] that process. Yet, in their own ways, they are committed to thinking through the mystery of how virtue remains intact, and retains its power as a signifier for Englishness, at moments when it is neither self-evident nor integral.

Chapter 1 explains the core dilemma of English political virtue by examining how Henry Neville and other English writers in the mid-seventeenth century make a case for a moderate republicanism that conserves ancient principles of liberty while also embracing an aggressive approach to global trade. English republicans saw their national virtue as both a product and a sign of good governance, yet they were torn between seeing their political structures as determined by climate and history or open to change through improvement. The English saw themselves as uniquely poised for progress, given that they were free from the oppressive despotism of the French and Islamic empires and not yet to the point of luxury that might signal the impending downfall of the mighty Chinese. For Neville and his fellow republicans, England's future depended upon its successful negotiation of a classical conflict between preserving the political virtue of liberty and pursuing imperial glory through conquest and trade. What Neville's critics have largely ignored, however, is the extent to which his fascination with the "despotical" Eastern rulers of antiquity and with the "absolute" monarchies "of the Persian, the Mogul, the king of Burma, [and] China" in his own day influenced his thinking about English liberty.[87] By resituating Neville's popular 1668 pamphlet fiction, *The Isle of Pines,* in its neglected Indian Ocean setting and in the context of his own and his contemporaries' political tracts, the chapter reassesses Neville's important insights concerning the paradoxes of English liberty. In depicting an enslaved African woman who moves between global commodity markets, *Isle* highlights England's morally dubious participation in Indian Ocean and transatlantic networks of trade. For Neville, who believed in the power of trade and the importance of liberty as keys to England's greatness on the global stage, virtue is neither a timeless ideal nor a self-evident action. Instead, it is an aspect of political identity that must be negotiated and defined anew with each shift in global power structures and commercial relationships.

Chapters 2 and 3 examine how this core belief in England's virtuous liberty gets reiterated, through strategic representations of Eastern empires, at new moments of political uncertainty. Chapter 2 addresses concerns surrounding England's succession crisis by reading John Dryden's heroic tragedy *Aureng-Zebe* (1675) in context of scholarship about early modern commensurability between East/West political theories of virtue and interest. While Neville qualifies his idealization of the East's commercial promise, others saw in "despotic" Eastern political institutions an admirable and much-needed pragmatism. Anticipating Sir William Temple's 1690 *Of Heroic Virtue,* a comparative description of how political virtue manifests itself in different times and places, Dryden illustrates an aggregate of virtuous qualities, rather than a single positive *or* negative model for England: his portrait of virtue is embodied not only by his eponymous Mughal prince but also in a bold Morat and a pragmatic Indamora, both of which characters take on Aureng-Zebe's displaced Machiavellian qualities. In the end, as Dryden echoes his French source François Bernier's language of "fortune" and "revolution" to predict India's decline, he also affirms that any nation's success—even England's—may have less to do with innate virtue than with what Machiavelli identified as the unpredictable work of fate.

Chapter 3 picks up the story of England's slide from liberty into license and luxury at a new moment of moral and political crisis surrounding the South Sea Bubble and the rise of Sir Robert Walpole. Turning to Jonathan Swift's *Gulliver's Travels* and unfinished *Account of the Court and Empire of Japan,* two contributions to his 1720s anti-Walpole satire, I consider how Neville's concerns about the costs and consequences of pursuing political virtue persist into the eighteenth century. Notoriously skeptical about England's nascent imperial endeavors, both at home in Ireland and abroad, Swift satirizes the optimism of Augustan contemporaries like Defoe and Addison, and presents a dismal picture of human nature in the modern age. Focusing on Swift's references to "virtue," particularly in regards to the Houyhnhnms—who vaguely resemble exemplars from the past (ancient Sparta and Athens) *and* the East (a conflated China and Japan)—this chapter argues that Swift's admiring nods to other times and places allow him to underscore a distinctly Protestant, Anglo-Irish virtue while maintaining his scathing critique of England's unvirtuous behavior. In book 3, just before Gulliver sails to Luggnagg, a fictional island "about an hundred Leagues distant" from Japan, he takes a side trip to Glubbdubdrib, an "Island of *Sorcerers* or *Magicians*" whose governor invites Gulliver "to call up" from the dead any historical figures he would like to interrogate.[88] After spending time "beholding the Destroyers of Tyrants and Usurpers, and the Restorers of Liberty to oppressed and injured Nations" (167), Gulliver finds himself "disgusted with modern History" (169), which he sees as marked by the betrayal and degeneration of England's "pure native Virtues" (172). Immediately after this episode, Gulliver sails to Luggnagg and then on to Japan, where he contrasts the admirable civility of the Japanese with the perfidious self-interest of the Dutch. Gulliver's ruminations in Glubbdubdrib provide a neglected context for the satire's final section, in which Swift depicts Gulliver's interactions with the eminently virtuous Houyhnhnms. While critics often read Houyhnhnmland as either utopian ideal or parody of virtue, I argue that Swift deploys a deliberately elusive definition of virtue that emphasizes both providential agency and human effort; in the end, it is virtue's very polyvalence that lets Swift offer his satirical "travells" as "admirable Things" that might "wonderfully mend the World."[89]

Following these first three, chronologically organized chapters, which offer sustained close readings of how political virtue claims operate in a single primary text, the final two chapters expand and complicate this story of virtue with a faster-paced attention to key argumentative threads that reverberate across the century. Chapter 4 traces the gendered discourse of chastity, examining how politico-economic definitions of virtue evoked by Neville, Dryden, and Swift get complicated by what Bernadette Andrea has called England's "genealogy" of "feminist orientalism."[90] In their depictions of English liberty, both Neville and Swift allude to the importance of female chastity in upholding what is otherwise a predominantly masculine notion of virtue. David Hume complicates this idea in his later *Treatise of Human Nature*, where he explains that the notion of female chastity is as crucial a Western strategy for perpetuating its patriarchal order as it is a constructed one.[91] Reading three texts from different genres—including Mary Pix's play, *Ibrahim, The Thirteenth Emperour of the Turks* (1696), Charlotte Lennox's novel, *The Female Quixote* (1752), and Jemima Kindersley's travel *Letters from the Island of Teneriffe, Brazil, the Cape of Good Hope, and the East Indies* (1777)—in the context of Hume's point about the "artificial" virtue of chastity and later debates about chivalry and sexual virtue voiced by Edmund Burke and Mary Wollstonecraft, I argue that the trope of the Eastern seraglio, in conjunction with the deferring work of romance, gave women writers a way to reconcile expectations of bodily chastity and political action. In this regard, feminist orientalism provides a literary strategy for articulating how chastity can function as a form of political virtue. Highlighting what is at stake in conservative defenses of chivalry, these writers show that their perspectives on freedom are rooted in a particular place. In their overt comparisons of West and East, they highlight the potential freedoms of constraint while at the same time displacing that constraint into the generic form of romance.

With continued attention to the voices of women writers and generic appropriation of Eastern spaces, chapter 5 considers how writers exploit the genre of the oriental tale to reconcile contradictory notions of virtue-as-ideal and virtue-as-action as England moved into a position of global power by the end of the eighteenth century. As the dilemma envisioned by Restoration-era republicans came to fruition—that is, as Britain's rising global preeminence merely underscored, for many, its lack of a solid civic foundation—the discourse of virtue continued to evolve. This final chapter frames a pair of pseudo-oriental tales, Samuel Johnson's 1759 *Rasselas* and Ellis Cornelia Knight's 1790 sequel, *Dinarbas,* in the context of John Brown's *An Estimate of the Manners and Principles of the Times,* Adam Smith's *Theory of Moral Sentiments,* and Catharine Macaulay's treatise on the "accidental revolutions" of global history. As storytellers, both Johnson and Knight use the abstract form of the oriental tale to craft a narrative of national integrity; they represent their call to "conscious virtue," or patriotic duty, as a solution to England's politico-cultural decline into moral lethargy. To answer the call of "duty" means learning to "read virtue right," in Macaulay's words, which is a task of learning how to be virtuous by balancing competing interests as citizens of a nation and citizens of the world. In both *Rasselas* and *Dinarbas,* however, the interplay between ideal and action remains unresolved, illustrating the ongoing deferral of virtue itself.

By the mid-eighteenth century, to speak of English virtue is to acknowledge what John Brown calls in 1757 a "crisis" in England's "manners and principles," particularly the "public spirit" that once gave it strength.[92] At the same time, to speak of virtue is to engage this present crisis by connecting beliefs about England's future potential to beliefs about its foundational principles of political liberty. This story of Englishness often plays out through costly compromises, as writers like Neville and Swift make painfully clear, especially insofar as the story is dependent upon imported things and ideas from elsewhere: Addison's "Pyramids of China" and the "Workmanship of Japan," "naturalized" and imitated until they signify English "splendour"; Islamic republicanism and Confucian wisdom and the impressive civility of heathen Japan's courts. In this regard, the instability of English virtue reflects and reorders the dynamic spatiotemporal networks in which philosophy meets praxis. By reiterating a tripartite definition of virtue as excellence, purity, *and* providential efficacy, writers acknowledge others' strengths while also reframing them into a carefully historicized and continually revised narrative of exceptional English strength.

In their own partial and incomplete ways, each of the writers I examine anticipates the theory of history Hegel would later make explicit in his posthumously published *Lectures on the Philosophy of History*. "Nations are what their deeds are," Hegel writes, and in the end "every Englishman will say: We are the men who navigate the ocean, and have the commerce of the world; to whom the East Indies belong and their riches."[93] This purpose—this telos—drives each individual English person's sense of virtuous identity and value. "A Nation is moral—virtuous—vigorous," Hegel continues, "while it is engaged in realizing its grand objects," and "the relation of [each] individual to that [national] Spirit is that he appropriates to himself this substantial existence; that it becomes his character and capability, enabling him to have a definite place in the world—to be *something*.... In this its work... the Spirit of the people enjoys its existence and finds its satisfaction." It is both the genealogy and the costs of this "work" that *Orienting Virtue* explores.

1

"OUR LUSTS GAVE US LIBERTY"

Mercantile Might and English Republicanism in Neville's *Isle of Pines*

> Custom taking away shame (there being none but us), we did it more openly, as our lusts gave us liberty. . . . For we wanted no food, and living idly, and seeing us at liberty to do our wills, without hope of ever returning home made us thus bold.
> —Henry Neville, *The Isle of Pines* (1668)

IN *AREOPAGITICA*, HIS 1644 ADDRESS to Parliament protesting a restrictive licensing act that had been passed the previous year, John Milton describes the "vast city" of London as "the mansion house of liberty, encompassed and surrounded with [God's] protection."[1] It represents "a nation not slow and dull, but of a quick, ingenious, and piercing spirit, acute to invent, subtle and sinewy to discourse" (742), a nation filled with "men ever famous and foremost in the achievements of liberty" (725). Milton goes on to identify two causes for this uniquely English liberty: first, he points to the "virtue" of England's "mild and free and humane government," made up of "lovers" and "founders of our true liberty," thanks to whom the English have been freed from "oppressive, arbitrary, and tyrannous" prelatical authority (745). And, second, he points to a God who "reveal[s] himself ... as his manner is, first to his Englishmen" (743), freeing them to pursue "our richest merchandise, truth" (741). Milton describes England's God-ordained liberty as both a cause and an effect of virtue.[2] On one hand, liberty is an essential precondition for intellectual improvement and moral good, insofar as it enables people "to know, to utter, and to argue freely," deploying their God-given reason on behalf of the common good (746). On the other hand, Milton argues, England's political "virtue" depends upon its citizens' freedom to think and speak freely: "If every action which is good or evil ... were to be under pittance and prescription and compulsion," he writes, then "virtue [is] but a name" (733).

In the vacuum of political and religious authority that emerged in 1649, the language of "liberty," frequently opposed to that of "tyranny" and "despotism," took on broad significance, as people questioned anew what it meant to be subject and what it meant to be free. As they articulated their nation's desire to achieve prosperity and sustain it into modernity, many Restoration-era writers and thinkers found themselves grappling with a dilemma: the commercial endeavors that promised to advance England's global standing also threatened to undermine its ancient constitutional liberties and send the nation into a tailspin of decadent consumption that had ruined far greater, even exemplary, empires of the past. In this chapter I trace how the rhetoric of "liberty" became intertwined with that of "virtue" in the work of Restoration-era republican thinkers, to the extent that liberty came to function as both a precondition and an essentially English sign of moral-material virtue. To illustrate the troubling stakes and significance of such political rhetoric, I then turn to Henry Neville's *Isle of Pines* (1668), a popular work of pamphlet fiction that highlights how English republicans recognized and displaced the human costs of mercantilism in their efforts to develop a viable—and virtuous—political model for the age of expansion and empire. More than simply a way to justify self-interest, I argue, the tripartite notion of "virtue" as human excellence, moral purity, and divine efficacy also helped early modern thinkers conceptualize the shifting dynamic between a political subject and his sovereign. For Neville, a staunch republican and an active member of parliament, virtuous political identity was not just a matter of pitting Machiavellian virtù or neoclassical ideals of civic virtue against stereotypes of oriental or French absolutism or the feminized virtues that Addison would later extol in his idealized "Citizen of the World." To be virtuous, as Neville saw it, was to reconcile old and new ideals—to maintain England's ancient liberties in the face of violent threats while also proving that these liberties were deserved and remain sustainable in a modern, mercantile world. Highlighting the difficulty of this synthesis project, Neville's dystopic tale prompts readers to consider how a moral ideal of liberty can be driven, and potentially undermined, by a lust for material things. Specifically, Neville's references to the history, customs, and wealth of the Indies suggest that English "liberty" is, at least in part, a rhetorical construct designed to accomplish contradictory goals of maintaining a mythic legacy of the freeborn Briton while assimilating the wealth of an allegedly despotical East.

"LIBERTY" AND THE ENGLISH CONSTITUTION

Praise for England's unique and divinely ordained liberties formed a constant refrain across the eighteenth century. Arthur Young, an English agricultural writer and a keen observer of British socioeconomics, writes in 1772 that "the birthrights and privileges of Britons . . . form a system of liberty, so happily tempered between slavery and licentiousness, that the like is not to be met with in any other country of the globe."[3] The "system" he describes was as familiar and essential to his readers as it is to Americans today: it ensured freedom of "person and property" (so that, as Young quipped, a man's "house is his castle"), "the liberty of the press," the principle of habeas corpus, and so on (50). Young's description of the freeborn Briton, which rang so true in the Age of Revolutions, was "rooted in a [much older, fifteenth-century] jurisprudential tradition that emphasized the role of law as a restraint on the power of the Crown," explains Jack P. Greene.[4] Sir John Fortescue had established in his posthumously published *De Laudibus Legum Angliæ* (1543) that "all human law" can be divided into three categories:

natural law, custom, and statute. While the "Laws of England, as far as they agree with, and are deduced from the Law of Nature, are neither better nor worse ... than the Laws of all other states or kingdoms," he states, English "customs"—and thus, potentially, English statutes—are "the very best," far superior to those of other nations.[5] The Elizabethan Sir Edward Coke agreed, calling "even the Magna Charta and other important statutes in the constitutional tradition 'but a confirmation or restitution of the common law.'"[6] According to these early jurists, the rights or "liberties" enjoyed by English subjects were deeply rooted in England's common law. Liberty is inherited rather than earned, they argued, for it is the "product of time, continuous usage, and the quiet and common consent of the people," rather than legislation.[7] Reinforcing the notion that the English enjoy liberties because they, unlike people of other nations, are destined to be free, Young reiterates in his *Political Essays concerning the Present State of the British Empire* the great "contrast between the liberty enjoyed by the British nation, and the arbitrary power under which so great a part of the world at present groans" (21). Summing up a long-standing narrative about the divine "blessing" of British exceptionalism, he attributes such exceptional liberty both to "the climate of the British isles," which "confers all the vigour and courage" for which Britons are known (7), and to the "superiority" of "mixed monarchy, or the British constitution" (22).[8] He calls for "warmest gratitude to Heaven for blessing in so peculiar a manner these happy kingdoms" and credits "the steady valour of our patriotic ancestors" with preserving liberty for "the present and future ages" (22).

Writers often contrasted this ideal of English liberty with the torpor of other, non-Protestant nations, especially the alleged despotism of Catholic Europe and the stereotyped tyranny of Islamic rulers. For example, Young echoed generations of Englishmen in singling out as particularly lacking in liberty the "Great Mogul" of the Ottomans—a "despicable potentate"—and his subjects, along with the "slothful inhabitants" of the world's torrid zone (6). Notably, though Young was writing in the wake of Ottoman decline, his rhetoric is not all that different from that of his predecessors, who tended to conflate distinct Eastern empires in order to make a point about the contrast between

English liberty and Eastern absolutism. Indeed, Henry Neville had observed over a century earlier that there is little difference between the "despotical" Eastern rulers of antiquity and the "Persian, the Mogul, the king of Burma, China, Prester John; or any other [of] the great men under those princes" of his own day, who are so like "the ancient monarchies of the Assyrians and Persians" that he finds it "needless to say any more of" them.[9] Neville's contemporary and friend, James Harrington, had a similar perspective on the absolutist tendencies of Eastern governments, claiming that, unlike "the Roman monarchy [and] that of Israel . . . the Turkish is the most perfect [monarchy] that ever was" because it is absolutely "pure" (that is, absolutist), rather than "mixed" (like the ancient British constitution). While Harrington specifically targets the Turks in his attack on despotism, he attributes the difference between an oppressed East and a free West to "the different genius of the nations," more broadly and collectively. "The people of the Eastern parts," he goes on to write, "scarce ever knew any other condition than that of slavery," whereas "these of the western . . . had such a relish of liberty, as through what despair soever could never be brought to stand still while the yoke was putting on their necks, but by being fed with some hopes of reserving to themselves some part of their freedom."[10] Even when constrained or restricted by external forces, Harrington suggests, the English maintain their innate claim to liberty. In this regard, he notes, "the people of the Eastern parts" have a twofold problem: not only have they suffered under tyrannical rulers but they are also generally incapable of forming or maintaining a better government for themselves. The English are free, in other words, even when they appear to be constrained; by contrast, any freedom obtained or enjoyed by people in the East is inevitably temporary or otherwise limited.

The widely held notion that liberty is a distinctively—even exclusively—English quality can be traced back through England's past via the powerful myth of the Norman Yoke. Christopher Hill has described this idea as it took shape in seventeenth- and eighteenth-century Whig historiography: "Before 1066 the Anglo-Saxon inhabitants of this country lived as free and equal citizens, governing themselves through representative institutions. The Norman Conquest deprived them of this liberty, and established the tyranny of an alien King and landlords. But the people did not forget the rights they had lost. They fought continuously to recover them, with varying success. Concessions (Magna Carta, for instance) were from time to time extorted from their rulers, and always the tradition of lost Anglo-Saxon freedom was a stimulus to ever more insistent demands upon the successors of the Norman usurpers."[11] This story of ancient and continuously preserved Anglo-Saxon liberties resonated with revolutionaries during the English Civil Wars and Glorious Revolution and with self-styled patriots in the Walpole era and beyond. Meanwhile, royalists developed a different theory of the Norman Yoke in order to reinforce their belief in *jure divino* and ensure the monarch's political and religious authority. According to this alternate narrative, "pious Normans had had a valuable disciplinary effect upon the dissolute Anglo-Saxons" by bringing order where there had been anarchy.[12] Running through both the patriot-Whig and royalist-Tory versions was the question of property ownership—that is, of whether a ruler has a God-given and thus legitimate right to conquer, possess, and do what he wishes within his kingdom. If, for example, "the King owned his title to conquest, and consequently owned all the property in the realm, then he also had a right to arbitrary taxation"; however, if "the sanctity of property and representative institutions were part of [the common English] inheritance" from time immemorial,[13] then the people themselves had a right and a responsibility to "struggle for preserving the property whereof they were in possession," as eighteenth-century "commonwealthman" John Toland put it.[14]

Whether prioritizing political order or freedom of conscience, free markets or controlled trade, seventeenth-century writers and thinkers agreed that England's distinctive liberty was a virtue worth preserving. Yet they often struggled to define and practice their inherited liberty. If English writers generally agreed that liberty was the antithesis of tyranny, there was a wide range of opinions within mainstream political discourse regarding how liberty should be worked out in practice. Thomas Hobbes, for example, situated liberty within his rigid philosophy of sovereign power, arguing that a man exercises liberty when he willingly gives up a portion of his freedom to act as he pleases, for the sake of collective order. Deploying a quasi-Calvinistic logic, Hobbes avers in *Leviathan* that men can act only according to their God-given "appetites"; thus, "*Liberty* and *Necessity* are consistent" rather than antithetical, for "did not [God's] will assure the *necessity* of man's will . . . the *liberty* of men would be a contradiction, and impediment to the omnipotence and *liberty* of God."[15] By contrast, members of more radical sects such as the Levellers and Diggers believed that the English legacy of liberty mandated political revolution with the goal of instating popular sovereignty and effecting a socialist redistribution of wealth.[16] Others saw political liberty as a primary catalyst for the nation's economic growth. The subtitle of Henry Parker's 1648 essay *Of a Free Trade,* "A Discourse Seriously Recommending to Our Nation the Wonderful Benefits of Trade," included a line about "Setting Forth Also Most Clearly, the Relative Nature, Degrees, and Qualifications of Libertie, Which Is Ever to Be Inlarged, or Restrained according to That Good, Which It Relates To." And in the wake of the Glorious Revolution of 1688, numerous essays linked political liberty and commerce as the dual engines of national prosperity. Charles Davenant, for example, who was, like Parker, a vocal proponent of mercantile policy, argued that "the foundation of all" national "safety, ease, wealth, and prosperity" was a commitment to "the liberties of the people."[17]

The rallying cry of "English liberty" was particularly resonant in the latter half of the seventeenth century, when "representative institutions were everywhere in Europe (except in the revolutionary Netherlands) being suppressed."[18] Writing in the midst of the Exclusion Crisis, and in response to Sir Robert Filmer's 1680 *Patriarcha,* a treatise defending the divine right of kings, republican Algernon Sidney went so far as to mock the assumption "that the Assyrians, Medes, Arabs, Egyptians, Turks, and others like them, lived in slavery, because their princes were masters of their lives and goods: whereas the Grecians, Italians, Gauls, Germans, Spaniards, and Carthaginians, as long as they had any strength, virtue, or courage amongst them, were esteemed free nations."[19] Whatever "the intention of our ancestors," Sidney points out, and whatever protections they meant to set in place, the reach and rights of English monarchs have come to drastically and dangerously limit the Englishman's freedom, until he has become no better than his oppressed foreign foils. John Locke's 1689 *Two Treatises of Government* went on to denounce Filmer's absolutist principles and lay the groundwork for modern liberal thought. Arguing that "the State of Nature" is both "a State of perfect Freedom" and "a State also of Equality," Locke avers that because people are divinely endowed with reason and rights, individuals must be free "to order their Actions, and dispose of their Possessions, and Persons as they think fit, without the bounds of the Law of Nature."[20] Guided by reason and empowered by right, an individual has the capacity to act freely to realize their best interests.

For each of these thinkers—who, with very different motivations and rationales, identify freedom as essential to individual and national success—liberty is by no means synonymous with the absolute autonomy of an individual will. As Locke makes clear, the "state of Liberty . . . is not a State of Licence"; for instance, no individual has "liberty to destroy himself" or others.[21] Rather, the virtuous "state of Liberty" indicates a capacity for action that is foreordained and blessed by God yet constrained and directed by natural law for the ultimate good of the whole. Whether referring to popular representation, free speech, or individual will, "liberty" became shorthand for a distinctive trait that God instills and preserves in the English people across centuries of conflict and conquest (even before the Normans, Fortescue points out, the Britons had been subjugated by the Romans, the Saxons, and the Danes). As these writers suggest, while liberty is a privilege uniquely bestowed on the English people, it is not to terminate on them; instead, they have a responsibility to steward and preserve this liberty for posterity. In this chapter of English history, however, the true test of liberty would come not on the battlefield but in the global marketplace. To the extent that liberty functions as both precondition and sign of English political virtue, writers must consider how such liberty sustains and proves itself in an increasingly global modern milieu.

THE ISLE OF PINES AND ENGLISH REPUBLICANISM

The remainder of this chapter turns to Henry Neville's *The Isle of Pines* as an example of a text that allegorizes the decline of England's civic virtue by illustrating the difficulty of maintaining English liberty in global contexts. *Isle of Pines* appeared in London in the summer of 1668 in the form of three successively—and anonymously—published pamphlets. The first consisted of a man named George Pine's original account of being shipwrecked while sailing to the East Indies as a bookkeeper aboard the *India Merchant;* the second contained one Henry Cornelius Van Sloetten's account of discovering an island, years later, that was peopled with Pine's numerous progeny; and the third and final pamphlet, ostensibly authored by Van Sloetten, included Pine's letter, Van Sloetten's account, and one Abraham Keek's introductory letters vouching for and framing the text. To seventeenth-century readers steeped in Richard Hakluyt's *Voyages and Discoveries* and Samuel Purchas's *Hakluytus Posthumus,* the claim that a new island had been discovered was both riveting and believable, though this piecemeal publication sparked speculation about the tale's genre and credibility even up to the mid-nineteenth century.[22] Dubbed "the most celebrated hoax of the later seventeenth century," *Isle* has been variously interpreted as a utopian sexual fantasy, a political allegory, and an account of English colonial anxiety.[23] In that Neville identifies core instabilities—of gender, race, violence, and law—that troubled English republican ideals during the age of expansion and empire, his tale is all of these. Yet critics have paid scant attention to the "lusts" for "Eastern commodities" that drive both the *India Merchant* crew's failed 1589 attempt "to settle a factory" in the East Indies and the Dutch merchants who stumble upon an island colony of "naked" English Pines seventy-eight years later.[24] In what follows I examine how *Isle*'s Indian Ocean setting complicates Neville's treatment of English republicanism insofar as politics intertwines with racial thinking and imperial ambition. With its genre-bending form, *Isle* transcends the parochial political debates that characterized Neville's earlier satirical pamphlets and foregrounds an ineluctable link between post-Restoration political theory and England's commercial endeavors.

Henry Neville spent much of his career, both before and after the Restoration, actively participating in the quest to define and practice a robustly modern republicanism that would revive and implement classical political principles in a commercially ambitious England. For Neville, republicanism was both an antipatriarchal political discourse that denounced civil and ecclesiastical tyranny and a pragmatic framework within which politicians sought to catalyze a national "reformation of manners."[25] Heavily influenced by Machiavellian thought, Neville and other republicans, including Algernon Sidney and Marchmont Nedham, saw liberty as an essential "precondition" for cultivating the "moral good," or virtue, that would elevate the nation as a whole and eventually lead to its "future end in glory."[26] They worried, however, that, as Machiavelli had argued, the preservation of liberty and the pursuit of *grandezza* were fundamentally irreconcilable goals. The preservation of liberty required an agrarian structure, whereas empire demanded expansion overseas. And while only free people could pursue glory through expansion, the pursuit of empire, if unchecked, would beget vices such as luxury and sloth that would in turn lead a republic to its decline and its citizens into corruption and servitude. Influential republican theorist James Harrington sought to apply Machiavelli's ideas to English politics in his *Commonwealth of Oceana* (1656). Given that "empire is founded upon dominion," Harrington argues, and that "dominion is property," "the people of Oceana, in proportion to their property, have been always [and, he implies, only] free."[27] According to Harrington, England will only achieve stability and order by throwing off monarchical oppression, revitalizing the ancient constitution, and returning to agrarian roots (like ancient Sparta), rather than by pursuing commerce (like Venice) or imperial expansion (like Rome).[28]

While, as several critics note, *Isle* works on one level as political satire—depicting a decline in civic virtue at the hands of a rapacious patriarch in order to target the *jure divino* sovereignty espoused by Sir Robert Filmer and other Stuart loyalists—Neville is not solely concerned with describing England's political degeneration at the hands of a corrupt monarch or with theorizing timeless ideals of civic virtue.[29] And while he echoes Harrington in asserting that the "alteration of property . . . is the only corruptor of politics,"[30] he shows himself more interested in finding a viable alternative to English decline than in "resurrect[ing] an agrarian and non-capitalist" past.[31] Given early modern England's burgeoning mercantilist push for profitable discovery and expansion, the impasse between liberty and empire took on added urgency for pragmatic republicans who, like Neville, believed that "liberty remained the key to greatness."[32] In response to J. G. A. Pocock and others who associate Neville with a Harringtonian, neoclassical republicanism, revisionist historians have argued that Neville and his contemporaries in the mid-seventeenth century were self-consciously synthesizing the ostensibly competing priorities of antiquity and modernity: civic virtue and self-interest, property and commerce.[33] As Vickie Sullivan contends, theirs was "a version of Harringtonian republicanism that rests on a more liberal foundation," insofar as they sought to achieve the grandezza of republican Rome without repeating its demise.[34]

These progressive seventeenth-century republicans saw trade, in particular, as a feasible and exciting solution to the impasse Machiavelli had identified between empire and liberty. According to David Armitage, by the time Neville was writing, political theorists were suggesting that "commerce had so altered the maxims of republican politics that [this] dilemma might either be resolved, or, at least, overcome."[35] Both economically and politically, engaging in commerce became a necessary and promising (if potentially dangerous) obligation rather than a choice. Speaking to fellow members of Parliament in 1658, Neville observed that "England, indeed, cannot subsist without trade. . . . Therefore, our question will be" how to "advance our interest, either for the strength or for the trade of this nation."[36] In light of examples such as the "economically vibrant" Dutch Republic, in particular, English republicans hoped that a "maritime empire could enrich [their] nation, render it stable in the arena of international power politics, and offer greatness without endangering liberty."[37] Given Neville's political contexts, it is hardly surprising that *Isle* situates events that might otherwise be interpreted as allegorical or ironic in a realistic context of intercontinental transit and trade. Replete with the empirically verifiable detail—dates, topographical references, and ethnographic data—that initially led Neville's audience to believe it a true story of discovery, *Isle* concludes with the Dutch merchant-narrator Henry Cornelius Van Sloetten's account of leaving the Pines' island and stopping in India, Madagascar, and other commercial ports en route back to Amsterdam. While *Isle*'s publication history and the fact that Neville apparently intended it as a hoax certainly complicate straightforward interpretations of the tale's politics, *Isle*'s concluding travelogue offers a telling glimpse of the political, economic, and moral stakes of the *India Merchant*'s voyage.

Recontextualizing *Isle* and its treatment of English "liberty" within a seventeenth-century global trade network requires that we also account for the text's provocative racial dynamics. Indeed, insofar as the commercial enterprise that promised a way of reconciling England's dual pursuits of liberty and empire proved inseparable from an expanding transoceanic slave trade, mercantile trade was a costly solution. As Jonathan Scott points out, neither the tension between agrarian and commercial economies nor their mutual dependence on slave labor was unique to modernity.[38] Yet as early modern republicans debated the meaning and implications of liberty in its political, civil, and ecclesiastical contexts, they inevitably modified their understanding of slavery as well.[39] For many neoclassical republicans, slavery signified a political condition wherein individuals or states were subjected to others through conquest or internal tyranny; liberty signified freedom from coercion and dependence on another's will or governance. As Susan Dwyer Amussen puts it, "Liberty meant, most immediately, that English men were free and possessed rights guaranteed by law," whereas slavery "was a metaphor frequently used as the antithesis of freedom to condemn the illegitimate use of power."[40] However, she notes, this political discourse (which was prominent in London as well as in England's colonial outposts) frequently elided a "real set of social relations that denied not only freedom but also personhood to a class of people. The relationship between these two dimensions of the term 'slavery'" posed contradictions "that the English and their colonists faced and more often avoided."[41]

Written at a moment when this rhetorical liberty/slavery dichotomy intersected with emergent notions of race and European economic ambitions, *Isle* reflects how "the liberties of Englishmen and the law of slavery . . . evolved simultaneously and as part of the same process."[42] Neville's character of Philippa, who plays a significant role in *Isle*'s dystopic plot, shows how slavery and republicanism go hand in hand, insofar as this global trade enables a solution to the political issues Neville addresses even as it calls into question republicanism's fundamental ideals. Besides the English bookkeeper George Pine, the survivors of the *India Merchant*'s fateful voyage include the shipmaster's daughter, two maidservants, and "one negro female slave" named Philippa (*Isle*, 194). Philippa's presence on the East Indies–bound ship compels us to examine how Neville's depictions of race and slavery complicate our understanding of his engagement with contemporary political debates about republican liberty and empire. Indeed, even as the text considers how and to what effect the English might follow in the footsteps of their successful Dutch counterparts—in establishing and maintaining a vibrant republic, in building up a maritime empire via trade, and in tapping into the treasures of the East—it also reveals an exclusionary racial logic that marks Philippa and her mulatto descendants, the Phills, as enslaved byproducts of European liberty. *Isle*'s global context, which both frames and shapes its plot, invites us to rethink Neville's republican vision not as one concerned solely with provincial politics but as one that recognizes and seeks to address the profitable inequities of European mercantilism.

EUROPEAN MERCHANTS AND INDIAN OCEAN TRADE

Isle's Dutch narrator highlights England's tenuous place in a seventeenth-century supply chain that included European merchants vying for Eastern luxury exports amid a thriving intra-Asian trade. Neville's depiction of English inferiority, represented by the Pines' nakedness, their lack of husbandry and technological prowess, their failed political-juridical structure, and an inability to control unruly citizens, signals England's impotence in relation to the successful Dutch colonizer-merchants.[43] While the English Pines describe their newly discovered island in conventional utopian terms—as "very pleasant, being always clothed in green, and full of pleasant fruits . . . ever warm"—they also perceive the woods as "full of briars and brambles" and other obstacles to cultivation (*Isle*, 205). By contrast, when the Dutch explore a "never inhabited" part of the same island, they find "a free and clear passage to us, without the hindrance of bushes, thorns and such like stuff" (205). To the Dutch, who possess both a successful colonial strategy and a strong republican political structure, the Pines' island appears to be a "fertile country" ready for their use (205). Moreover, while both the Elizabethan English and the Restoration Dutch merchants set out to capitalize on "the great advantages arising from the Eastern commodities," and while shipwreck keeps the English ship from reaching the East Indies, Van Sloetten's ship successfully reaches India after leaving the Pines' island (194). By describing the Dutch merchants' successful activity in Indian Ocean ports, Neville acknowledges a mutual European fantasy of unfettered trade with the East even as he accurately indicates Dutch preeminence over other Europeans in Asia and Africa.

Yet *Isle*'s Indian Ocean frame reflects long-standing Anglo-Dutch trade rivalries in Southeast Asia rather than inherent or irreparable English inferiority.[44] Following a late sixteenth-century breakdown in England's political relationship with Portugal, Europe's primary supplier of spices, the English East India Company (EIC) and Dutch East India Company (VOC) found themselves competing for access to and control over the lucrative spice trade and its island sources.[45] After being forced out of this trade in the 1620s and dealing with the costly aftermath of its own Civil War, post-Restoration England was ready to regain commercial traction in the East Indies. By the time Neville was writing, two Anglo-Dutch Wars and multiple English Navigation Acts had forced the Dutch, along with England's continental neighbors, to recognize the island nation's unrealized but "exceptional capacity for maritime and colonial expansion."[46] In light of shifting intra-European allegiances and the increasing importance of Eastern goods to English lifestyles, *Isle*'s depiction of Anglo-Dutch cooperation and friendship is telling. By minimizing real, oft-antagonistic rivalries, Neville invites his readers to see past the patriarchalism running its course on the Pines' island and consider England's potential to expand its empire via Eastern trade. Toward this end, he demonstrates how the Dutch excel at commerce and conquest while apparently maintaining their republican value of liberty. To the extent that Neville's depiction of Dutch success is also a visionary blueprint for England, we might read in his text a temporary—and strategic—conflation of the English and Dutch narrators.

Van Sloetten's ethnographic commentary and detailed log of his ship's route, ostensibly about Dutch mercantile success, also offer an account of how England might emulate the Dutch Republic's successful Eastern trade in order to enrich the nation and invigorate English republicanism. As he recounts his ship's progress after leaving the Pines' degenerate island, Van Sloetten describes a forced landing at "Cambaia, a part of the East Indies, but under the government of the great Cham of Tartary" (*Isle*, 208). From there, the ship sails to Calicut, its intended destination and "the chief mart town and staple of all the Indian traffic," where the merchants spend "a full month" "unload[ing] a great part of our goods" (209). On its return voyage home, the ship "coas[ts] along several of the islands belonging to India," crosses paths with "two Portugal ships," gets "chased by a pirate of Argiere," stops among the "very unhospitable and treacherous" people of Madagascar, spends "the Christmas Holy-days" on "the Island of St. Helens," and docks briefly at the Spanish-ruled Canaries before arriving back in Amsterdam (209–10). This detailed description, often neglected by *Isle*'s critics, highlights the broader mercantile and Indian Ocean contexts within which Neville situates his fictional English island. Van Sloetten's attitude toward the East throughout this framing travelogue is a mix of admiration and self-interested superiority. While he recognizes the value and importance of Indian commodities to Europe's luxury markets, he focuses on documenting "the strangest, and indeed most barbarous" of Indian "customs" and the unhealthy "air of that place" for European constitutions (209). Moreover, in a telling remark for Dutch and English republicans alike, he observes that Indian "men and women imitate a majesty" in their bearing and take pains to maintain a long-lasting tradition of policing bloodlines so as to ensure that their rulers possess "true Royal blood" (209). Van Sloetten's observation about the Indian monarchy becomes more significant in the context of Neville's and Harrington's own observations about the inherent flaws in Eastern governments.

Meanwhile, through his Dutch narrator, Neville articulates England's anxious cognizance of the perils, as well as the promise, of Eurasian trade. Van Sloetten's references to the Portuguese and to Algiers's Barbary pirates remind readers of England's hostile Catholic rivals and the ongoing threat of Islamic slavery terrorizing European Christians who pass through Mediterranean waters.[47] Moreover, his reference to "the great Cham of Tartary," or the Qing emperor, serves to remind readers of Asia's control over markets the English were struggling to engage. The narrator seems keenly aware of early modern England's supplicant position in a global economy "dominated by Asian production, competitiveness, and trade."[48] As the fictional travelogue attests, seventeenth-century Asian markets served as the hub for "merchants of all nations" (*Isle*, 209). For the English in particular, seeking to solidify their place in this global marketplace, the East functioned as a "fantasy space for mercantile capitalism," "promising both an insatiable market for European exports and a vast, inexhaustible, storehouse of spices, luxury goods (from tea to textiles), and raw materials."[49] By the 1660s, however, this promise was hardly fulfilled. Not only did a Dutch monopoly keep English merchants out of the Spice Islands, but the English were also excluded from Chinese and Japanese markets and limited to trading with the Ottoman, Persian, and Mughal Indian empires. Even in these more accessible markets, they were quick to exaggerate and overestimate the reciprocity of trade.[50] While urbane Europeans from Paris to London to Lisbon coveted Eastern exports—from pepper and spices in the early seventeenth century to Indian calicos and Chinese tea and porcelain by the century's end—they had little to trade in return apart from gold or silver bullion, which was both costly to transport and crucial to war-drained domestic coffers. Forced to compete with one another in the precarious yet vital Eurasian trade, European merchants sought to minimize their costs by engaging in "country trade," or the lucrative reexport between Asian markets—bartering for Japanese bullion at a central Asian port, for example, in order to purchase commodities that might be transported to another Asian market and sold at a profit.[51]

Underscoring the fantasy of Euro-Asian reciprocity, Van Sloetten does not describe the type of goods his men spend "a full month" trading in Calicut. Nor does *Isle* offer any explanation for Madagascar's commercial significance as a port of call. Yet the Dutch ship's brief stop in Madagascar offers a clue about the link between commerce in general and the slave trade as a particular form and byproduct of it. Historically, late seventeenth-century Madagascar was a locus for a transoceanic slave trade that connected an established Indian Ocean slave network to new demands from American plantations.[52] Quick to capitalize on lucrative opportunities to provide intercontinental transit for enslaved people, European merchants purchased enslaved Malagasy (along with Indian, Southeast Asian, and other African people) from Arab and African traders and exported them for sale in both Indian Ocean and Atlantic markets. In this way, they could profit as middlemen in the Indian Ocean "country trade" while also attempting "to establish a plantation economy on the American model in the Indian Ocean."[53] For the most part, the Dutch VOC sent these enslaved people East, "to work as domestic servants, artisans, and laborers at their headquarters in Batavia, at strategic commercial emporia such as Malacca and Makassar, on the plantations they established in the 'Spice Islands' of eastern Indonesia, at their stations in coastal Ceylon, and at its settlement at the Cape of Good Hope."[54] The EIC, by contrast, traded some people in Indian Ocean markets,[55] but transported far more to plantations in the Americas.[56] In this regard, while the rapid increase in New World demand for slave labor differed in kind and scale from Asian demand, seventeenth-century slavery was truly a global enterprise. And while the Atlantic trade has received far more scholarly attention than has its Indian Ocean counterpart, historians have recently and compellingly argued that the two networks were inextricably linked.[57] Judging by the numbers alone, mid-seventeenth-century England was focused on obtaining laborers for Caribbean plantations; however, some Englishmen who admired the Dutch Republic's thriving commercial empire also saw the profit to be made by exploiting African and Asian laborers in the East.[58] Even as the transatlantic trade increasingly exploited Africa to serve New World plantation economies, the East remained a market destination for enslaved people throughout the seventeenth century. In short, Richard B. Allen argues, "European slave trading in the Atlantic world did not occur in isolation from what transpired in the Indian Ocean world—and vice versa."[59]

As a well-connected politician, Neville would have been well aware of slavery's importance as a political, economic, and moral issue for England. For alongside a theoretical commitment to liberty, many English republicans were preaching the practical outworking of liberty through trade. And England's commercial success in a global trade network depended on its continued and increasing participation as an intermediary between two flourishing slave economies: the new world of the West Indies and the ancient world of the East. Indeed, England's participation in the slave trade—in conjunction with access to New World mines and plantations—allowed it, at long last, to break into an economy long dominated by merchants from the Gulf of Arabia, Surat, and the Malabar Coast. It is hardly surprising, then, that England's increasing commercial engagement with the East correlated with the rise in transatlantic slavery as, over the course of the seventeenth and eighteenth centuries, England moved from primarily transporting labor to transporting the products of forced labor (at first, large quantities of American silver, and, by the eighteenth century, the cheaper American sugar and textiles that eventually allowed England to undersell Eastern suppliers).[60] In short, the same "widespread faith in the benefits of trade" undergirding England's Eastern fantasies and invigorating mid-seventeenth-century republicanism also tempted the English to follow the Dutch Republic's lead in exploiting and justifying the profitable inequities of a transoceanic slave trade.[61]

RACE AND SERVITUDE IN *ISLE OF PINES*

Given the economic realities of Neville's world—one in which England vied with other colonial and commercial powers for new markets, control over trade routes, diverse commodities, and cheap sources of labor—the dark injustice of the slave trade is implicated in the broader monarchical-patriarchal inequities *Isle* addresses. These inequities, the text suggests, are hardly erased by mercantilist measures to mediate the impasse between republican liberty and imperial grandezza. Disseminated in 1668, *Isle* stands at a transitional moment in European thinking about African slavery. Despite a "cumbersome and inefficient" process by which colonial ordinances were approved in London, the 1660s saw the codification of numerous laws governing the treatment of enslaved Africans in the Americas.[62] These punitive legal codes effectively created a double standard for English justice, with one for citizens and another for slaves. Indeed, by 1688, the government in Barbados had synthesized various laws and practices into a comprehensive and widely influential legal code that "acknowledged slavery as a status" and "an institution" and situated enslaved people "entirely outside the laws of England."[63] As "one negro female slave" who remains on the outskirts of Pine society, providing sexual and domestic service to George Pine and yet, unlike the other women, never becoming his wife (*Isle*, 194), Philippa embodies these tensions and transitions in European thinking about slavery. She stands at the historically significant crossroads between East and West, between domestic slavery and plantation slavery, between England's position as a globally insignificant island nation and its position as a commercial power enriched, in part, by the products of slavery, from spices and sugar to tobacco and tea. At the same time, this "slave" and her descendants haunt Neville's text as a reminder of the costs of this transition (194). Indeed, Philippa's presence on the island and her role in the *India Merchant*'s voyage accentuate how "the enslavements of African and Asian peoples create[d] a serious moral predicament for [European] opponents [of slavery] and apologists alike ... torn between gain and godliness."[64]

With the notable exception of Philippa, Neville elides any direct reference to slavery's role in the trade circuit *Isle* describes—one that involved, whether directly or indirectly, European merchants, African coasts, Asian markets, and American plantations. Yet situating *Isle*'s dystopic plot, and the racial dynamics contributing to it, within a global economic network allows us to explore how Neville's political satire is undergirded by a racially inflected logic of law and order. While it is Philippa who beguiles and the Phills who rebel against their English Pine counterparts and are swiftly singled out for punishment, the logic by which they become the impetus and scapegoat for political disorder remains implicit. The Phills play a symbolic role in the narrative, as their otherness, marked by explicit and stereotypical ascriptions of race, serves to consolidate English identity. Yet Neville is silent about why the Phills are singled out for punishment and about how, exactly, racial violence factors into a republican social order. Indeed, his juxtaposition of realistic, detailed geographical descriptions with narrative silences concerning the island's racial dynamics troubles any straightforward interpretation of his political ideals. However, when we consider the Pines' island—and the Phills' role on that island—in the broader context of early modern trade routes and the intercontinental slave trade on which they depend, we see that *Isle* acknowledges the constitutive inequities of mercantilism only to displace them onto the commercially superior Dutch Republic and Eastern empires.

Before discussing this displacement, I turn briefly to unpack *Isle*'s depiction of Philippa and her descendants. Starting with Philippa, Neville portrays three generations of Phill servitude and exclusion, transgression and punishment, in a way that foregrounds the inequities of slavery in a colonial context. Shortly after the shipwreck, as "idleness" sparks in George Pine "a desire for enjoying the women," he engages in sexual intercourse with each of his four female companions; only Philippa's desire is described as being outside a normative moral order (*Isle*, 197). Tapping into European stereotypes of libidinous Africans and natural repugnance, Pine writes that he dallies with Philippa only under cover of night, for "my stomach would not serve me" to do it otherwise (198). He retroactively ascribes to Philippa desirous and deceitful motivation, claiming that she "longed also for her share" with the intent "to beguile" (198). While Philippa becomes part of Pine's sexual entourage, she is the only woman treated as neither "person" (195) nor "wife" (200). And, as Pine points out in his account of their first night on the island, when "the blackamore being less sensible than the rest, we made our sentry," Philippa's supposedly less acute capacity for sensation, thought, and emotion justifies her role as a servant to the others (196).

If Philippa's racial difference precludes her integration into Pine society, this exclusion becomes more pronounced and more violent in subsequent generations. As a new generation of Pines yields to the desire that consumed their late patriarch and succumbs "to whoredoms, incests, and adultery," their leader Henry Pine decides that such "sin" must now be punished (201). After it is determined that one man should die for all the wrongdoers, John Phill is "proved guilty of divers ravishings and tyrannies" and "thrown down from a high rock into the sea." Passively describing the "execution being done upon him," the narrator does not specify whether "the rest [who] were pardoned" are Phills or by what standards (and by whom) John is "proved guilty" (202). Immediately after the execution, Henry Pine supplements his father's original "commands" with a set of "good and wholesome laws" designed to define, prohibit, and redress further "wickedness" (193). He then delegates the responsibility and authority for "prosecution" to representatives from each tribe (203). Despite these measures, the cycle of Phill transgression and violent expulsion reoccurs in the third generation, when Henry Phill is accused of ravishing the governing Pine's wife and leading an insurrection. By this point, the Pine governor "[finds] his authority too weak to repress such disorders; for where the hedge of government is once broken down, the most vile bear the greatest rule" (207). Only with the Dutch visitors' help are the Pines able to squelch rebellion and restore order by once again "explod[ing]" (203) the Phill offender from their midst (208).

One generation after John Phill's execution and the subsequent introduction of law, the new leader, William Pine, offers an explanatory analogy: "Now as seed being cast into stinking dung produceth good and wholesome corn for the sustentation of man's life, so bad manners produceth good and wholesome laws for the preservation of humane society" (202). William leaves out of his biblical allusion exact equivalents to the act of casting [seed] into dung and to "bad manners," thereby affirming that John Phill's punishment ("casting") precedes the enumeration of law.[65] Rather than punishment existing as a response to broken law, then, an ex post facto law justifies predetermined punishment. Moreover, as God's ostensibly natural law is filtered through a Pine governor and his representatives, divine and human sovereignty—insofar as they coalesce in a legal regime—become one and the same. The source of all "mischiefs," William states, is a "neglect of hearing the Bible read ... according to my grandfather's [George Pine's] prescription" (201). And while blasphemy against God is punishable by death, a person who defames the governor is "exploded from the society of the rest of the inhabitants" (203). Obedient people are protected and nourished within a morally and socially ordered community, while the disruptive and "vile" are banished from it (207).

Collectively, the Pines' treatment of the Phills indicates a contradiction between republican ideals of justice and liberty and the force of law. Yet Neville's depiction of violence on his fictional island prompts a key interpretive question: Why does the lapse in Pine values of "justice and sincerity" disproportionately affect the Phills (201)? That is, why are the Phills consistently marked as "most vile," blamed for a breakdown in Pine governance, and singled out as the only tribe not denoted by the surname of "the 'English Pines,'" which George initially proclaims to be "the general name of the whole" (200)? While most recent scholarship on *Isle* at least cursorily considers the relationship between *Isle*'s political agenda and its racial subtext, critics do so only after classifying the pamphlet fiction as either satire, or allegory, or travelogue. Yet Neville crafts a generically hybrid text in order to articulate a complex political problem and potential solution. If we read *Isle* as political satire—and, per Elliott Visconsi, as "more interested in solving the political problem of rape than in assigning racialized blame for the act"—then the Phills become victims of a patriarchal Pine regime that relies on an antiquated, "unsophisticated," and inequitable rule of law.[66] Read satirically, the Phills' excessive and degenerative sexuality mirrors the process by which an immoral patriarch's libertine appetites return to haunt, degrade, and potentially destroy the commonwealth.[67] By contrast, as historical allegory, *Isle* appears to pit Charles I (as the "tyrannical" John Phill) against a benevolent constitutionalist ruler like Henry Pine, who seeks to "use justice and sincerity amongst [the people], and not to let religion die" (*Isle*, 201).[68] Recognizing that "in multitudes disorder will grow" (201), Pine rulers follow Machiavellian principles by encouraging population growth while using "terrifying executions" to check overweening ambition.[69] Read allegorically, the Phills lose any sign of the racial identity that Neville describes in such detail. Finally, if read as a colonial travelogue, the tale's depiction of miscegenation and recurring Phill insurrection reflect deep-seated anxieties about the proportion of white to African or native people in England's colonial outposts. As racial violence operates constructively in *Isle*, according to an insidious logic that links Phill lineage to transgression and punishment, the meaning of justice is obfuscated and deferred.[70]

Of course, *Isle* lends itself to all of these interpretations. However, whether dismissing Neville's depiction of racial difference as stereotypical and inconsequential or focusing on it as central and prescriptive, none of these readings takes into account how *Isle*—and its treatment of Pine inequity—reflects republicanism's broader economic concerns and the mercantile context in which Neville and others hoped these concerns might be resolved. Nor do they take into account the interrelation and politico-economic significance of mid-seventeenth-century transatlantic and Indian Ocean slavery. Indeed, given England's participation in an Afro-Eurasian trade network (and the slave trade feeding this network), Philippa's status as a "negro slave" on board the *India Merchant*, along with her and two of her progeny's subsequent exclusion from Pine society, is more telling than her racial lineage—significantly, she and her descendants, unlike the other Pines, are not free.[71] In *Isle*, which explores the possibilities and pitfalls of commerce as a way to revitalize English republicanism, slavery works within a global structure of commodity trade. Consequently, race is neither *Isle*'s focus nor a negligible factor, for it is both part of the problem Neville addresses (patriarchal inequity and national servitude) and part of the solution he proposes (commerce). If trade offers a way to reconcile expansionist policies with vaunted English liberties, it does not do so without compromise and cost.

In light of this complexity, Neville's depiction of servitude on the island also becomes important. The shipwreck with which George Pine's narrative opens represents a traumatic rupture in the social order because it abruptly erases an established class hierarchy that privileges the aristocracy. As the survivors rebuild their lives and culture on the island, Pine and his former master's daughter remain cut off from their lineage and the maidservants from their families; only Philippa—who, as a "negro female slave," had been an utterly marginalized subject in England—finds herself in a position to enjoy greater equality (194).[72] After the "company" labors together to build shelter, there seems to be "nothing else to do" (199) but to enjoy "idleness and a fullness of everything" the island provides (197). Yet by the time the Dutch visit and notice "prince and peasant here faring alike," there is a class structure in place that seems to replicate that which existed before the shipwreck (192). The ruling Pine's wife has two maidservants, just as her father did in the first generation. The Dutch refer to William Pine as "the Lord of that country," comparable (though materially "inferior to") the "gentry in England" (206). And they remark twice on the "number of servants" ("about a dozen") that attend William "after a more royal manner than ever we saw him before" (206–7). Nowhere in the text does Neville comment on how this hierarchy emerges or explain who comprises the servant class. And while Henry 'Sparks' Pine (descendant of one of the original maidservants) delegates equal authority for "the prosecution of . . . laws" amongst the four tribes, we see no evidence of either a democratic or a racial division of labor (203).

What purpose, then, does this depiction of servitude serve within the text as a whole? According to the Machiavellian narrative, servitude marks the inevitable decline of a republic that pursues greatness above security. Thus, perhaps we might read the emergence of a servant class on the island as indicating English decline due to patriarchal excess; because of tyrannical leadership, in other words, the English Pines are beginning to regress toward a more primitive and less participatory way of life. However, unlike the "mischief [that] began to rise" among the people a generation earlier (for which only John Phill, "the second son of the Negro-woman," is punished), Neville's English narrator neither judges servitude nor describes it as a sign of "the stronger seeking to oppress the weaker" (201–2). In light of Philippa's overdetermined role as a "negro slave" (a phrase that signifies her racialized status and productive function) and the Phills' repeated "explo[sion] from [Pine] society" (203), we might consider Neville's depiction of servitude not only as a classic example of political tyranny but also as indicating an emergent racial logic of slavery.[73] The development of a class hierarchy appears to reinforce the seemingly natural order that stands at *Isle*'s beginning: the original shipmaster's daughter, Sarah English, bestows her name upon George Pine's progeny; the "two maidservants," both of whom Pine marries, serve as reproductive breeding machines; and Philippa, the "slave," supplies scapegoats for punishment. Neville is silent about who serves as Philippa's counterpart at the end of the tale—that is, who takes Philippa's place as the "slave" who serves the other islanders—though it is consistently her descendants who remain simultaneously essential to and excluded from Pine society. In this way, the Phills embody a troubling contradiction for Neville and his readers. For in a parallel colonial reality, the bonds of servitude that *should* affect the English Pines (according to the Machiavellian trajectory for imperially ambitious republics) are being shifted onto a group of racial others who enable English expansion in the first place, thereby absorbing its consequences and alleviating its costs.

NEVILLE'S SOLUTION: TRIANGULATION AND DISPLACEMENT

By contextualizing *Isle*'s political agenda and racial subtext within an early modern trade network that links together African slavers, New World plantations, European merchants, and Indian Ocean markets, we see that African slavery is a crucial yet sublimated component of England's commercial aspirations and, consequently, of republican thinking. Moreover, the corrosive social disorder that plagues *Isle*'s racially diverse society—a disorder whose logic remains on the threshold of articulation in the text—is simultaneously a domestic problem for the English. Contrary to what *Isle*'s title and narrative structure imply, as they subordinate a realistic travelogue to a satirical tale of parochial politics, what occurs on the fictional island is by no means divorced from what takes place in the Calicut markets or on the detour to Madagascar. The apparent disconnect that appears, however, as Van Sloetten and his crew leave the English Pines behind indicates one way in which *Isle* conceives of England's global role and its attempt to reconcile a growing commercial capacity with complicity in the accompanying inequities of slavery.

By considering the role and function of Philippa and the Phills as key Pine islanders, *Isle* highlights two triangulated relationships. The first situates England in relation to the Dutch (as colonial rival and fellow republic) and to the East, while the second conflates the English and the Dutch to think about European mercantilism in terms of New World resources and Eastern markets. In each triangle, Africa is both the excluded term and the unexplained—yet crucially sustaining—space of labor. With this elision in mind, Van Sloetten's concluding query about how "time will make this Island known better to the world" contains a double resonance for Neville's English readers (212). Since colonial acquisition is a primary means by which England might expand and become better known, the question of what it will take for its colonies to become fitting specimens of Englishness, rather than bastions of savagery, is essential. But the real problem for the English, Van Sloetten suggests, is closer to home: while those "naked people" on the island "retai[n] a great part of the ingenuity and gallantry of the English nation ... they have not that happy means to express themselves" (212). They retain a capacity for English virtue but have lost their ability to practice or act upon it. As a politician who is invested in reversing this cultural aphasia, Neville uses *Isle* to consider how the English might protect and expand their national interests in a manner that is both profitable and virtuous. Even as he affirms in his later political work Van Sloetten's description of the "courteous, noble and debonair spirit, wherewith [the] English nation (especially those of the gentry) are very much indued" (192), Neville appears to recognize that modern Britain's future will be shaped not by attempts to recover its ancient constitution, to "fin[d] in the historical past a concrete moment of sovereign origins,"[74] or to "safeguard its liberty" at the expense of expansion, but through efforts to mitigate the nation's protracted moral decline by pursuing a commercial agenda that promises prosperity and promotes liberty for the era to come.[75]

At the same time, *Isle* suggests that while patriarchalism fosters political tyranny, mercantilism promotes inequities of a different sort. Indeed, the servitude and promiscuity riddling the fictional island represent more than just the degradation to which absolute monarchical government drives a nation. For these vices are tied to "the depraved nature of mankind" (201). And in their distinctly racialized form—represented by Philippa—they signify the broader consequences of a republican project that seeks to reconcile universal liberty with the grandezza of empire. In response to these dilemmas, *Isle* partially displaces the troublesome contradictions of mercantilism onto England's Dutch rivals and the Eastern empires that dominate the early modern global economy. By contrasting the English Pines' weakness with the commercial expertise of Van Sloetten and his crew, *Isle* reminds readers of the Dutch Republic's proven success at pursuing profitable expansion while maintaining a form of domestic liberty. At the same time, it partially displaces onto the Dutch responsibility for the inequitable byproducts of this lucrative circuit to and from the Indies, including slavery.[76] Moreover, by situating his imaginary island in a recognizable Indian Ocean trade network, Neville implicates in this global system the "eastern absolute princes" whose coveted "Eastern commodities" the Europeans chase.[77] To Neville's republican readers, the East remained a locus of fear and desire insofar as it represented both an infamous seat of absolutist tyranny and a source of those same "Asiatic luxuries" that drove ancient Rome to its demise and offered England a chance to avoid that fate by reconciling liberty and empire through commerce.[78] If, then, *Isle* satirizes English weakness, it also contrasts England to the mercenary Dutch Republic and the "despotical" East, recasting England as a competitive (albeit marginal) supplier in the global marketplace and as a potential (albeit once again monarchical) republic whose commercial activity may preclude or at least temper the potentially negative repercussions of expansion if carried out in a manner and society that is equitable, tolerant, and genuinely free.[79]

In the end, *The Isle of Pines* is not simply concerned with denouncing what transpires on the Pines' degenerate island, for it highlights, too, the significance of an intercontinental route along which the island serves as an incidental, even accidental, stop. In this sense, the tale offers a complex exploration of how, in George Pine's words, "our lusts g[i]ve us liberty"—not only at home, through patriarchal excess, but also in markets abroad (*Isle*, 198). In *Isle*, Neville juxtaposes a vision for English prosperity with a circumspect exploration of the costs and consequences of following the ancient Roman and early modern Dutch republics in pursuing Eastern commodities or, in the case of the Dutch, exporting a New World model of plantation slavery to the East. But by employing satirical argument and forward-looking fantasy, Neville demystifies patriarchal absolutism only to offer an equally vexed solution. For while he believes that England can and must "become ... an empire for liberty," he leaves open the possibility that the path to this empire may create new inequities and render liberty itself an ironic accomplishment.[80]

Neville's fable illustrates how England's virtuous liberty is both proven and destabilized by its global interests, insofar as trade solves the modern republican dilemma while stoking new and insatiable desires. As England's position in the world became more powerful, in subsequent decades, these desires continued to shape its national rhetoric of virtue. In his celebratory 1721 dedication to Harrington's *Oceana*, the freethinking philosopher John Toland would explicitly analogize Harrington's fictional republic to modern-day England, attributing London's status as "the largest, fairest, richest, and most popular city in the world" to "the inestimable blessings of Liberty, which has chosen her peculiar residence, and more eminently fixt her throne in this place."[81] At last, Toland suggests, England, now become Great Britain, has arrived at grandezza, with her population size, urban aesthetic, overflowing coffers, and global reputation serving as tangible evidence of a divinely endowed capacity for, and a faithful defense of, liberty. Rather than advocating a return to classical principles of civic virtue, as Harrington did, or proposing a measure of caution, like Neville, Toland celebrates a forward-looking fantasy of English imperium that elides the reality of Eastern strength. The next chapter further examines this powerful fantasy of English greatness by turning to the work of John Dryden. While Dryden approaches the problem of civic virtue from a different political perspective than Neville, he similarly fuels his dramatic depiction of virtue—focused, in response to the political crisis of his moment, on the heroic virtue of an individual ruler—with stereotypes of Eastern absolutism.

2

"STRIKING SAIL" IN SATIRE
Heroic Virtue and the Mughal Machiavelli in Dryden's *Aureng-Zebe*

I confess, I have only represented a practical virtue, mix'd with the Frailties and Imperfections of Human life.
—John Dryden, dedication to *Aureng-Zebe* (1675)

IN HIS DEDICATION TO *AURENG-ZEBE,* first performed in 1675 as the last heroic tragedy of his career, John Dryden deploys a maritime image of "striking sail" in order to develop an analogy of courtly virtue. Fools, he writes, though they pass as "solid men," give wit "no more Quarter, than a *Dutchman* would to an *English* Vessel in the *Indies;* they strike sail where they know they shall be master'd, and murder where they can with Safety."[1] Dryden uses his analogy to satirize widespread dissembling and disunity in Charles II's court as England's succession crisis was building in the 1670s. With his image of Dutch dissembling in contested seas, he also frames the tragic portrait of heroic virtue that follows in terms of England's carefully calculated interests in an ever-shifting global sphere of influence. To "strike sail," in nautical parlance, means to lower the topmast in salute, surrender, or submission. One strikes sail in response to rough seas or unfavorable winds—or, as Dryden suggests, to flatter superiors, as fools stifle "natural antipathy" to "fawn and crouch to Men... whom they cannot ruin." In the English court, Dryden observes, obsequity is commonplace while heroism is hard to spot. Even if he does see it at a distance, a "reasonable man... can hardly approach Greatness, but as a moated castle; he must first pass through the mud and filth with which it is encompassed," wading through knaves who take the "title of honest fellows" without having the character to back it up. In Dryden's analogy, though, the lowered sail is an ambiguous signifier, in part because naval weakness is situational: in different seas, murderers might be victims, and victims could be victors. In this sense, to strike sail may mean to give a mock salute, to at once acknowledge and undercut a known superior.

With its dual application, Dryden's maritime analogy reveals his broader concerns about the gap between a nation's virtuous principles and its external reputation. By comparing courtly fools masquerading as "solid men" to rival Dutch and English vessels in the Indies, Dryden highlights how the ubiquitous behavior of dissembling at court obscures important leadership qualities of "Greatness." Given Dryden's stated aim in writing *Aureng-Zebe*—to represent English interests by portraying "practical virtue"—and his controversial subject of a contemporary Mughal emperor, he frames this problem of dissembling as one of domestic policy with global resonance. Dryden stops short of suggesting that dissembling itself is unvirtuous, or that greatness and political deception cannot coexist. It is this complicated portrait of political virtue that this chapter unpacks. Through his literary experiment with Machiavellian politics on a global stage, Dryden invites readers to reconsider the role of pragmatic self-interest in discussions of heroic virtue and national greatness. In the process, he holds up a contemporary foreign empire as partially exemplifying admirable pragmatism; at the same time, however, he corrects for any potential threat to English exceptionalism by splitting the historical Aurangzeb's admirable qualities among his decidedly flawed dramatic characters.

In its focus on Dryden, this chapter picks up on the dilemma Neville and his fellow republicans had been working through—that of how to reconcile civic virtue and self-interest, domestically and abroad, during what Pocock has called England's "Machiavellian Moment." Dryden addresses this problem by representing the figure of an extraordinarily excellent ruler whose heroic virtue ensures the greatness of his state. I argue that Dryden's final heroic tragedy advocates for English interests not by affirming a specific or self-evident English virtue but by interrogating the meaning of heroic virtue itself. To the mind guided by reasonable interest, in the wake of the Commercial Revolution, virtue had become somewhat fluid and mobile—manifesting itself, for example, in the qualities of civility and courtesy required to lubricate trade and diplomatic relationships in Eastern courts.[2] Meanwhile, with England's ships striking sail at sea, fighting to prove the nation's greatness by gaining market share, the concept of heroic virtue itself was being reworked to signify economic affirmation of moral worth. Insofar as material prosperity remained a highly contingent enterprise, subject to the whims of fortune and fate, virtue defined in this way remained an unstable national ideal.

Following in a long tradition of Western dramatists who look outside of England—and specifically to Eastern princes—to find models of heroic virtue, Dryden adapts his source material on the historical Mughal ruler Aurangzeb in order to offer a timely model of political virtue for English viewers.[3] But insofar as his play portrays virtue in globally resonant and distinctly Machiavellian terms, rather than that of provincial politics, it is deliberately ambivalent toward Aurangzeb's rule rather than condemning Eastern despotism or encouraging English fantasies of colonizing India. In this regard, *Aureng-Zebe* underscores the ongoing deferral of English political virtue at a moment of national crisis. Given the historical Aurangzeb's reputation for so-called Machiavellian qualities of dissembling for personal gain, some critics have examined how Dryden displaces these historical qualities onto the fictional Aureng-Zebe's brother Morat, leaving Aurang-Zebe himself, altered and anglicized nearly beyond recognition, to play the part of a positive exemplar for England's Charles II.[4] Yet Dryden's keen recognition of England's global interests, alongside his commitment to represent "practical virtue," invites us to read his revisionary Mughal hero not as a rejection of Machiavellian pragmatism but as a fictional foray into the possibilities of realist statecraft. By reading Dryden's portrait of heroic virtue in light of what Sanjay Subrahmanyam has called "cultural commensurability" between early modern cultures as well as of recent reevaluations of Aurangzeb's legacy and Islamic political ethics, we can see how Dryden's salute to an Eastern exemplar signals his recognition that great nations need leaders who embody their complex interests *and* can shape-shift to fulfill them.[5] Rather than dismiss the historical Mughal's strategic dissembling as unvirtuous, Dryden maps Aurangzeb's heroic qualities onto different characters in the play (including his fictional love interest, Indamora) in order to consider the merits of pragmatism for Mughal and European politicians alike. At the same time, Dryden echoes Machiavelli himself in emphasizing how providential "fortune" both limits political agency and necessitates a turn to pragmatic politics. In staging this dilemma, Dryden anticipates Sir William Temple's prediction about the global revolutions of heroic virtue and leaves open the possibility that such virtue works differently in different times and places. In the process, he offers a slippery salute—playing the fool, so to speak—to those who practice virtue in culturally different ways.

DRYDEN'S MIDDLE WAY IN POLITICS AND POETRY

In his dedication, Dryden describes *Aureng-Zebe* as a testament to English "virtue," a term he reiterates forty-five times between the dedication and the play itself. "As a Poet," he writes, "'tis my Duty to give testimony to Virtue" by offering "images of virtue" that "Honour . . . my King, my Country, and my Friends." Dryden goes on to explain his subject and aims: first, he claims, the "Story [that follows is] *English*, and neither too far distant from the Present Age, nor too near"; second, he affirms that his dedicatee, a distinguished naval commander in the Second Anglo-Dutch War, embodies virtues of courage and bravery that showcase England's greatness abroad yet are sorely lacking at home, in court; and third, he clarifies, the real "Heroes of the Poem" are Charles and his brother. Dryden aims "to represent to [the Crown] images of their warlike predecessors; as *Achilles* is said to be rouz'd to

Glory, with the sight of the Combat before the ships." Of course, despite these claims, the play is not about an Englishman: Dryden's portrait of virtue (and of Charles's "warlike predecessors") comes in the guise of Aurangzeb, the reigning Mughal emperor from 1658 to 1707. Dryden's choice was historically motivated: the Mughals had weathered a succession crisis of their own that offered a parallel to what would soon culminate in England's Exclusion Crisis, as Country Party Whigs sought to keep Charles II's Catholic brother and heir, James II, from obtaining the English throne. The real Aurangzeb was one of four princes who had vied for his father's throne, and his tactics for resolving crisis and restabilizing the empire were instructive.

As scholars have noted, Dryden takes dramatic liberties with this history. His plot revolves around the competing claims of the aging emperor Shah Jahan and two of his usurping sons, Aureng-Zebe and Morat, to the "captive queen" Indamora. The play ends tragicomically, with Morat's reform and subsequent death, his faithful widow Melesinda's act of sati (in a fictional displacement of actual Hindu practice), the jealous Empress Nourmahal's own self-immolation, the happy marriage of Aureng-Zebe to Indamora, and the restoration of order to the troubled empire. Dryden's most radical and sustained revision is to the titular character of Aureng-Zebe, a historically Machiavellian middle son whom Dryden renders moderate, winsome, dutiful, and loyal—a hero who "sums [others'] virtues in himself alone" (*AZ*, 1.92). In the play, Aureng-Zebe is characterized by rivals and advisors alike as a prince "sway'd by no strong Passion." He is "temperate" and "weighed." To his many virtues he "adds the greatest, of a loyal son," which positions him to uphold his father's "sinking state." Meanwhile, as he faces factions and jealous rivals on every side, he laments that virtue itself has become "friendless and forsaken," and that virtue's "Indian air is deadly to thee grown" (98). The play emphasizes, in other words, how Aureng-Zebe possesses singular virtues that, in conjunction, contribute to and signify the *greatness* of his empire. Yet it also depicts him as torn between honor and love, filial loyalty and personal ambition; again and again, as Agra's governor Arimant puts it, "prudence interest weighs" in him (95). Meanwhile, Aureng-Zebe's brother Morat is dismissed as an unvirtuous son—a "Machiavel," as one critic puts it—whose martial skill is undermined by his unmoderated passion.[6]

Given the seemingly clear contrast between Morat's Machiavellian behavior and Aureng-Zebe's prudent temperance, critics have often focused on the latter's political virtue. In his introduction to the play, Frederick M. Link observes that Dryden alters the historical plot in order to render Aureng-Zebe recognizably virtuous: while "the distinguishing traits in [his immediate source] Bernier's portrait are cleverness and deviousness," Link argues, Dryden's virtuous hero "could not usurp the throne" without betraying his character—"his moral defects had to be eliminated" so that he could "be rewarded with private as well as public success, with love as well as power."[7] It is for this reason that Dryden invents a love interest for Aureng-Zebe in the figure of Indamora, whose name neatly reflects England's own desiring attitude toward India. According to Link, Dryden's protagonist "is endowed with virtue" to such an extent that the play "is not an exploration of character . . . but a play demonstrating the proper conduct of a prince" whom "we are to admire . . . as an ideal . . . paradigm of a governor."[8] Similarly, Michael Alssid calls the play "a 'panegyric'" meant "to establish lucidly and emphatically the poet's ultimate ideal, his 'mirror' of the great monarch whose private happiness is fused to the public good."[9]

By contrast, Derek Hughes calls Dryden's play a portrait of failed heroic virtue. Tracing Dryden's departure from various influencing models, particularly the "strict rules of moral virtue" of the French romances, Hughes argues that "Dryden's heroic plays portray the inevitable disparity between ideal aspiration and mundane reality."[10] "Against the Eden of the Platonics he set all the sad variety of an impaired and imperfect world," writes Hughes, portraying heroes who succumb to "indomitable and hopeless passion"; in this reading, Aureng-Zebe represents one of Dryden's "naïve idealists."[11] For Hughes and other critics who emphasize Dryden's unheroic heroes, the key question is whether Dryden seems to believe in the possibility of heroic virtue at all. The notion that true virtue is its own reward seems to clash with Aureng-Zebe's example, insofar as his "desire to make virtue profitable produces only a series of naïve and quickly frustrated strategems," as any "rewards are secured by pragmatic compromises that run counter to his plans."[12] To some extent, then, according to Hughes, what Dryden represents is a heroism that is not "strictly, technically, and pedantically virtuous."[13]

Despite such critical skepticism, however, Dryden's work stands out for its earnest and explicit interrogation of virtue discourse. As a politically minded playwright, Dryden was clearly concerned with bridging the conceptual gap between virtue and self-interest by portraying individuals who deploy their excellence in the service of public good. Arthur Kirsch identifies the problem of heroic virtue—namely, the notion that a hero must exhibit human frailty in order to be admired—as one Dryden had long wrestled with; but he also contends that *Aureng-Zebe* represents a significant shift in Dryden's oeuvre. In his earlier plays, Kirsch argues, Dryden attempted to portray the French Cornelian "concept of [heroic] *gloire* in a form that would be effective on the English stage."[14] In other words, Dryden was committed to a theatrical practice in which virtue and glory (loosely mapped, in contemporary terms, as morality and interest) are not at odds. *Aureng-Zebe* breaks this model, Kirsch argues, insofar as its protagonist fails to embody "the enormous capacity for passion of all Dryden's previous heroes"; Dryden's Aureng-Zebe is eminently temperate, while "all the marks of heroic virtue which he lacks are appropriated by Morat" and "stigmatized as unmistakable evidence of villainy." In "split[ting] the hero" and dividing his qualities between the two characters, Dryden "irrevocably undermines the heroic ethos which had animated his earlier plays."[15] With Aureng-Zebe as his ostensible hero, Kirsch contends, Dryden leaves us not with heroic glory but with private "virtues of love and piety," sentiment, and compassion—and, significantly, for Kirsch, these private virtues are accompanied by "no corresponding emphasis upon public responsibility."[16]

Kirsch raises a pertinent question: Does Dryden's final heroic drama represent his abdication of public responsibility, in a political and poetic sense? Dryden's lifelong political commitments would suggest otherwise. Throughout his long career as a public poet, he explored questions of heroic virtue—what it looks like and how to cultivate it— as a way of responding to political and moral crises in England. As

Joseph M. Levine notes, Dryden's poetic contemporaries Thomas Rymer and William Temple both believed "that the modern world had declined in its morality, that it had become less refined and virtuous," and that "the modern drama [had] failed in its form . . . [and] in its substance, that is to say in its representation of nature, manners, and morals."[17] They believed, too, that "it was still the obligation of the poet to try to purge and reform it," especially through "classical example."[18] While Dryden had yet to work out his own position on the ancients versus the moderns, he agreed with his peers on poetry's moral power and saw his political identity and poetic work as ineluctably linked. Despite his fascination with the past, Dryden was keenly aware of the need to adapt and respond to present political realities, and he believed in the power of poetry to inspire political action. Dryden's "middle way" mentality might be understood in light of the pressures he faced throughout his life, as a public poet and civil servant, to conform to the political party or individual then in power.[19] Yet, while Dryden cared deeply about cultivating civic virtue at a moment of national division, Levine makes clear that "Dryden's views and personality remain frustratingly elusive."[20] Like Neville before him, Dryden was trying to "reconcile ancient principles with modern circumstances."[21] Using satire to imagine and illustrate different ways of being in the world, Dryden portrays virtue as a tool for adapting to shifting political realities.

DRAMATIZING THE MACHIAVELLIAN CLASH BETWEEN "PRACTICAL VIRTUE" AND FORTUNA

Aureng-Zebe demonstrates Dryden's concern with the specific "political virtue" of prudence. Used in the Machiavellian sense, David B. Haley writes, "prudence, [or] practical wisdom, is rooted in praxis"—in other words, it is "the gift of finding out and expediting the common good," and it is a gift designed to "reaffirm our political freedom."[22] For Dryden, Haley argues, "the great secular experiment of the Interregnum" was a failed one, for it was a time of "false freedom" rather than true liberty.[23] Dryden's disillusionment extended to the restored monarchy; while he did not subscribe to republican ideals, he was nonetheless influenced by the Machiavellian ideas circulating in his political circles.[24] For instance, Niccolò Machiavelli had emphasized the significance of the *occasione,* an historical moment of upheaval, confusion, and instability that pitted *Fortuna* against the virtù of a ruler and his citizenry. As Haley notes, "The 1650s in England were the *occasione* for radical innovation in the historical constitution and, more radically still, in godly rule"; Dryden himself "considered the *occasione* of 1649 a crisis from which the nation was rescued by traditional authority and providence, not by civic *virtù* and prudence."[25]

In *The Prince,* his treatise on the nature of political power, Machiavelli does not eschew political virtue so much as he reimagines it for Italy's moment of chaotic disunity. Keenly aware that "the temper of the multitude is fickle," Machiavelli argues "that while it is easy to persuade them of a thing, it is hard to fix them in that persuasion" without resorting—or being willing to resort—to "force."[26] In "consider[ing] what ought to be the conduct and bearing of a Prince in relation to his subjects and friends," he is a pragmatist and realist, far more interested in describing "the real truth of things" than in entertaining "an imaginary view of them" (39–40). Machiavelli goes on to describe what would become his notorious brand of political virtue, arguing that "the manner in which we live, and that in which we ought to live, are things so wide asunder," that "any one who would act up to a perfect standard of goodness in everything, must be ruined among so many who are not good" (40). Realistically speaking, Machiavelli continues, "it is impossible for [a Prince] to possess or constantly practice" all of the "qualities that are reckoned good" (e.g., generosity, courage, chastity, courtesy, devout belief), "the conditions of human nature not allowing it" (40). For this reason, he explains, the prince "will find that there may be a line of conduct having the *appearance of virtue,* to follow which would be his ruin, and that there may be another course having the appearance of vice, by following which his safety and well-being are secured" (40, emphasis added). With this reality in mind, he argues, "it is essential, therefore, for a Prince who desires to maintain his position, to have *learned how to be other than good,* and to use or not to use his goodness as necessity requires" (40, emphasis added).

Machiavelli articulates the collective and national stakes of such princely pragmatism, as he represents his divided Italy as "our country, left almost without life, [who] still waits to know who it is that is to heal her bruises" (69). It is clear to Machiavelli that nations who want to be great need leaders who demonstrate their virtue through *prudent* choices, rather than "qualities that are reckoned good" (40). The key, according to Machiavelli, is for the prince to understand what each moment of crisis requires of him, so that he can combat the powerful but not all-encompassing force of "Fortune, who displays her might where there is no organized strength to resist her, and directs her onset where she knows that there is neither barrier nor embankment to confine her.... A Prince who rests wholly on Fortune is ruined when she changes," he contends, so the mark of prudence is knowing "how to adapt... to these changes" (66–67). Machiavelli deploys biblical metaphors at the end of his treatise to argue that the prince who prudently adapts to "the character of the times" and the changing forces of Fortune will, ideally, work in conjunction with Providence to accomplish his task of effecting unity for the glory of the nation. It is in the prudent prince's attitude and actions, he believes, that "we see... extraordinary and unexampled proofs of Divine favour" (69). Just as it was for Moses, he enthuses, "the sea has been divided; the cloud has attended you on your way; the rock has flowed with water; the manna has rained from heaven; everything has concurred to promote your greatness" (69). Given such clear signs of divine aid and providential agency, Machiavelli concludes, "what remains to be done must be done by you; since in order not to deprive us of our free will and such share of glory as belongs to us, God will not do everything himself" (69). In sum, human excellence is requisite but not sufficient for rulers who aim to shore up and ensure their nation's greatness.

Dryden's play illustrates Machiavelli's argument that a ruler's political pragmatism allows him to resist the inexorable force of Fortune—and it is this Machiavellian strain in *Aureng-Zebe*, I argue, that complicates readings of the play that focus on whether Aureng-Zebe functions as Dryden's ideal monarch. As Aureng-Zebe learns, through Indamora, how to reconcile public and private forms of virtuous interest, we see that political excellence manifests itself as the cultivated ability to read others properly, to adjust to fluctuating circumstances, and to make appropriate compromises. Meanwhile, Dryden's frequent references to "Fortune," "Fate," and "Heaven" evoke another aspect of Machiavellian pragmatism.[27] According to Machiavelli, "heaven's decrees" oppose both the interests *and* the prudence of men. For Machiavelli, in other words, a character's active "virtue," or virtuous agency, is situational rather than fixed; thus, it is always a temporary and uncertain quality. This opposition between human agency and the impersonal force of Fortune is the very problem Machiavelli seeks to solve by emphasizing a ruler's pragmatic virtù. Similarly, in Dryden's play, the rhetoric of fortune renders human claims to virtue unstable, not only at the level of plot but also at that of English-Mughal interactions. In the play, the rhetoric of virtue serves not only to signal human excellence in action but also to signify the unearned rewards of fortune. It is this second, more passive manifestation of virtue that compensates for Aureng-Zebe's personal failures. In the end, it is neither Aureng-Zebe's innate virtue nor Morat's innate villainy that triumph; instead of human action, it is nebulous Fortune—Machiavelli's divine "decrees"—that favors Aureng-Zebe and allows him to possess Indamora and all she represents.

On one level, Dryden defines virtue as an individual recognition and fulfillment of one's role and responsibility, manifested through ongoing work to resist (or at least properly modulate) one's own passions and interests. Virtue, in this sense, is represented as human action driven by a will to fulfill one's public duties over and against any personal interests that would get in the way. For instance, the Emperor blames his decline in power on his "frailer Virtue," an abdication of responsibility that allows him to pursue Indamora, betray his son, and abandon his throne. He refers to "Virtue" as one of several strategic tools that, along with "disdain [and] despair," he "oft ha[s] tri'd" in his dealings with others (*AZ*, 1.96)—yet it is a tool that he claims proves impotent in the face of his stronger desire, which causes him to "swerv[e]" from virtue's path

(2.113). The Emperor personifies virtue to accentuate its frailty, crying, "I feel my Virtue struggling in my Soul, / But stronger Passion does its pow'r controul" (3.124). As Arimant puts it, the Emperor's virtue is "opprest," though "still alive" (1.96). Arimant collapses "Virtue" into a list alongside "Prudence" and its antithesis of "Interest," admitting that even his own "Virtue, Prudence, Honour, Interest, all / . . . fall" before "Beauty, [which] like Ice, our footing does betray" (2.103). Aureng-Zebe, by contrast, has a "Strong Virtue" that "struggles still" yet "Exerts itself, and then throws off the Ill" (1.101). Aureng-Zebe's strength and struggle are equally indicative of his moral state. When Arimant observes that "prudence interest weighs" in the eminently virtuous prince, he refers to how Aureng-Zebe balances his competing responsibilities as private lover to Indamora and public heir to the emperor's throne. However, Aureng-Zebe's "prudence" is situational; it reflects his particular role as son and subject, a role in relation to which filial loyalty is the "greatest" virtue of all (1.91). But interest, too, is situational: Aureng-Zebe's personal interest in Indamora directly flies against his father's personal interests, leading the emperor to make unwise public demands. Arimant's phrasing thus opposes two situational terms to each other; neither filial "prudence" nor personal "interest" is fixed. As Aureng-Zebe learns to reconcile these competing manifestations of virtue within himself, he must also learn to read and interpret others' claims to virtue as similarly situational.

If the Emperor finds his reserves of "virtue" impotent and "frail," Dryden's female characters wrestle with virtue's illegibility, insofar as their visible virtue—in the form of physical chastity—is misread as manipulation. When Nourmahal cries foul on her husband's infidelity and insists that her "known Virtue is from Scandal free," the Emperor responds by mocking her "pompous Chastity." Angered at her true accusations, he cries that "such Virtue is the Plague of human Life," a "shrill sound of Virtue" rather than the thing itself (2.108–9). In contrast to the outspoken, ambitious, and openly self-interested Nourmahal, Melesinda responds to her own husband Morat's infidelity by attempting to demonstrate what she calls a virtue more than "vulgar"—that is, more than a "shrill sound" (5.166). While any woman can maintain "pompous

Chastity," Melesinda loyally loves in the face of rejection, throwing herself on her cruel husband's pyre in an act of virtuous self-sacrifice. In what Balachandra Rajan has called a "parody" of Melesinda's virtuous act, the play ends with Nourmahal, too, burning up in passion.[28] Underscoring his skepticism about traditional meanings of virtue, however, Dryden frames such embodied female chastity as one imperfect form of virtue among others. Bridget Orr points out how Dryden's representations of sati reveal his ambivalence: if the heroic play assumes "a broad human equivalence between the noble representatives of civil nations," here we are "challenged by a more powerful sense of ethnic difference."[29] Yet Dryden's portrayal of this foreign custom is more than mere showcasing of ethnic difference; sati, according to Dryden, is a powerful but misunderstood expression of virtuous action. In the play, Melesinda and Nourmahal are doubly punished—first, for men's infidelity, and second, for their own naïveté in believing their expressions of virtue to be legible markers of feminine value.

Given his aim to show "images of virtue" befitting "the honour of [England]," Dryden realizes that his critics may find fault with this scene of sati. He reassures readers by emphasizing that what looks like virtue in one context may take a different form at home: "Those Indian wives are loving fools," he writes in his dedication, "and may do well to keep themselves in their own Country, or, at least, to keep Company with the *Arria's* and *Portia's* of old Rome." By contrast, he reiterates, "some of *our* ladies know better things" (emphasis added). But what are these better things? Rather than fixed, innate qualities, the most legible and efficacious form of virtue seems to be the prudential ability to hold competing values in tension—and specifically, the ability to balance self-sacrifice with calculated interest. Of the women in the play, it is Indamora who insists that inner virtue and external fame can work together seamlessly. At first, Indamora's virtue is also misread by the one whose opinion matters most, as Aureng-Zebe accusingly claims that her "Virtue [has] turn'd Vice, and [her] Faith inconstancy" (*AZ*, 1.99). Yet Indamora escapes the fire that consumes the other women, in part because she has learned to think of virtue not as a performance of chastity but as a pragmatic political tool. Critics like John A. Vance have called Indamora "the moral force behind the play."[30] And yet her moral vision often manifests itself through her deliberate dissembling; her virtue plays out in acts of diplomacy and interpersonal savvy, rather than mere bodily loyalty. When Arimant accuses her of being "cruel and unjust," saying, "Your Empire you to Tyranny pursue," Indamora replies, "Should not I my own advantage see?" (3.116). She also calls out Aureng-Zebe for misreading her character, eventually helping him to see how her apparent dissembling serves as a sign of the way she uses her ability to read others in order to show her faithfulness to him. Morat, Arimant, and the Emperor also learn from Indamora how to reframe their interests in more pragmatic and public-oriented ways. She teaches them not that personal interest is incompatible with traditional displays of virtue but that one must dissemble, at times, in order to reconcile one's virtuous persona with individual and collective interests.

At one point, in a moment of anger at Aureng-Zebe for his jealousy and mistrust of her virtue, Indamora prepares to walk away, saying, "Now, with full sails, into the Port I move [alone!],/And safely can unlade my Breast of Love;/Quiet and calm" (4.146).[31] To love him, she suggests, would mean surrendering her interest, since returning to their relationship may require her to "tempt the second hazard of a wreck." In this moment of Indamora's careful calculation, Aureng-Zebe's fortunes are uncertain—however, just lines later, she "strikes sail," forgives him, and returns to his arms. This moment is one of several where Dryden represents his characters as ships to be guided in relational seas, calm or tempestuous, political or amorous. When Aureng-Zebe, whose "Virtues shine too bright" for his "frailer" father to bear, faces his father's jealousy, he likens himself to a ship who seeks in Indamora—futilely, at first—a "calm harbor" for his "tempest-beaten soul" (1.97–98). She is the prize that he desires and that, steered rightly, he achieves. Later, Aureng-Zebe's reformed brother Morat admits to Indamora that, misdirected in his own pursuit of power, he has "Sail'd farther than the Coast, but mis'd my Way." For Morat, arrival at port means achieving the "Fame, [he] in vain ... courted long" (5.51). But Indamora chides him for his "Lust of Pow'r," implying that his desire for fame is too tainted by interest and insisting that "true Renown is still with Virtue join'd." Morat professes a change of heart, saying, "You show me some[thing] I ne'er learnt before." With his dying breath he thanks her, saying, "Now you have giv'n me Virtue for my Guide." Yet Morat admits that his readiness to "Command... By Virtue" is a "distant Prospect of a Shore,/Doubtful in Mists"—and so it is Aureng-Zebe, not he, who will take the ruling role (5.151). According to Morat's use of the maritime metaphor, the proper captain of the state ship is not a person, but what Morat calls the "Guide" of Virtue, working alongside a "ballast" of Honor. By personifying "Virtue" as a political agent, in this scene, Dryden represents the political virtue of a leader not as a fixed set of qualities but as a practiced ability to read situations rightly and balance, without renouncing, competing interests—as Aureng-Zebe does, as Indamora counsels Morat to do, and as she admirably attempts to do herself. None of the characters embody such virtue perfectly, but Dryden splits his portrayal of political pragmatism among them: Morat acts boldly upon his convictions; Indamora is a keen and careful reader of others; and Aureng-Zebe is the one who is loved by the people and thus able to bridge competing value systems for the good of the community.

Together, Dryden's characters of Morat, Indamora, and Aureng-Zebe exemplify how the play wrestles with the Machiavellian clash between virtuous agency and the impersonal force of fortune. Arimant further emphasizes the opposition between virtue and fortune *and* the stakes of India's succession crisis when he cries, "What Heav'n decrees, no Prudence can prevent" (1.90). "Fortune," he claims, "has in her hand the greatest stake" in "the Empire of the East" (1.89). At various junctures of Aureng-Zebe's battle for control of his father's empire, the language of fortune reinforces that the outcome of the battle has less to do with the heroic virtue of an individual ruler and more to do with how individual acts reveal broader, unpredictable forces beyond human control. Indamora laments that fortune is not on her side, exclaiming that, since "Sullen Planets at my Birth did shine" and "threaten every Fortune mixt with mine.... Who knows what adverse Fortune may befal?" (1.99). Indamora hopes Melesinda will find her own freedom, but knows that can only happen "if Heav'n be just, and be to Virtue kind" (3.119). Shortly thereafter, Nourmahal's maidservant Zayda gives credit to "Fortune" for having "from Morat this day remov'd / The greatest Rival," even though Aureng-Zebe has a "virtue [which] through so dark a cloud can shine" (3.125). And Arimant describes the situation between Aureng-Zebe and Morat thus: "Fortune seems weary grown of *Aureng-Zebe,* / While to her new made Favourite, *Morat,* / Her lavish hand is wastfully profuse" (3.120). Meanwhile, Aureng-Zebe himself uses the language of fate to explain his discouragement in battle, saying,

> How vain is Virtue which directs our ways
> Through certain danger, to uncertain praise!
> Barren and aery name! thee Fortune flies.
> . . . .
> The World is made for the bold impious man;
> Who stops at nothing, seizes all he can. (2.115)

Each of Dryden's characters must wrestle with seeing this opposition of virtue and fate as a clash of their own agency with situational factors beyond their control or knowledge. As they use virtue claims to represent acts that are ultimately determined and even thwarted by circumstance, those claims further undermine any stable definition of virtue as human excellence or chastity. Even Indamora, seeking to help Morat recognize that "all greatness is in Virtue understood," tells him:

> There's joy when to wild will you Laws prescribe,
> When you bid Fortune carry back her Bribe:
> A joy, which none but greatest minds can taste;
> A fame, which will to endless Ages last. (5.150)

Pitting fortune against virtue, Indamora indicates to Morat that, insofar as he reforms into a virtuous man, he can fight fortune with his own agency. She hopes to make him believe that rational "laws" (and lawmakers) can establish virtue in the empire, over the "wild will" of immoderate individuals who are carried away by "Fortune" and "her [corrupting] bribe." But in this moment Indamora minimizes a truth she elsewhere seems to grasp: in fact, fortune does not work in the way she describes, and "fame" is not necessarily—or even usually—"endless." Earlier conversations in the play reinforce that fortune is fickle and unpredictable; it does not answer to human goodness or laws, but rather confounds them, thus demanding ingenuity, dissembling, and strategic pragmatism on the part of any would-be political hero.

Dryden diverges from Machiavellian discourse by distinguishing fortune from Protestant providence, and it is in part this distinction which allows him to make his claim that *Aureng-Zebe* illustrates a distinctly English virtue. Dryden does not take the "secular perspective of Machiavelli and Harrington, in which providence is merely immanent," Haley notes; rather, from Dryden's perspective, "providence shows directly its care for the nation."[32] Machiavelli himself incorporates the language of providence into his discussion of Fortuna. However, as Haley argues, Dryden's "real interest lay in a broader mimesis of providence, whose special care England had been."[33] In this regard, insofar as the impact of Fortuna extends beyond the fate of an individual to the fame of a nation, "Dryden's prudential heroes . . . are not victors in a contest with Fortuna" but rather "the beneficiaries of a divine dispensation."[34] It is his belief in this "divine dispensation" that allows Dryden to both acknowledge and correct for political commensurability between England and the Mughal Empire, as he looks ahead to England's future. But several questions remain. If Fortuna does shape Aureng-Zebe's ability to practice heroic virtue, how exactly does Dryden fulfill his dedicatory promises "to give testimony to Virtue" for English readers? In other words, what is the virtuous role of dutiful English rulers and citizens? Moreover, if heroic virtue ends up looking a good deal like Machiavellian virtù, in the play, in what sense does situationally defined heroism fit English expectations and ambition? What is it that sets English virtue apart, particularly if the task of reconciling older aristocratic honor codes with newer commercial virtues was facing would-be rulers across the early modern world, not just in England or Europe? Finally, given that the historical Aurangzeb was also navigating new notions of virtue—striving to reconcile martial with mercantile values and to rule in such a way that united his own religious and secular commitments, as well as his diverse Muslim and Hindu constituencies—what exactly is "English" about Dryden's vision of political virtue?

A closer look at how the Machiavellian and Mughal contexts for Dryden's play intersect will provide a more nuanced lens for understanding Aureng-Zebe's supposedly "failed" virtue. Until recently, many critics considered Dryden's dramatic representations of virtue in terms of his contributions to heroic drama, without considering the global contexts for his national commitments. But Dryden follows Neville and others in representing England's distinctive qualities in terms of shifting global dynamics—specifically, in *Aureng-Zebe*, the relationships between England, its European rivals (especially France and the Netherlands), and an infamous Mughal emperor. Dryden was keenly aware of England's global contexts, recognizing that English manifestations of political virtue were contingent on fluctuating global dynamics, both in terms of art (such as French poetics) and economic interests (such as superior Dutch ships at sea).[35] Shawn Lisa Maurer and Nandini Bhattacharya argue that *Aureng-Zebe* responds to these contexts by featuring an emergent *feminized* virtue appropriate for a newly mercantile and middle-class milieu. For example, Maurer argues that we see in the play a model of virtue that is more mercantile than martial, as "Aureng-Zebe, and subsequently the emperor, enact a code of masculinity that resolutely opposes traditionally warlike, antagonistic, indeed aristocratic attitudes toward both familial and male homosocial relations."[36] Bhattacharya contends, meanwhile, that to the extent Aureng-Zebe embodies "essentially ideal feminine virtues," he is "emasculat[ed]" in the service of Dryden's "attempt to portray a nonwestern culture as essentially more fragile and vulnerable" than an England intent on colonial expansion.[37] But to what extent does the fictional Aureng-Zebe's "feminized" virtue depend upon the Mughal landscape and its historical actors? Moreover, to what extent is Dryden's depiction of "English" virtue similar to or different from Mughal notions of political virtue? Like Neville, Dryden operated in a sphere of political reality and was attuned to the interplay of individual and national virtue on a global stage. He was a poet of "political reflexivity," who thought carefully about statecraft in its different contexts, from absolutist governments to patriarchal and constitutional monarchies.[38] As Dryden's characters show, political pragmatism requires compromises demanded by context—in other words, it requires a willingness to strike sail to superior challengers. Such pragmatism was a political skill at which the historical Aurangzeb excelled. It was also a recognizable aspect of realist statecraft, an approach to politics whose virtues were being debated by early modern European and Asian states alike. It is to this broader discourse I turn next.

GLOBAL STATECRAFT AND A MIRROR FOR PRINCES: BERNIER'S MUGHAL MACHIAVELLI

Much has been written about Dryden's adaptation of Mughal history for English purposes. The best postcolonial readings, as Ros Ballaster puts it, recognize the play's "ideological work . . . in turning India into a territory for English consumption, but also the ambivalence which haunts a play that takes events from recent history in a distant part of the globe and turns them into an allegory" for England.[39] Balachandra Rajan, for example, has argued that Dryden's choices to alter the plot and anglicize his hero demonstrate disrespect for Mughal history. As a complete inversion of his Mughal counterpart, the fictional Aureng-Zebe serves as an antihero and a negative example for English monarchs. Meanwhile, Rajan contends, Aureng-Zebe's "captive bride" Indamora is aptly named, as his object of desire aligns with England's own: the play reflects imperial lusts and ambitions only partially fulfilled by East India Company (EIC) ships loading calicos and unloading bullion in India's bustling ports.[40] Nonetheless, Mita Choudhury contends, "interpretations of [the play] as either an 'example' or a 'parallel' would be problematic because, whether Dryden understood it or not, contemporary English politics was in no way similar to the politics of the Mughal period in India."[41]

Despite the lack of direct parallels, *Aureng-Zebe* includes aspects of commensurability that deserve parsing. While Dryden certainly does not portray Aurangzeb as a straightforward model for Charles (positive or negative), neither does he "recast Aurangzeb as an embodiment of a kind of universal heroic virtue," as Choudhury suggests.[42] Indeed, Dryden's play presents a more complicated picture of England's relationship with India than binary readings of West and East allow. One reason for this complexity is Dryden's own appreciation for cultural difference. David Bruce Kramer argues in *The Imperial Dryden: The Poetics of Appropriation in Seventeenth-Century England* that even as "Dryden often invokes, restates, and reworks the myth of English invincibility, both poetic and military," he is also "aware of the relative strengths of [other] countries and writers" and "acutely conscious of the means and forms by which countries—and poets—measure their strength."[43] In this regard, Dryden's plays function as "fables of foreign wealth" to demonstrate how other "cultures may produce individuals who possess virtues their conquerors lack."[44] As Dryden "considers what types of knowledge might be peculiar to other cultures, he often represents pagan religions not as fraudulent shames ... but as a valid but lesser means of knowing"—and, in this sense, Kramer suggests, "Dryden's representations of the clash of cultures may be read not only as a way of discussing his views of gaining power over others, but as a means of considering the mixed virtues of the losing side and in what consists the loser's wealth."[45] Dryden's ability to hold multiple perspectives in tension underscores his remarkable ability to see and represent "potential human greatness in the enemy" on a different side of a partisan conflict.[46]

Reading Dryden's portrayal of India in light of his dedicatory emphasis on "practical virtue" invites us to consider how his shifting definition of heroic virtue was shaped by global relationships that were also in flux. Dryden does indeed modify his historical source beyond recognition—perhaps, as Rajan and others suggest, because he is looking ahead to a world he hopes will be dominated by Britain's navy and EIC. Yet in the uncertainty of his own moment, he exhibits curiosity about how an infamous ruler from elsewhere handles tricky political situations and defines heroic virtue. Geoffrey C. Gunn has argued that "Asian forms of governance offered a sounding board for European Enlightenment thinkers"—and indeed, with his choice of a complex and controversial dramatic subject, Dryden largely avoids acquiescing to negative "caricatures of Islamic polities."[47] Contextualizing his play in light of contemporary Mughal India's *strength*—not just in economic or military terms but also in terms of political ethics—provides a different framework for understanding how his fictional hero embodies heroic virtue on the English stage.[48] Rather than eliminating the historical Aurangzeb's ostensibly *unvirtuous* Machiavellian qualities in order to refigure the Mughal hero for an English audience, Dryden's specific choice of historical figure draws into focus a transnational interest in Machiavellian pragmatism *as* a form of heroic virtue—not a particularly English form, per se, but a form with potential to be adapted for English purposes.

The historical Aurangzeb—whose legacy remains controversial to this day—exemplified how the political act of striking sail could be deployed to achieve strategic alliances between rivals. While in Dryden's account the rival factions are familial, the historical ruler was known, too, for navigating competing religious and state interests and Muslim and Hindu allegiances. In her recent reassessment of Aurangzeb's legacy, Audrey Truschke argues that, "for Aurangzeb, morality fell well within state authority and the broader duties of a king to safeguard the welfare of those he ruled."[49] John Richards adds that the historical Aurangzeb was keenly aware of his own role in global affairs: his religious "[zeal] was tempered by highly developed political and diplomatic instincts" and respect for "secular trend[s] ... of economic growth and vitality."[50] It was his ability to hold personal religious fanaticism and political savvy in productive tension that set him apart from his rivals. It was also this tension that contributed to Aurangzeb's legacy as a so-called Machiavellian ruler, as Dryden knew from his primary source, the French physician François Bernier, who spent several years in the employ and company of the Mughal court. While Peter Craft contends that "throughout Bernier's history, Aurangzeb's Machiavellian strategies are exposed and condemned," Bernier in fact seems somewhat sympathetic to the complexity of the Mughal court he visited and to Aurangzeb's rationale for his governing priorities and behaviors.[51]

On one hand, Bernier admired Aurangzeb's unique qualities; on the other, he believed that these qualities were not appropriate for French (or other European) rulers and their citizens. He explains in his *History of the Late Revolution of the Empire of the Great Mogul* that Aurangzeb possessed two key qualities that elevated him above his brothers and best qualified him to rule: first, Bernier writes, he is "much more judicious, understanding the world very well"; and, second, given that he is "reserved, crafty, and exceedingly versed in dissembling," he knows best how to look out for "his interest."[52] Bernier affirms that Aurangzeb's skill at dissembling (a skill in which he surpassed his also artful brothers) was crucial to his successful reign. Bernier writes, "so true 'tis, that *he who knows not to Dissemble, knows not how to Reign*," recognizing that only through such masterful dissembling was Aurangzeb able to take and maintain control of his father's kingdom (34). Bernier goes on to partly justify Aurangzeb's behavior to his French readers, suggesting that while the Mughal's Machiavellian tactics appear to violate what Bernier sees as distinctly *European* customs, he nonetheless demonstrates leadership qualities that are important for aspiring empires like France to note. In his conclusion to the *History*, Bernier makes this prediction about his readers:

> Most of those, who shall have read my History, will judge the ways, taken by Aureng-Zebe, for getting the Empire, very violent and horrid. I pretend not at all to plead for him, but desire only, that before he be altogether condemned, reflexion be made on that unhappy custome of this state, which leaving the succession of the crown undecided, for want of good laws, settling it, as amongst us, upon the eldest son, exposeth it to the conquest of the strongest, and the most fortunate, subjecting at the same time all the princes born in the Royal Family, by the condition of their birth, to the cruel necessity either to overcome, or to reign by destroying all the rest, for the assurance of their power and life, or to perish themselves, for the security of that of others.... I am perswaded, that those who shall a little weigh this whole history, will not take Aureng-Zebe, for a barbarian, but for a great and rare genius, a great states man, and a great king. (285–86)

Notably, Bernier defines heroic virtue situationally—that is, he acknowledges that Aurangzeb behaves in "violent and horrid" ways precisely *because* such behavior is necessary, due to an "unhappy custome" of eschewing certain "good laws" and thereby reducing the stability of the kingdom to a game of survival of the fittest. However, Bernier's superlative praise for Aurangzeb extends beyond his moment of victory in the succession to his later reign—he is not only the "strongest, and the most fortunate" of his brother princes but also "a great and rare genius ... states man, and ... king." With such descriptors Bernier separates the greatness of Aurangzeb as a "rare" individual from the systematic decay of Asiatic states that he takes as the broader topic (and title) of his work.

Bernier draws several lessons from this history, both about the endless wealth of the Indies as well as appreciation for his own nation, and the extent to which France's fortunes depend upon the individual at its helm. He writes, "'Tis in the Indies ... where I learned the felicity of France, and how much this kingdom is obliged to your cares" (289). After all, the wealth of Aurangzeb is in part an illusion and mirage, "yet should I not believe him in effect and truly so rich, as the world rings of him" (320). The problem with the Mughal Empire, for Bernier, comes down to a lack of proper distribution of excessive wealth and property, which, he believes, is "the main foundation of whatever is regular and good in the world" (346). He notes that "vast estates" and towns alike "go so wretchedly and palpably to ruine" (329); the arts fail to flourish (330); and "traffick languishes" (332), at least from the trade-minded perspectives of those in France, England, and Holland. Bernier extends his judgment of the Mughal Empire to its neighboring nations, asserting that, while there are some distinctions between Asian states, these differences are "really but a slight matter; those three states of Turky, Persia and Indostan, for as much as they have all three taken away the *Meum* and *Tuum* as to land and propriety of possessions ... cannot but very near resemble one another: they have the same defect, they must at last, sooner or later, needs fall into the same inconveniences, which are the necessary consequences of it, *viz.* tyranny, ruine and desolation" (336). Bernier ties together these disparate examples by reasserting European ideas about property: "Far be it therefore," he writes, "that our monarchs of Europe should thus be proprietors of all the lands, which their subjects possess. Their [European] kingdoms would be very far from being so well cultivated and peopled, so well built, so rich, so polite and flourishing as we see them" if they followed the example of Aurangzeb or his fellow rulers (336). In fact, if Europe follows in the footsteps of "states" such as "Turky, Persia, and Indostan," Bernier continues, "there would soon be kings of deserts and solitudes of beggars and barbarians ... because they [who] will have all, at last lose all, and who, because they will make themselves too rich, at length find themselves without riches, or, at least, very far from that, which they covet after, out of their blind ambition and passion of being more absolute than the laws of God and Nature do permit" (345). Recognizing that he is making a future prediction rather than describing a present reality, Bernier openly defers the moment when his prediction will come true, "confess[ing] that *we are not like to see in our days that total ruine and destruction of this Empire, we are speaking of* ... because it hath neighbors" that are not powerful enough to rise up and resist (341, emphasis added). According to Bernier, it is the weakness of other, "neighbor[ing]" empires that props up Mughal strength for the foreseeable present.

In the 1670s, English ambivalence toward the Mughal ruler and his policies paralleled Bernier's complicated portrait of Aurangzeb. In one respect, the English could agree with Bernier that Mughal political structure was not well suited for longevity. In prefatory remarks to a 1671 English edition of Bernier's *History*, Bernier's self-described "English interpreter" echoes the author in pinpointing specific flaws in imperial policy that render the Mughal emperor unable to subjugate and unify his disparate constituents. The translator, Henry Oldenburg, a German-born secretary for London's Royal Society, also reiterates Bernier's peeved description of how the wealthy Mughals keep bullion out of global circulation, noting that there are "vast quantities of gold and silver, circulated through the world, and conveyed into Indostan, and there swallow'd up, as in an abyss" (xi).[53] However, he echoes Bernier's praise for Aurangzeb, commenting on the "depth of policy and craft ... used by Aureng-Zebe, the heros [*sic*] in this history" (viii) and noting the subservience of various "neighbors of the empire of Mogol"—including not only "the Usbec-Tartars" but also "the Dutch of Suratte"—who "demeaned themselves towards the new emperor" for the purpose of "securing and improving their trade" (ix). Oldenburg also extols "Aureng-Zebe's singular Prudence, and indefatigable pains in managing the Government himself" (ix) and comments on how "generously Aureng-Zebe recompensed those, that had faithfully served him in these revolutions" (x).

Dryden himself echoes the ambivalence expressed by Bernier and his translator. As Peter Craft has pointed out, Dryden's representation of Aurangzeb was motivated by both national and personal interests, given that he needed to avoid jeopardizing his patron Charles II's trade interests with the Mughal emperor.[54] Indeed, the historical Aurangzeb was more than a political genius who knew when and how to strike sail to others; he was also a trade partner for England and a figure worth striking sail *to*. Returning to Dryden's prefatory image: English ships were striking sail, so to speak, not only to the Dutch in the Far East but also to Mughal armies closer to home. After a 1635 treaty with Portugal and ongoing negotiations with Mughal officials, England's East India Company (EIC) was able to establish itself in Surat, which served as a hub for the textile trade. The EIC faced "a period of contraction and difficulty" between the 1620s and 1660s, as trade was disrupted by the Civil Wars and "Dutch competition . . . became increasingly formidable."[55] By the 1670s, after trade had resumed and the EIC regained Crown support, England's India trade had surpassed that of the Dutch, who had turned their sights to the Far East.[56] But the EIC's "relations [with the Mughals] were particularly tense in 1674," Bridget Orr explains, and "the internal dynamics of India's ruling dynasty were of immediate concern to the English as the EIC was expanding its operations" there.[57] Even as late as 1688, P. J. Marshall points out, the Mughals retaliated against the English, who "waged war against the Mughal empire in 1688–89 by seizing ships off western India, only to have the Surat factory closed and Bombay blockaded."[58] Marshall goes on to note that the EIC "liked to contrast their own [practices] with the violent coercion and enforced monopolies allegedly practiced by the Portuguese and the Dutch"; what kept them from military action, however, "was not any principled rejection of war as an instrument of trade . . . but a realistic calculation of costs and benefits."[59] Pragmatic policy was couched in moral language, but, in reality, England was striking sail to the Mughals for calculated purposes of economic and political gain.

Largely missing from the critical conversation on Dryden's adaptation of Mughal history is an exploration of how such political realism, and the recognition that heroic virtue includes "great" acts of pragmatic "prudence," informed shifting discourses of political virtue and ethical governance well beyond England. The historical Aurangzeb may have been following Mughal custom to some extent, as Bernier notes, but he was also navigating broader political and economic shifts. Bernier documents the workings of a complex and cosmopolitan court, recognizing how Aurangzeb attempted to continue—and, in some cases, depart from—his predecessors' commitment to integrating subjects from different cultural and religious backgrounds into a unified empire. While Aurangzeb is known for his newfound, and sometimes brutal, commitment to Islamic piety, historians have contended that his motivation was largely political rather than religious. In his work on the Mughals' development of a political culture that practiced "strategies of cultural accommodation in the lands where they spread their faith and established their power," Muzaffar Alam argues that these "strategies [were not] simply the result of a banal pragmatism" but showed "evidence of an intellectual—even moral—transformation resulting from such accommodation."[60] Alam explains how Nasirean ethics, drawn from medieval Persian texts, were incorporated into Mughal politics, contributing to the ruling elites' emphasis on religious tolerance and cultural integration. Islamic political discourse melded religious and secular notions of governance (e.g., joining Nasirean ideals of cooperation and justice to Quranic sharia law) that were also inflected with specific customs and norms from both Mughal and Hindu cultures. According to Alam, "Islam's politics endeavoured to narrow the bridge between communities" and initiate "a kind of dialogue with the worlds it reached—and reached out to."[61]

Insofar as Dryden depicts his historical hero accurately, as a figure whose conflicting desires and responsibilities inform his realist statecraft, his play is inflected with what Sanjay Subrahmanyam has called "cultural commensurability" between East and West.[62] In the realm of Islamic ethics, such thinking can be seen in the "mirror for princes" genre, which offered guidelines and advice for rulers and to some extent intersected with the realist politics of Machiavelli himself.[63] In *No Virtue Like Necessity: Realist Thought in International Relations since Machiavelli,* Jonathan Haslam situates Machiavelli in a conversation about political virtue and realist self-interest stretching back to Augustine and Aristotle; he notes that this conversation was a global one—with threads in India, China, the Middle East, and Europe—that had implications for international relations. Realist political thought, which Haslam describes as having a tripartite emphasis on reasons of state, a balance of power enforced by war, and a protectionist balance of trade, had a long legacy in "Islamic cultures" that anticipated Machiavelli's and, later, Hobbes's ideas.[64] It was in the Islamic world, Haslam argues, "not in Italy, that the 'mirror of princes' literature first appeared and it was here that the overriding demands of religion were first challenged in the name of secular priorities."[65] It is within this tradition of realist thought, too, that compromise becomes a recognizable act of heroic virtue—not just compromise between religious and secular traditions or between motivations of passion versus reason, but also compromise between lip service to moral ideals and the far more pragmatic "primacy of reasons of state."[66]

In addition to examining how Machiavelli's work was informed by Islamic political thought, recent studies have traced how his ideas of political virtue were circulated and received in Islamic and broader global contexts.[67] As Kaya Şahin puts it, "Machiavelli transformed the ancient Roman *virtu* into a form of practical and pragmatic rationality," in ways that paralleled what was happening in the Islamic Ottoman and connected empires.[68] Meanwhile, according to Linda T. Darling, "Middle Eastern political literature definitively shows" that "the transition to early modern politics took place in a complex of interrelated states and was associated with new modes of transportation and communication, new senses of identity and belonging, and new ideologies of unification and competition"—in other words, "forces that were not unique to Europe."[69] This recent scholarly emphasis on the commensurability between Middle Eastern and European political discourses reframes Dryden's global commitments in broader and more productive ways than a focus on isolated English politics or Eurocentric prejudice allows. Indeed, the succession crisis Dryden dramatizes was concerned with questions about how rulers should interact with subjects, as well as how they should handle the interests—and, per Bernier's concern, the property—of the state. While Dryden's concerns were not exactly the same as those of his Mughal contemporaries, his sympathetic use of a Mughal model in the wake of a similar crisis draws in, rather than excludes, these global resonances. In this regard, Dryden's eponymous hero represents a politically sophisticated, vibrantly cosmopolitan, and visibly wealthy Islamic society, and his play, with its political analogues for an English audience, takes part in a genealogy of advice to rulers that stretches back to Aristotle. Dryden's choice not only of an Eastern exemplar but of Aurangzeb specifically (the same Aurangzeb whom one Venetian traveler called "that Machiavelli") invites us to read his play as engaging Mughal notions of statecraft and Machiavellian pragmatism.[70] It also demonstrates a degree of respect for pragmatic prudence that plays out as bold political savvy and a tolerance (even if a dissembling one) for different cultures and customs. In sum, rather than dismissing the Machiavellian qualities of Dryden's anglicized Aureng-Zebe as *unvirtuous,* as critics have tended to do, we can see tenets of Machiavelli's pragmatic thinking in Dryden's complicated portrayal of heroic virtue itself.

In his anxieties about "dissembling" at the English court, Dryden echoes Bernier's ambivalence about realpolitik. Unlike Bernier—who sees Aurangzeb as a political genius and a "great" individual, yet effectively negates his example for French readers by suggesting that cultural differences will lead to the Mughal empire's eventual "ruine and desolation"—Dryden frames Aurangzeb's story as one about English "virtue."[71] Yet he deploys a similarly compensatory narrative strategy for distinguishing between an individual of rare heroic virtue and the declining state that individual represents.

RESOLUTION THROUGH REVOLUTION: SIR WILLIAM TEMPLE ON HEROIC VIRTUE

These debates about the pragmatic, Machiavellian qualities that Dryden ostensibly writes out of Aurangzeb's character were shaping broader conversations about heroic virtue. In his 1690 essay *Of Heroic Virtue,* English statesman Sir William Temple speaks to the imaginative framework for Mughal India that Dryden's play appears to dramatize. According to Temple, heroic virtue denotes not rigid adherence to a set of classical rules but rather a way of being in a constantly shifting world, similar to that which Dryden himself embodies in his pragmatic approach to poetry and politics. Temple sees Aurangzeb, whom he calls "the great Mogul [of] our age," as a prime example of how the Mughal Empire fits into the broader schematic of heroic virtue.[72] Temple's argument, which frames the Mughal hero's virtuous qualities in light of what Machiavelli referred to as fortune, or what Temple calls the accidental revolutions of global history, reiterates Dryden's own vacillating between appropriation and admiration.

In his essay, Temple dissects and lauds the "virtue" of four non-European nations or regions: China, Peru, Scythia (or Tartary), and Arabia. He defines "heroic virtue" itself as that quality "said to arise from some great and native excellency of temper or genius, transcending the common race of mankind in wisdom, goodness, and fortitude," and deployed in the "general good" and political advantage of their countrymen (304–5). Thanks to Confucius, Temple notes, the Chinese excel in such universal virtues as "courtesy or civility" (324), while their government in practice "excel[s] the very speculations of other men," from "the republic of Plato [to] the Utopia's, or Oceana's of our modern writers" (332). But while China's virtues are most evident, Temple does not focus exclusively on them—in fact, he goes on to qualify his praise of China, noting that "other sorts" of learning and knowledge, including "astrology and physic, and chemistry" (322), "are either disused or ignoble among them" (325). Instead, he states that even "outlying" or "barbarous" empires have their forms and degrees of virtue. For instance, he declares that not only the Peruvian Incas but also the barbarous Scythians and "the Mahometan empires," though they "were not raised like others, upon the foundations, or by the force of heroic virtues," have their "Princes, in whom some beams at least of that [virtuous] sun have shined" (384). He then highlights the very Mughal hero Dryden dramatizes, putting Tamerlane and his successor Aurangzeb, the "great Mogul [of] our age," on par with Oliver Cromwell as heroes, albeit both "of the fanatic strain" (373).

Temple's definition of heroic virtue and singling out of Aurangzeb highlight two pertinent points about cultural similarities and differences. First, Temple underscores virtue's universality in terms of human nature, contending that all countries in all ages boast "Princes, in whom some beams at least of that sun [of virtue] have shined," so it is only "jus[t] . . . to mention . . . those who appear to have shined the brightest in their . . . ages or countries" (384). But he also emphasizes that because heroic virtue manifests itself differently in different times, places, and cultural milieus, for different purposes, we must learn what virtue is by surveying both exemplary and cautionary models from global history. In order to develop and mature, he writes, virtue must always be "ennobled by birth . . . cultivated by education," and "*assisted by fortune*" (306, emphasis added). Given these criteria, he notes, certain forms of virtue "shall not perhaps be paralleled in other countries or times" (448). For instance, he says, "science and arts have run their circles, and had their periods in the several parts of the world"; for the time being, they have moved "from East to West," though he speculates that, due to the inevitable "revolutions of empire," they may at some point in the future return eastward (449).

What is particularly striking about Temple's essay is not necessarily his West-centric historiography but rather his acknowledgment and prediction that different countries' "fortunes" will continue to cycle. To the extent that England's own claim to heroic virtue is linked to its empirically validated successes, he suggests, its virtue may disappear or radically change in the future. Acknowledging that progress may give way to regress, Temple asks: What if "our first flights seem to have been the highest?" (458). On one hand, Robert K. Batchelor points out, Temple situates his "praise of Confucian values" in "a universal context that included lawgivers like Mango Copac in Peru" and offers "a relatively conventional... statement about the virtue of top-down ancient political models."[73] On the other hand, Temple identifies England's current moment as a uniquely global one that blends "Dutch and French versions of modernity [with] Moroccan, Mughal, and Qing ones."[74] Accordingly, he seeks to craft a viable definition of "heroic virtue" that takes into account England's achievement, character, and national role vis-à-vis different times and places. For this reason, Temple defines virtue both as an attribute marked by nonnegotiable and universal qualities (such as birth, education, fortune) and as one contingent upon certain geographical variables (such as climate and political custom). As Haslam puts it, Temple is a realist: "Whereas others, notably Hobbes and Cumberland, had seized upon one aspect of the nature of man as his essential characteristic and built a system of politics upon that ground, Temple, much the political practitioner, saw a duality, with behavior ultimately determined by circumstance."[75] For Temple, the rhetoric of heroic virtue is a way of framing, and in some sense reconciling, universal ideals of greatness with shifting economic realities and differences of custom.

While Dryden's dramatic hero may possess some prudence, his lack of Machiavellian traits has led critics to conclude either that Dryden's portrait of virtue *fails* (insofar as Aureng-Zebe embodies what Dryden calls a "practical virtue," marked by human frailty, rather than the rare greatness of Temple's heroic virtue) or that the anglicized Aureng-Zebe represents a radically new form of virtue associated with the West and its commercial priorities. Yet the recurring language of "fortune" and "fate" throughout the play does more than echo the conventions of Greek tragedy. Such language also works against any effort to pin virtue down to a set of fixed qualities, ancient or modern; instead, it underscores the instability and even illegibility of "practical" virtue and the ways in which "heroic" qualities must be defined situationally and circumstantially. In some sense, Dryden's Morat is Temple's "temporary" and "dimly shining" hero, marked by militant might, who is moderated and reformed *too late* and thus supplanted by an "imperfect" hero who is favored by fortune's shifting wheel. As Indamora tells Morat, "Yours is a Soul irregularly great.... A Sun which does, through Vapours, dimly shine" (*AZ*, 5.151). The very qualities Dryden's anglicized Aureng-Zebe lacks on-stage—namely, the captive Indamora's pragmatic rationality and the dissembling boldness of the dispossessed Morat—are qualities that England's real-life Mughal counterpart was celebrated for possessing, and qualities he was using to shape Mughal statecraft at a moment when the definition and stakes of political virtue were up for global debate. The question of what type or mix of political virtue(s) would actually *work* to elevate and sustain one nation's interests on the world stage had yet to be decided—as Temple makes clear, the wheel of fortune was *still turning*, its final stopping point deferred and impossible to predict.

Insofar as virtue is defined as innate qualities or willpower on a character's part, in Dryden's play, virtuous agency does not seem powerful enough to thwart or deter the forces of fortune. But insofar as virtue is defined as the pragmatic balancing of specific interests with a recognition of Fortune's whims, it can indeed be rewarded. In this sense, what looks like "inconstancy" on Indamora's part can be reframed as her strategic reckoning with the uncertainty of fortune. Indamora's definition of virtue wins out, in the end. But she—like India itself, under the historical Aurangzeb's reign—is a realist. The fictional Aureng-Zebe's failure of feminized virtue, then, brings us back to Temple's argument on the revolutions of fortune, the global implications of these revolutions, and the different forms heroic virtue takes in different places and seasons. Just as Temple acknowledges that no one can predict whether East or West will stay at the top of Fortune's wheel in coming ages, Dryden's play does not leave his readers with a stable claim to English virtue. Instead, it acknowledges the historical Aurangzeb's rare greatness as an individual and leaves open the possibility of a future shift in power on the global scale. Dryden simultaneously affirms a degree of cultural commensurability while echoing Bernier's zero-sum game argument about India's wealth and prediction of decline. The moral of Dryden's story about heroic virtue is twofold, then, inviting viewers to admire the bold pragmatism and ambition of each individual "*Heroe* of an Age" while acknowledging the inexorable and unpredictable role of fortune in privileging one empire over another (*AZ*, 1.95).

STRIKING SAIL IN SATIRE: RECOGNIZING THE INSTABILITY OF "PRACTICAL VIRTUE"

Dryden's dramatized relationships mimic the moves of a ship at sea—its frequent striking of sail, switching of flag, navigating the shifting of current. A ship's decision to strike sail is always calculated: the captain weighs their strength against another's and makes a move accordingly. Magnified from individual relationships to the level of the court, and from there to the state, we see a similar need for calculation at work. In his essay "Of Popular Discontents," Temple writes, "The comparison between a state and a ship has been so illustrated by poets and orators, that 'tis hard to find any point wherein they differ. . . . The similitude holds, and happens alike to the one and to the other."[76] The link between ship and state makes sense in a global moment propelled by trade, given shifting geopolitics and ongoing debates about maritime sovereignty.[77] The analogy is particularly useful to Temple in making a case for national unity in safely steering the state-ship. "If the Captain, the Master, the Pilot" is on the same page as the crew, he writes, then a ship can be steered with skill and care; "just so in a state," since "nothing, besides the uniting of parties upon one common bottom, can save a state in a tempestuous season" (66). Temple goes on to claim that "our nation is too great, and too brave to be ruined by any but itself" (64). Much as Dryden had cited the might of England's navy, in opposition to the Dutch, as proof of the "Vertues . . . of the English poets,"[78] Temple identifies a two-fold guarantee of national greatness in "the greatness of our naval forces" and "the balance of our neighboring powers"; "to this [balance]," he writes, recognizing the stakes, "all differing opinions, passions, and interests should strike sail, and, like proud swelling streams, though running different courses, should yet make haste into the sea of common safety" (64–65).

Returning to the nautical image with which this chapter opened: Dryden's suggestion that one strikes sail in the tempest—which he characterizes as a maze of interests, inside and out—not just to save face but to preserve self *and* nation from those one "cannot ruin," underscores that virtue is globally situational. As his stated purpose is to scold the unvirtuous (the witless, the Dutch) and to affirm the great (king, country, and friends), Dryden uses his metaphor to comment on courtly politicking and the power dynamics of global trade. His reference, in the dedicatory epistle, to a cornered "English vessel in the Indies" draws these maritime relations into the frame of the play: in the sea-space of the Indies in the wake of the Third Anglo-Dutch War (which had ended in Holland's favor the year before), the Dutch are like those fools at court, for they pass as "solid men" while persisting in dissemblance, greed, and gratuitous violence. The play is itself a mock salute, in this sense, and a triangulation of English, Dutch, and Mughal qualities that satirizes pieces of all three. Given England's shifting relations with European rivals and Eastern allies—sometimes refraining from action, sometimes turning to aggression—striking sail seems a necessary skill. Whether at the parochial level of mockers at court or at the global level of encounters in uncertain seas, striking sail is a pragmatic act of sizing up and responding to others, with a salute of surrender or a seizure of goods. If, in *these* seas, we are besting the Dutch, while in *that* sea they are besting us, then our monarchs need a model for virtue that "rouz[es] to Glory" in conciliatory ways. The witty insider may see that, translated onto an English stage, Aurangzeb's troubling traits become clear in their absence, through the inversion Rajan posits. We (English viewers) know we are not tyrannical or tyrannized, *as they are,* just as we know we are not (like the Dutch) murderous fools. The displacement works not because of any stable analogy—between us/them, or English/Dutch, or England/India—but because, as Temple describes, we understand virtue to take different forms in different times and places.

At a moment of uncertainty in English politics, Dryden articulates how difficult it is to find a clear—and clearly moral—vision for how England might function and flourish in a rapidly changing world. Rather than simply using a Mughal monarch as a negative exemplar for English political virtue, Dryden's play looks outward to depict a mix of qualities requisite for greatness, including some that are unavailable or unadmired at home. As Orr, Rajan, and others suggest, Dryden's play is certainly invested in England's nascent imperial project, including the submission of a feminized Orient and possession of its boundless riches. But it is also interested in broader questions of what constitutes virtuous greatness and what sets apart—in Arimant's words—each nation's "heroe of an age" (*AZ*, 1.95). Some of these questions remain unresolved: if "True Greatness, if it be anywhere on Earth, is [only] in a private Virtue," as Dryden asserts in his dedication, then how will such greatness be recognized in and rewarded by a world that privileges "Pomp and Vanity"? For instance, what if the greatest and most powerful of world leaders possesses only the pragmatic virtue of Machiavellian ambition? And if a Mughal princess's unlikely sati can be seen as virtuous in her fictional world, then what else might be reimagined as virtuous for an (English) worthy cause? In Dryden's play, one of virtue's functions is to check baser instincts: a desire for revenge, or a lust for pleasure or profit. We see Aureng-Zebe's virtue in his moderation, his ability to control desire and bide his time. But moderation does not define heroism. Aureng-Zebe wants the kingdom and Indamora, too; he desires internal stability plus foreign riches. He is unwilling to give up either reward and in fact sees them as intertwined. By considering how Aureng-Zebe maintains his identity as son (marking his filial virtue, per Maurer) and as emperor (marking his inheritance of global prestige), Dryden is not so much enacting a fantasy of conquest as he is exploring how forms of virtue intersect.

In the end, Dryden contends, his play represents not ideal but rather "practical virtue, mix'd with the Frailties and Imperfections of Human life." Admitting that perhaps he could have found "images of virtue" that resonate better with his audience, Dryden emphasizes that the poet has license to change, to try again, to modify these images to better suit them for national purposes. Dryden's willingness to keep seeking better and more complete pictures of virtue for the nation underscores his recognition that seas change, literally and politically. If it matters who is at the helm, to guide and unify, then that guide, as Morat states, is not a single person—whether England's Charles or James, or India's Aurangzeb—but rather virtue itself, in its aggregate, fictional, and ever-morphing form. Virtue steers the state-ship, as it does, to varying degrees, the characters in Dryden's play. But what *exactly* that virtue entails—and to what extent English viewers can learn lessons from foreign emperors—remains unclear. To *be* virtuous or at least to be *seen* as such, it seems, is to have the Machiavellian ability to strike sail, knowing how and when to temper passion and bridle ambition. For disordered states (as for men in love, or witless fools), it is better to strike sail than to be like Arimant, who, in his own words, is like those "Mariners [who] mistake the promis'd Coast: / And *with full Sails*, on the blind Rocks are lost" (*AZ*, 2.104, emphasis added). The problem for Arimant and Dryden's other disappointed figures is not that virtue cannot align with interest, but that their interests are too often unmoderated and unrealistic. "Practical virtue," then, is not the lack of dissembling but a mark of one's ability to gauge when and whether to strike sail and defer glory for another day.

The next chapter turns to a new moment of crisis and to the work of Jonathan Swift, who, like Dryden, makes his case about England's political virtue—and the lack thereof—through a vivid picture of "the Frailties and Imperfections of Human life." Swift eschews Dryden's taste for and belief in the heroic. However, like Dryden, he looks eastward in his quest to find and aggregate his own "images of virtue" that let him simultaneously satirize England's hollow virtue claims and hold up his own, provocatively imagined ideals.

3

RECOVERING THE "TRUE SPIRIT OF LIBERTY"
Gulliver's Travels in Sparta and Japan

Patriotism must be founded in great principles, and
supported by great virtues.
—Henry St. John, Viscount Bolingbroke, *The Idea of a Patriot King* (1738)

IN BOOK 3 OF *GULLIVER'S TRAVELS,* just before Jonathan Swift's eponymous protagonist sails to the fictional East Asian island of Luggnagg, and from there to the actual island of Japan, Gulliver takes a diversionary side trip to Glubbdubdrib, an "Island of *Sorcerers*" whose governor, a skilled necromancer, invites him to call up his heroes from the dead.[1] While Gulliver's other travels take him to exotic geographical locations, real and imagined, his brief stint in Glubbdubdrib allows him to travel back in time and "gratify that insatiable desire I had to see the World in every Period of Antiquity" (167). In the "five days" Gulliver spends "in conversing with . . . the antient learned," he observes a magnificent victory by Alexander the Great, admires Brutus of Rome for his "consummate Virtue" (166), and summons "some *English* Yeomen of the old stamp," sometime bearers of England's "pure native Virtues" (172). As he "behold[s] the Destroyers of Tyrants and Usurpers, and the Restorers of Liberty to oppressed and injured Nations" (167), Gulliver finds himself more and more "disgusted with modern History" (169). Not only have historians mixed up the heroes with the villains, he notes, but in fact the very definition of virtue has been forgotten, in part because modern readers have few true examples to emulate. He laments that England, in particular, is marked by the betrayal and degeneration of its "pure native Virtues" (172). "Once so famous for the Simplicity of their Manners, Dyet and Dress, for Justice in their Dealings, for their true Spirit of Liberty, for their Valour and Love of their Country," he says, the English have acquiesced to greed and corruption, leaving foundational principles behind (172). In the process, their renowned "native Virtues" have been sullied and forgotten, "prostituted for a piece of Money by [the Yeomen's] Grandchildren" (172).

Keeping in mind Gulliver's Glubbdubdrib sentiments, along with his "insatiable desire . . . to see the World," this chapter picks up the story of virtue-as-liberty in the early eighteenth century, when Swift joined British patriots in seeking to stem the slide from liberty to license that they perceived was being institutionalized under Sir Robert Walpole's regime. With continued attention to what Neville highlighted as the costs of pursuing "native" liberty to its logical end, this chapter examines Gulliver's reference to England's "pure native Virtues" in light of Swift's vision for recovering these qualities. Progress, Swift suggests, driven as it too often is by self-interest, has produced crises of national character in England and Ireland alike. England's vaunted liberties—rooted in common law and custom and enshrined in the Magna Carta—increasingly serve to cover up consumption and greed. Swift, who dictated that his own gravestone epitaph would memorialize him as a "champion of liberty" for his native Ireland, wished that England could recover its lost virtue, restore its ancient constitution, and stabilize its increasingly barbarous language. Meanwhile, frustrated by England's colonial policies at home, he gave voice to the "vigorous assertion by Irish protestants of their entitlement to the same constitutional liberties and civil rights as Englishmen."[2] For Swift, English liberty—the basis and enabler of all civic virtue—was both a political principle to uphold and a divine inheritance to preserve.

Throughout *Gulliver's Travels*, Swift wrestles with the possibility that the "true Spirit of Liberty" is an irrecoverable ideal from the past.

In light of how, throughout his oeuvre, Swift mocks and mourns the unrelenting lurch toward modernity that threatens older values and structures, critics have often read the *Travels* as a satire of travel and the travelogue.[3] It is wanderlust, Swift seems to suggest, or the uncontrolled desire for movement toward what lies next or beyond, that is responsible for virtue's decay in England and Ireland. Indeed, throughout the *Travels* he satirizes the sort of virtue-as-progress that Addison's Mr. Spectator celebrates—one characterized by fanciful stock market bubbles, cruel colonial plantations, and the arrogant optimism of Royal Society scientists. And yet, I argue, insofar as Swift filters his vision of England's foundational principles and future potential through a distinctly global lens, *Travels* is also generated by the desire for movement that he satirizes. Indeed, the "virtue" Swift foregrounds in the *Travels* both emerges out of and depends upon traffic between times and places.

For the most part, Gulliver travels to places that appear only on fictional maps: Lilliput and Laputa, Balnibarbi and Brobdingnag. Yet despite Gulliver's dismissive statement that "we" (the English) "have not the least interest" in the places and peoples he encounters en route, the text is clearly interested in England's ongoing quest to engage with foreign empires, particularly those in the East (246). Each of the four books begins with Gulliver setting out for an actual Eastern locale: the Levant, Surat, the East Indies, or the South Seas. Gulliver describes several of the fictional peoples he encounters as nebulously "Eastern," and Swift alludes to different cultures and customs of Eastern peoples, from the remarkable order of the Chinese alphabet to the superiority of Japanese civility. In a way that European nations (and England, specifically) have not, Swift suggests, Eastern empires have to various degrees resisted the corrupting tide of progress to preserve their cultural beauty and political order. For this reason, as Gulliver seeks to revitalize England's "pure native virtues"—a task to which Swift himself, despite his notoriously pessimistic outlook on the world, was genuinely committed—he must travel through time and space. In the course of his travels, he collects exemplary models of virtue from the ancient world (Rome, Athens, and Sparta) as well as from the Eastern empires whose wealth and longevity the early modern English admired. In this regard,

Swift's tale presents collected examples of the virtues Gulliver claims in Glubbdubdrib he wishes modern readers still had, along with an analysis of their relevance as models for present-day England. By the end of the *Travels,* however, Swift echoes Neville's fear that the global traffic of things and ideas is a double-edged sword, that the line between liberty and license is ever evolving, and that England's "pure native virtues" are neither pure nor necessarily native.

THE LEGACY OF LIBERTY IN AUGUSTAN ENGLAND

As Gulliver implies in his distinction between a "true Spirit of Liberty" and its ostensibly false counterpart, liberty remained a crucial yet contested watchword in the early decades of the eighteenth century. By this point, the fear of patriarchal absolutism that had sparked the violence of the Civil Wars and, later, the Exclusion Crisis and Glorious Revolution, had faded into collective memory. Republican ideals did not disappear, however, but were instead revised, reiterated, and folded into a carefully preserved yet adaptable tale of England's divinely endowed quality of political liberty. As John Philip Reid contends, "The doctrinal truism that the British had a monopoly on liberty, and that their liberty was perfect" was frequently used to deride other nations for perceived tyrannies, to justify the spread of English customs to colonies abroad, and both to "legitimat[e] the existing social and constitutional order [and] preserv[e] it inviolate."[4] By the early eighteenth century, Reid notes, "liberty" had become a ubiquitous and highly useful "abstraction as [much as] a practical constitutional principle," and writers across the newly partisan Whig-Tory political divide deployed the term to rally support for their respective causes and ideals.[5]

As in Neville's day, the rhetoric of liberty encoded certain Enlightenment contradictions. For example, many who endorsed Locke's liberal doctrines of rights and reason did not interpret the truism of natural liberty as a mandate to curtail British expansion or abolish slavery. Instead, they pointed to England's legacy of God-given liberty as both a cause and an effect of their nation's growing stature on the world stage.

Swift's friend and fellow satirist Alexander Pope illustrates some of the tensions shaping the Augustan landscape in his 1712 poem *Windsor Forest*. After a period of "savage laws," "severe" kings, and "cities laid waste," his speaker declares, "Fair Liberty, Britannia's Goddess," has "rear[ed] her cheerful head" and returned from a dormant state to "lea[d] the golden years."[6] British liberty is ineluctably linked to the nation's global fortunes, the speaker suggests: at long last, "Rich Industry sits smiling on the plains,/ And peace and plenty tell, a STUART reigns" (41–42). Pope published *Windsor Forest* shortly after Queen Anne, with help from Swift and other pamphleteers, finished negotiating the Treaty of Utrecht that ended the War of Spanish Succession. He was one of the many poets, Whig and Tory, who joined in celebrating the "Tory Peace" that restored Europe's balance of power and quenched, once again, the threat of Franco-Catholic tyranny. As Dryden had done in *Annus Mirabilis,* Pope calls to his readers' minds searing memories of past violence in order to articulate his vision of Britain's future grandezza. "What tears has Albion shed" due to its "dreadful series of intestine wars," exclaims the speaker, before prophetically describing England's "future navies" (222) and overseas "realms commanded" (32). In his allusion to "the golden years" of Augustan Rome and his speaker's trenchant hope that "slav'ry be no more" (407), Pope hints at his ambivalence regarding the violent transatlantic trade in human lives that accompanied England's newfound "peace and plenty." Indeed, Britain's rising status on the world stage went hand in hand with its new and lucrative access to the Asiento, Spain's portion of the African slave trade. To some extent, Pope echoes Neville's fear that England risked following in ancient Rome's steps as a liberty-loving but slave-owning society that was doomed to fall by the sword of its own success.

While concerned, on some level, with the transatlantic trade, Swift was more invested in combating what he perceived to be the political fallout of a rising credit economy—a crisis that he saw affecting London and Dublin alike.[7] It was the South Sea Bubble crash of 1720, in particular, Jonathan Lamb contends, that forced Britons to confront the "illusion" on which their newly capitalist economy was founded, "namely the compatibility between private and public interest in a romance of commercial expansion."⁸ In the wake of the crash, Walpole's rise to power, and subsequent social and political corruption, numerous pamphleteers and satirists published tracts criticizing the English people for betraying their republican ideals and abdicating their responsibility to promote public good. Meanwhile, as the rapid rise of Walpole's Whigs led "to the exclusion of many previously entrenched political groups," J. G. A. Pocock explains, this shift in power also catalyzed the formation of an opposition group "variously known by such epithets as 'country,' 'Commonwealth,' and 'patriot' ideologues."⁹ This loosely united and multifaceted party comprised "dissatisfied elements of both rural gentry with Tory antecedents and urban merchants and artisans with Dissenting connections and radical leanings."¹⁰ Despite differences of opinion and belief, members of the opposition party—known as "Real Whigs," or "Old Whigs," as opposed to Walpole's followers—shared a common goal: they hoped to renew what Gulliver calls their nation's "pure native virtues" by finding "an antidote to [the] disease in the constitution."¹¹ England's "true Spirit of Liberty," they believed, was worth fighting to preserve against overweening politicians and the sort of public corruption that eroded and eventually toppled even such an ardently pro-liberty empire as ancient Rome had been.

The Augustans wrestled with a problem similar to that which Neville had addressed, decades earlier: How might England reconcile its past and present values (civic virtue versus self-interest, and agrarian stability versus commercial prosperity) to pave the way for Great Britain's future global influence? In order to make their nostalgia productive, opposition writers worked to locate within the British Isles a superior capacity for virtuous liberty. They often framed liberty as both a past and present action and a future ideal that was divinely endowed and thus guaranteed to last. For example, Henry St. John, Viscount Bolingbroke, a Tory politician-philosopher and Swift's friend, published treatises urging readers to contemplate the link between British liberty and material success. "If liberty be that delicious and wholesome fruit on which the British nation hath fed for so many ages, and to which we owe our riches, our strength, and all the advantages we boast of," he writes, "the British constitution is the tree that bears this fruit, and will continue to bear it."¹² In calling for a return to Britain's ancient constitution, which was grounded in classical ideals, Bolingbroke and other English patriots acknowledged that commerce was an inevitable and even beneficial feature of modern society. In his *Idea of a Patriot King* (1738), Bolingbroke paradoxically accounts for England's current crisis of character—the qualities it lacks—in terms of its essential and enduring traits. Not only does "the situation of Great Britain, the character of her people, and the nature of her government, fit her for trade and commerce," he writes, but indeed "her climate and her soil make them necessary to her well-being."¹³ He explains that some rivals, particularly the Dutch Republic, which was, like England, "a nation of patriots and merchants," have simultaneously improved in industry and maintained their liberty, whereas England's efforts have been "checked, diverted, clogged, and interrupted" by trade rivalries and war (275–76). Thanks to "our situation, our interest, and the nature of our strength" as an island nation, he continues, Britain will certainly rally, for it has the *potential* to improve and become greater than its rivals (278). All it lacks is a strong and principled leader, one with the vision and fortitude to reinvigorate the principles of old—specifically, for Bolingbroke, those practiced during Queen Elizabeth's reign. Such a "patriot king" would stand up to Walpole's regime and call the modern obsession with progress what it was: liberty gone awry.

Following Bolingbroke's lead, eighteenth-century "Commonwealthmen" invoked the legacies of past heroic figures in order to legitimate and inspire their efforts. For instance, writers such as Joseph Addison, John Trenchard, and Thomas Gordon celebrated the example of Cato the Younger, a Roman statesman known for his moral integrity, resistance to corruption, and opposition to Caesar's overreaching power.¹⁴ Others, like Swift's Gulliver, called up the memory of Cato's nephew, Brutus, in order to highlight the disintegration of English liberties. By giving voice to heroes from the past, the Augustans hoped they might cultivate the civic virtue that their predecessors had modeled.

"PURE NATIVE VIRTUE" AND SWIFT'S PROTESTANT PATRIOTISM

Swift himself was sympathetic to the Commonwealth cause, though his specific beliefs and allegiances have proven notoriously difficult for historians and critics to pin down. A political Whig, advocate of mixed government, and foe of absolutism, he also believed firmly in the value of aristocratic hierarchy and supported Queen Anne as Walpole's Whigs consolidated their power. As an Anglo-Irish Anglican cleric who affirmed individual "liberty of conscience," he also recognized—and feared—that too much freedom would lead to disorder, even anarchy.[15] A staunch advocate of Irish autonomy and a critic of England's brutal colonial policies, he nonetheless "considered English culture far superior to Gaelic" and supported England's civilizing mission as long as it took a moderate and benevolent form.[16] He was, as S. J. Connolly contends, "a man torn between contradictory impulses," one in whom "a deep suspicion of political power and of those who held it, combined with an equally deep antipathy towards those who sought to upset the established order."[17] In one sense, Swift's ideas seem antithetical to the republicans' revolutionary project. After all, he sought stability and order, not disruption and radical change, and he "regarded the events of 1641 and after with abhorrence."[18] At the same time, however, Swift was well versed in republican principles; his extensive library included republican thinkers like Harrington alongside royalists like Clarendon, and he cites Algernon Sidney alongside Locke and Molyneux.[19] He could not help but be inspired by republicans' intolerance for tyranny and decisive response to exploitation at the hands of political elites. As Caroline Robbins puts it, Swift's "awareness of the failings of governments and distaste for the pretensions of the great lent even to his unpolemical work a revolutionary character."[20] Like the republicans of the mid-seventeenth century, Swift was caught between nostalgia and progress, ideal and action; he was plagued by a dream of building a better future by restoring a lost past.

Like Neville and Dryden, Swift uses fiction to imagine a viable model of political virtue that reinvigorates past principles in order to deal with present problems. Skeptical anyway of modern writers' claims to see further and know more than their ancient predecessors, he realized that England had not—as his predecessors had hoped—"become... an empire for liberty."[21] Swift's clearest example was the sorry state of his native Ireland, whose Protestant inhabitants, he believed, were entitled to English liberties they were denied and refusing to claim. In the fourth of his *Drapier's Letters,* he urges his countrymen to claim and express their political virtue on the basis of national origin and religious belief, writing, "by the laws of GOD, of NATURE, of NATIONS, and of your own COUNTRY, you ARE and OUGHT to be as FREE a people as your brethren in England."[22] At the same time, Swift realized that while a nation can certainly repeat its historical mistakes, it cannot simply reinstate lost principles. For this reason, even as Swift uses the *Travels* to engage in contemporary debates about the relative merits of past and present, considering how his readers might learn from and imitate earlier examples from Rome, Athens, and Sparta, he combines this focus on the past with a vision of England's future vis-à-vis the empires of early modern Asia. In what follows, I trace Swift's two sets of examples—one from the past, the other from the East—to examine how Swift frames stable English virtue in terms of tenuous global networks. Virtue may or may not be possible to achieve in the modern age, Swift worries, but *if* England (and, by extension, Ireland) is to be virtuous again, it must look outside of its national borders and present moment for inspiration.

Before turning to these examples from the past and the East, we must examine briefly Swift's definition and use of the term "virtue" in the *Travels* and elsewhere. Given Swift's complex national, political, and religious loyalties, what does Gulliver mean when he laments England's loss of "pure native virtues"? Throughout his oeuvre, Swift defines virtue in a broadly neorepublican political sense. Virtue, he suggests, is the overarching civic quality that leads people to willingly sacrifice their individual interests for the good of the nation. Swift, who served as dean of St. Patrick's Cathedral in Dublin from 1713 until his death in 1745, preached that virtue was, above all, a quality of "Public Spirit."[23] In one of his sermons he writes, "Love of the public ... or love of our country, was in ancient times properly known by the name of virtue, because it was the greatest of all virtues, and was supposed to contain all virtues in it."[24] In other words, Swift suggests, virtue is both an ideal and an action, a sign of who one is and is meant to be. "Many great examples of this virtue are left us on record, scarcely to be believed... in such a base, corrupted, wicked age as this we live in," he explains. But these examples must be recovered, collated, and explained, before they can become useful. Swift's task, as Gulliver describes it in Glubbdubdrib, is to do exactly that, recasting the heroes of history most worthy of emulation in their rightfully visible places.

Of the forty-two iterations of "virtue" in *Gulliver's Travels,* approximately half appear in book 4, while the rest satirically underscore the *lack* of virtue at home and abroad. In book 2, for example, while singing "praises of my own dear native Country" to the giant-king of Brobdingnag, Gulliver describes England as a "noble Country, the Mistress of Arts and Arms... the Seat of Virtue, Piety, Honour and Truth, the Pride and Envy of the World" (*GT,* 89). The king listens skeptically as Gulliver describes England's fertile soil, temperate climate, "illustrious" Parliament, and noble citizens, "worthy followers of their most renowned ancestors, whose honor had been *the reward of their virtue,* from which their posterity were never once known to degenerate" (106, emphasis added). Later, in book 3, Gulliver watches a "visionary" debate among "political projectors" regarding the low likelihood of "persuading Monarchs to chuse Favourites upon the Score of their Wisdom, Capacity and Virtue" (158–59). In book 3, virtue takes on other meanings, scientific and political: Gulliver marvels at the "Magnetick Virtue" of the flying island of Laputa (143), for example, and listens to an "artist" insist that "the true seminal Virtue [of land is] contained" in its "Chaff" (154). Within Swift's satire, and insofar as the term refers to moral and cultural superiority and civic excellence, virtue is not to be found in England. By the time Gulliver tells the chief Houyhnhnm in book 4 that "difference in opinions" over petty topics such as "whether *Whistling* be a Vice or a Virtue" "hath cost many Millions of Lives" back home, Swift has rendered rather laughable (and equally tragic) the belief that "virtue" signifies a stable or absolute standard, moral or otherwise (207). Instead, he uses the term to underscore how often appearances trump substance in the nation he loves.

Critical discussions of "virtue" in *Gulliver's Travels* have largely focused on Swift's representation of the Houyhnhnms in book 4, including the fine line Swift explores between the human and nonhuman animal.[25] Nearly every critic of the *Travels* has wrestled with the question of whether Swift intended the Houyhnhnms to serve as virtuous ideals for his readers or as further objects of satire.[26] While in Houyhnhnmland, Gulliver rhapsodizes about "the many Virtues of [the] excellent Quadrupeds" (217). In contrast to the filthy, brutish, humanoid Yahoos, the "wise and virtuous" Houyhnhnms possess "a Constellation of Virtues"; they "are endowed . . . with a general Disposition to all Virtues," and they spend much of their time talking about virtue (250, 225, 234). They believe that "it is *Reason* only that maketh a Distinction of persons, where there is a superior Degree of Virtue" (226). After leaving Houyhnhnmland, Gulliver says that he wishes "to apply [the] Lessons of Virtue" he has learned from the Houyhnhnms and to "propos[e] their Virtues to the Imitation of Mankind" (249, 236). At stake in the debate about whether the Houyhnhnms function as virtuous ideals or comedic relief is the question of satire's overarching purpose, and of whether Swift intended the *Travels* merely to indict society or also somehow to reform it.[27]

In his assessment of *Gulliver's Travels* shortly after its publication in 1726, John Boyle, the Earl of Orrery, one of Swift's friends and earliest critics, denounced Swift's representation of Houynhnmland as "a real insult upon mankind" precisely because he saw it as a gross misrepresentation of the nature of virtue.[28] Regarding the Yahoos, Orrery writes that "the representation which [Swift] has given us of human nature, must terrify, and even debase the mind of the reader who views it," so that readers are ultimately "disgusted, not entertained; we are shocked, not instructed" (117). Meanwhile, he contends, the "virtuous qualities [of the Houyhnhnms] are only negative"—they are "brutes" without any "knowledge of letters," and it is only because "they are incapable of doing wrong, [that] therefore they act right" (120). True virtue, by contrast, must be tested and proven; without opportunity to prove their virtue, the Houyhnhnms cannot be truly virtuous. In an otherwise fine "romance," Orrery avers, Swift misses an opportunity to showcase such true virtue—that manifestation of human excellence and purity that has potential "to raise our idea of the Almighty by contemplating his works" and to demonstrate "the end and intention" of all God's creation. In other words, Orrery suggests, Swift's shortcoming lies not in failing to portray the Houyhnhnms as epitomes of virtue but rather in failing to portray any positive models of virtue at all. It is not necessary that the Houyhnhnms be figured as perfect, he writes; after all, "it is too certain, that no one individual has ever possessed every qualification and excellence: however[,] such an assemblage of different virtues, may still be collected from different persons, as are sufficient to place the dignity of human nature in an amiable, and exalted station" (120–21). *Vir* is an impossible ideal, a standard of excellence no individual can achieve, even after a lifetime of proper education. According to Orrery, however, Swift's pessimistic outlook on the world leads him to abdicate his writerly responsibility to portray what virtue *would* look like should it exist in composite form.

Despite what one more recent critic has called Swift's "bleak satiric disaffection" and "apocalyptic skepticism," however, Swift believed strongly in the power of individuals—and of words—to do something in the world.[29] While he famously wrote to Pope in 1725 that a primary goal "in all my labors is to vex the world rather than divert it," he wrote that same year to Charles Ford that he hoped *Gulliver's Travels* would "wonderfully mend the World."[30] In order for his satire to accomplish such mending work, Swift had to convey that virtue entails more than visible actions, failed or forsaken; it also bespeaks divinely endowed ideals that endure in the English political consciousness. In this regard, *Travels* presents precisely the "assemblage of different virtues . . . collected from different persons" that Orrery saw it as lacking. But insofar as Gulliver collects these examples of virtue from empires that were—and continue to be—as invested in the quest for global glory as was early modern England, his picture of excellence raises more questions than it answers about the nature and longevity of *English* virtue.

MODELS OF VIRTUE FOR HOUYHNHNMLAND: FROM THE PAST

In Glubbdubdrib, where he has the chance to travel back in time, Gulliver considers the extent to which three ancient civilizations—Rome, Athens, and Sparta—embody the "pure native virtues" that modern England lacks. Exhibit A is ancient Rome, where Gulliver describes seeing "Caesar and Pompey at the Head of their Troops" (*GT*, 166). After requesting "that the Senate of *Rome* might appear before me," he contrasts this ancient "Assembly of Heroes and Demy-Gods" to its "modern" counterpart of the English Parliament, which appears to be "a Knot of Pedlars, Pick-pockets, High-way-men and Bullies" (166). As he gazes upon these heroes from the past, Gulliver is "struck with a profound Veneration at the sight of *Brutus*," descendant of the founder of the Roman Republic, whose "Countenance" is so clearly marked by "the most consummate Virtue, the greatest Intrepidity, and firmness of Mind, the truest Love of his Country, and general Benevolence for Mankind" that even "*Caesar* freely confessed to [him] that the greatest Actions of his own Life were not equal by many Degrees to the Glory of taking it away" (166). Gulliver is most impressed by Brutus's role as one of history's greatest "Destroyers of Tyrants" and "Restorers of Liberty" (167). Amid false virtue that takes visible form as expansion and prosperity, Brutus stands out to Gulliver as possessing that "true Spirit of Liberty" that is, per Swift, virtue itself. But while Rome was graced with certain virtuous individuals (like Brutus), it could not maintain its collective virtue. Brought to its knees by a tyrant's overreaching ambition, Rome's fate was evidence of the problem of grandezza that Neville and his fellow republican theorists had pinpointed years earlier.[31]

On the other end of the political spectrum from imperial Rome, Gulliver turns to the democratic city-state of Athens. While in Glubbdubdrib, Gulliver suggests that one reason for England's lack of virtue is not simply what happened in its past but also how that history has been told. Here, Gulliver is looking not for exemplars of heroism and bravery but rather for those who can express their political ideals in ways that compel people to imitate and learn from the past. Consequently, he consults "those Antients... most renowned for Wit and Learning," pitting the classical Athenian "Heroes," Homer and Aristotle, against modern "commentators," or "Dunces" (168). Using Aristotle as his mouthpiece, he observes "that new Systems of nature were but new Fashions, which... would flourish but a short Period of time, and [then] be out of Vogue" (168). Gulliver accuses the modern commentators of "horribly misrepresent[ing] the meaning of those Authors to Posterity" and of relegating such "great Philosopher[s]" as Aristotle to the dustbins of history (168). Yet while Gulliver is attracted to the timeless wisdom of the Athenian philosophers, he sees Athens, like Rome, as one more flawed example of liberty gone awry. As a pure democracy, Athens lacks the checks and balances on liberty that could have kept its founder Solon's constitutional principles intact. Too much popular freedom rendered its great wits impotent. Alas, Swift points out in a 1701 tract, Athens eventually fell into "degeneracy" and succumbed to the same forces of luxury and effeminacy that brought Rome to its knees.[32] He suggests that human nature is the same regardless of political structure, with a propensity toward decay, though some sociopolitical systems are better than others at controlling that nature.

If Rome acquiesced to oligarchical tyranny and Athens to uncontrolled democracy because each abandoned its foundational principles, ancient Sparta exemplified for some in early modern England a golden mean of mixed government. Shortly after listening to Aristotle's dialogue with Descartes, Gassendi, and other modern philosophers in Glubbdubdrib, Gulliver grows hungry and "prevail[s] on the Governour to call up *Eliogabulus's* Cooks to dress us a Dinner" (*GT,* 168).[33] Gulliver ends up doubly disappointed with his fare: when the Roman cooks "could not shew [much] Skill," he is given "a Dish of *Spartan* Broth" prepared by "a *Helot of Agesilaus*"; however, unable to stomach Spartan austerity, he is "not able to get down a second Spoonful" (169). In his annotated edition of *Gulliver's Travels,* Albert J. Rivero proposes that the "black broth Gulliver finds so nauseating" symbolizes the Spartans' famously "simple, austere life," one that Swift "admired" and "used... as a model for the Houyhnhnms" (169n). At first glance, Swift does indeed appear to choose ancient Sparta as his model for the virtuous Houyhnhnms.

Like the Spartans and unlike the English, who, as Gulliver suggests, are caught up in "feed[ing] the Luxury and Intemperance of the Males, and the Vanity of the Females," the Houyhnhnms are eminently temperate (213). They are spare of speech, eschewing as "Evils" the "Controversies, Wranglings, Disputes, and Positiveness in false or dubious Propositions" to such an extreme extent that, in fact, Gulliver notes, "I have often since reflected what Destruction such a Doctrine would make in the Libraries of *Europe*" (226). Reflecting the ancient Spartan ban on keeping any written records, historical or legal, "the *Houyhnhnms* have no Letters, and consequently, their Knowledge is all Traditional," passed down from generation to generation in oral form (230). Houyhnhnm education is carefully controlled and always purposeful; the elders "train up their Youth to Strength, Speed, and Hardiness" through consistent, mandatory physical exercise (227). Like the Spartans, they are "cut off from all Commerce with other Nations" (230). And, like the ancient Spartans, the Houyhnhnms act not out of individual passion but out of a deeply ingrained commitment to uphold state values and thereby preserve a way of life. All public institutions, consequently, are designed to contribute to the collective good rather than to individual pleasure. Marriage, for example, is founded "not upon the account of *Love*, but to preserve the Race from degeneration" (226). Rather than forming intimate familial relationships, men and women are tasked simply to avoid "mak[ing] any disagreeable Mixture in the Breed" (227). As a result, "the Violation of Marriage, or any other Unchastity, was never heard of," and couples, once married, "pass their Lives with the same Friendship, and mutual Benevolence that they bear to all others of the same Species" (227). In Houyhnhnmland as in ancient Sparta, the "principal Virtues" benefit the community above any individual (226).[34]

As with each of Swift's allusions to the past, the Spartan model of virtue is complicated. In Sparta, as in each of the other "virtuous" societies of the ancient world, freedom is a relative, rather than absolute, state. The humanoid Yahoos function in Houyhnhnmland much as the Helots did within the Spartan state: as a repulsive and oppressed underclass of serfs.[35] As Plutarch observed, "In Sparta the freeman is more a freeman than anywhere else in the world, and the slave more a slave."[36]

Indeed, the Spartans' virtue of liberty was bought and preserved at a high human cost. In many ways, however, Sparta—known for its citizens' laconic brevity, martial masculinity, and rigid austerity—was a conservative's model of restraint. Drawing upon the work of Sir Thomas More, Niccolò Machiavelli, James Harrington, and Sir William Temple, along with classical thinkers such as Xenophon, Plutarch, and Plato, Swift and other eighteenth-century writers held up Sparta as a model of public virtue. As late as 1794, in his *Review of the Governments of Sparta and Athens,* William Drummond contrasts "Spartan virtues" ("the fortitude, the hardiness, the generosity, the abstinence, the modesty, and the frugality") with those of Sparta's rival, Athens, which was remembered for its citizens' commitment to the arts and sciences, along with a love of pleasure and wit.[37] Drummond's *Review* sums up the "nostalgic admiration for Lycurgan Sparta" that informed "the humanist tradition in which Swift was nurtured."[38] As Stephen Bygrave has argued, Sparta was admired among the eighteenth-century English not for its refined citizenry but for its cultural longevity, which the English attributed to Sparta's absolute commitment to enforce its foundational constitutional precepts. Because it never changed or developed, Bygrave explains, Sparta could not "therefore progress or decline (let alone fall)."[39] As Europe's "rustic or undeveloped other," Sparta functioned simultaneously as a model of restraint and as a useful foil for ostensibly more civilized and more ambitious nations.[40] On one hand, Sparta was an antithesis of progress. And yet, despite being a "'barbarous' or 'warrior' society" that lacked the refining influences of a vibrant public sphere, Sparta nonetheless possessed an admirable internal strength and consistency that let it pose a "successful resistance to modern, commercial pressures."[41] It is Sparta's reputation for restraint and longevity, in conjunction with Swift's own, conservative sentiments, that has led critics like Rivero to contend that Swift models Houyhnhnm virtue on the ancient Spartans.

Sparta lasted as long as it did because it resisted the siren call of luxury; however, as Swift and other politically savvy writers were well aware, luxury was an "inevitable corollar[y] of technological and commercial success."[42] After all, as Bernard Mandeville writes in his satirical *Fable of the Bees,* "the only thing [the Spartans] could be proud of, was, that they enjoy'd nothing."⁴³ In this regard, debates about the respective virtues of Sparta and Athens (as with republican-era debates about Rome) were debates "over modernity itself," as Bygrave asserts; "an agrarian, austere Sparta stood for stability and simplicity but was an oligarchy; a materialistic and refined Athens was commercial, urbanized and liberal."⁴⁴ According to Ian Higgins, for example, it is "nostalgia for such a world without finance corporations, credit systems, and East India Companies that Swift presents in the rural societies of Brobdingnag and Houyhnhnmland."⁴⁵ As Plutarch points out in his *Parallel Lives*, it was when "gold and silver money first flowed into Sparta" that "greed and a desire for wealth prevailed," eventually undermining the Spartan founder Lycurgus's brilliant constitutional order.⁴⁶ To read Swift's Houyhnhnms as modern-day Spartans is reductive in two ways, however. First, as Gulliver demonstrates by his overt distaste for "Spartan Broth," Spartan virtue had its costs and consequences. Cultural purity was preserved at the cost of family, comfort, and the right to an internal, private self; marriage had use value only, with wives regularly shared in common; children were educated exclusively by—and for—the state. The Spartans' commitment to liberty led them to isolate themselves, sealing their borders and shunning all foreign contact. Understandably, English moralists, historians, and politicians debated throughout the eighteenth century whether Sparta was an ideal to emulate, an extreme example to avoid, or simply an obsolete relic become irrelevant for modern, trading nations. Swift and his contemporaries realized, Pocock writes, that "if the Goths, Spartans, and early Romans had been *free and virtuous*, they had been neither enlightened nor polite."⁴⁷ In this sense, none of these societies could offer a viable model for an already-modern England to imitate.

A second problem with linking Swift's "pure native virtues" to a particular ancient model is that the past never functions as a straightforward reference. Each example of ancient virtue proves limited in the light of history: the temperate Spartans' resistance to luxury keeps them forever in a state of barbarity; the wise Athenians' love of pleasure leads to licentiousness; the courageous Romans' lust for conquest overextends and destroys their great republic. None of these examples could adequately address how economically powerful and highly civilized Eastern empires were shaping England's present fortunes as they had its past and would, likely, its future. As Swift was aware, Rome's push for imperial conquest, Athens's proclivity for assimilating luxury, and Sparta's isolationism represented distinct attitudes toward political structures and global relationships. If Addison and Defoe, in their fantasies of global reciprocity and English prosperity, elided realities of Eastern wealth, Swift's allusions to the past reverberate with anxious awareness that so-called native qualities are influenced by the traffic of things and ideas. In this regard, when Swift foregrounds sociopolitical systems from the classical past as examples for England's present and future, he is not simply being nostalgic for a past moment or obsolete structure. Much like Neville, decades earlier, Swift, Bolingbroke, and other "patriots" sought to reconcile their neoclassical admiration for the virtues of ancient civilizations—Roman courage, Athenian eloquence, Spartan restraint—with strategic visions for their own nation's future. It is in Swift's own turn to the global that we can see how he develops this past-future vision through his exploration of East-West contrasts and connections.

MODELS OF VIRTUE FOR HOUYHNHNMLAND: FROM THE EAST

In his admiration for the ancient past, Swift was reviving a much older quarrel about the relative merits of the "ancients" versus the "moderns." In his 1690 *Essay upon the Ancient and Modern Learning,* Swift's friend and patron Sir William Temple famously mocked the "moderns" of his age for perceiving themselves as "dwarfs standing upon a gyants shoulders, and seeing more or farther than he."[48] These ostensibly enlightened "moderns," Temple writes, fail to understand that ancient giants, too, were standing on the shoulders of learned men before them. Because of this modern myopia, he continues, "all that passed in the rest of our World before the *Trojan* War is either sunk in the depths of time, wrapt up in the mysteries of Fables, or so maimed by the want of Testimonies and loss of Authors that it appears to us in too obscure a shade to make any Judgment upon it" (4). In his own "The Battle of the Books," Swift defends and expounds upon Temple's ideas, calling him the "General of the *Allies* to the *Antients*" and a "Hero" in the fray of ideas.[49]

The quarrel regarding ancient and modern learning showcased differences and similarities not only between past and present but also between East and West. Temple, most notably, makes clear that the transmission of knowledge is not only a generational process that occurs across time, but also a global process that occurs across countries and continents. In fact, he predicts, in time we may see European learning regress, given that "Knowledge and Ignorance, as well as Civility and Barbarism, may succeed each other in the several Countries of the World" (*Essays*, 5). Temple goes on to trace Western learning back to its Eastern roots—namely, to such "remote and ancient Fountains as the *Indies* and perhaps *China*"—citing as his evidence the testimonies of Jesuit missionaries (12). The historical knowledge that has been lost in the modern age belongs to a time before, and a place apart from, that in which "so great a part of the World became Christian," he contends (4). The "ancients to those that are ancients to us" were not, as one might imagine, the Greek and Roman heroes that Gulliver calls up from the dead, but rather influential thinkers from Asia (15). Temple attributes the "seeds of all these Grecian Productions and Institutions" to "ancient Indian and Chinese Learning and Opinions" (14). Underscoring the West's debt of knowledge to Eastern intellects and traditions, he admits that while "it may look like a Paradox to deduce Learning from Regions accounted commonly so barbarous and rude," it is clear that the West's best ideas were "derived from [Eastern] fountains" (14).[50] For example, he explains, Pythagoras and Democritus "learn't the first Principles both of Natural and Moral Philosophy" when they "Travelled into [Chaldea] and India" (14). Lycurgus, the famous Spartan lawgiver, obtained "the Chief Principles of his Laws and Politicks, so much Renowned in the World" when he "likewise Travelled into India" (14). Most significantly, Temple reminds his readers, "near the Age of Socrates lived [China's] Great and Renowned Confutius" (13). Not only were the philosophers contemporaries, but Confucius had strengths that his Western counterpart did not: while "the Bent of the Grecian seemed to be chiefly upon the Happiness of private Men or Families," Temple notes, "that of the Chinese [was] upon the good Temperament and Felicity of... Kingdoms or Governments" (13). By emphasizing collective good above individual passion, Confucius was able to cultivate the sort of virtuous citizenry that Swift saw lacking in England and his native Ireland—to the extent that in its language, its moral doctrine, and its history, pure and stable for millennia, China appeared still to possess virtues England had lost.

In the *Travels*, Swift echoes Temple in suggesting that examples of virtue can be found in the interlocking worlds of the ancient past and the still-dominant East. The Brobdingnagians not only have a distinctly Laconic "stile" of speech that is "clear, masculine, and smooth," but they also "have had the Art of Printing, as well as the *Chinese*, time out of mind" (*GT*, 114). The Luggnuggs are "a polite[,] generous [and courteous] People," though they have "some share of that Pride which is peculiar to all *Eastern* Countries" (175). Those members of "the great Empire of *Japan*"—who, along with the Dutch, are the only real-world people with whom Gulliver interacts—are wealthier and far more civilized than the Europeans (182). And the "behaviour" of the virtuous Houyhnhnms is "so orderly and rational, so acute and judicious" (191), that Gulliver wishes they could be (as Leibniz had imagined, regarding the Chinese) missionaries "for civilizing *Europe*" (247). Indeed, in their painstaking isolation from foreign contact, commerce, and corruption, the Houyhnhnms follow not only the Spartans' example but also that of early modern China and Japan, whose isolation was legendary among European commentators and frustrating to ambitious English merchants.

For Swift, early modern China and Japan offer examples of orderly societies rooted in linguistic stability and cultural purity, two qualities that he sees as lacking in a morally and culturally bankrupt England. Running throughout the *Travels* is Swift's belief that the erosion of language reflects cultural decay.[51] Swift observes, for example, that the English language rapidly declined during the seventeenth-century Civil Wars. He faults the "Infusion of Enthusiastick Jargon" that "prevailed" during "the Usurpation" and the "Licentiousness which entered with the *Restoration*," which "from infecting our Religion and Morals, fell to corrupt our Language."⁵² If a lapse into license—an extreme, and therefore false, form of liberty—severed England's linguistic links to the past, a continued greed for foreign commodities perpetuated the erosion. Swift argues in his *Proposal for Correcting, Improving, and Ascertaining the English Tongue* that the ancient Romans' language declined for similar reasons: "The great Corruption of Manners, and Introduction of forein Luxury, with forein Terms to express it" went hand in hand with the renowned empire's fall (14). Despite his desire to stem further linguistic slippage, Swift did not share his predecessors' optimistic belief that a pure English language could be recovered. In Gulliver's description of Lagado, for example, Swift parodies the Royal Society's once-popular project to find a mathematical and thus "Universal Language to be understood in all civilized Nations" (*GT*, 158). The attempt to trace language back to its pure and transparent essence is a fool's errand, he suggests; instead, recognizing that linguistic decay is ineluctably linked to a crisis of moral and political character, one must resist corruption through social and political reform.

Unlike what Gulliver calls "our barbarous *English*," the Houyhnhnms' language is stable and consistent, much as the English perceived the language of early modern China to be (*GT*, 207). Whereas other empires have watched their native languages evolve and erode for different reasons (from "natural Inconstancy" for the French to foreign invasions in ancient Greece), Swift writes in his *Proposal*, "the *Chinese* have Books in their Language above two Thousand Years old, neither have the frequent Conquests of the *Tartars* been able to alter it" (16). Swift inherited his admiration for the Chinese language both from Temple and from Restoration-era predecessors such as John Webb, whose *Historical Essay Endeavoring a Probability That the Language of the Empire of China Is the Primitive Language* (1669) located in China the roots of a "transcendent representational system" that satiated Swift's "longing for a model of continuity, stability, and authenticity."⁵³ Regarding England's admiration for China, David Porter writes:

> In China [the English] discovered (or so they believed) a form
> of government that had endured, essentially unchanged, for

thousands of years and that had, furthermore, documented its achievements in countless tomes of meticulous historical records. Here was a state bureaucracy based on principles of wisdom, integrity, and respect for the past and known for its rational organization and efficiency. Here was an officially sanctioned moral doctrine that had for millennia promulgated values of virtue and obedience across an expansive empire while remaining untainted by violent sectarian dispute. And here, finally, was a peculiar form of writing that seemed to transcend the fatal transience and ambiguity of Western vernaculars to convey the timeless essence of ideas and things in themselves.[54]

China's combination of linguistic and cultural purity ensured fruitful ground in which the seeds of virtue might take root. Indeed, Bolingbroke describes the Chinese as a "people in whose minds a great veneration for their forefathers has been always carefully maintained."[55] To patriots like Bolingbroke, for whom words reflect character, the purity and stability of the Chinese language over time reflected the empire's orderly political structure as well as its citizens' devotion to practicing and preserving essential cultural values.

While Temple and Webb held up the Chinese as paragons of wisdom and virtue, others among Swift's contemporaries marveled at Japan's vast wealth and cultural longevity—effects of their successfully isolationist foreign policy—amid a rapidly changing world. Notably, Japan is the only real-world empire to which Gulliver travels. While en route to the East Indies, in an episode he recounts in book 3 of the *Travels*, his ship is attacked by "two Pyrate Ships [that are] Commanded by a *Japanese* Captain" and manned by a largely Dutch crew (*GT*, 130). Gulliver asks "a *Dutch-man*, who seemed to be of some Authority" on the ship, for mercy, "beg[ging] him in consideration of our being Christians and Protestants, of neighbouring Countrys, in strict Alliance, that he would move the Captains to take some pity on us" (130). The Dutch-man sneers at Gulliver's request, and it is the Japanese captain who helps Gulliver escape. "I was sorry to find more Mercy in a Heathen, than in a Brother Christian" who turns out to be a "malicious Reprobate,"

Gulliver remarks (131). Gulliver reiterates the contrast between the Dutch and the Japanese when he lands "at a small Port-Town called *Xamoschi*, situated on the *South-East* Part of *Japan*," and there meets the Japanese Emperor (183). Introducing himself as a shipwrecked "*Dutch* Merchant," he asks to forego "performing the Ceremony imposed on my Countrymen of *trampling upon the Cruxifix*, because I had been thrown into his Kingdom by my Misfortunes, without any intention of trading" (183). Despite questioning Gulliver's motivation, the Emperor allows him to pass safely through the city; Gulliver returns to England via Amsterdam shortly thereafter.

In *The Far East and the English Imagination, 1600–1730*, Robert Markley offers a compelling reading of the global economic tensions Swift foregrounds in this scene. Completely closed off to European missionaries and non-Dutch merchants from 1638 to 1853, Markley explains, early modern Japan posed distinct "challenges to Eurocentric views" of trade and global progress.[56] European commentators could not help but notice how "the Japanese rivaled or surpassed the English, French, and Dutch in their standards of living, technological sophistication, civility, business acumen, and military prowess."[57] Few eyewitness accounts of Japan had been published in English when Swift wrote *Gulliver's Travels*. One he would have known is Will Adams's account in Samuel Purchas's *Purchas His Pilgrimes*, written as Adams attempted to convince Japan's emperor of England's friendship while persuading him to let him leave the country and return home.[58] According to Adams, "The people of this island of Japan are good of nature, courteous above measure, and valiant in war: their justice is severely executed without any partiality upon transgressors of the law [and] they are governed in great civility."[59] He goes on to describe what he observes the Dutch are trading with the Japanese, noting particularly that Japan has no need of Holland's silver, for they have "much silver and gold to serve their turns in other places where need requireth." Indeed, Japan stood out in the early modern world as "a valiant and invincible Nation, [with] a polite, industrious and virtuous People, enrich'd by a mutual Commerce among themselves, and possess'd of a Country, on which Nature hath lavish'd her most valuable Treasures."[60] England's Protestant writers, in particular, struggled to fold evidence of heathen Japan's economic prosperity and exemplary civility into their worldviews. A proper mercantilist perspective rested on the assumption that mutually beneficial traffic between empires is essential to the global balance of power.[61] Yet the isolationist empires of China and Japan were evidently opting out of this East-West exchange of resources. In different ways, writers like Swift worked to piece together cohesive historiographical narratives that reconciled a persistent admiration of Eastern ideas, goods, and practices with a persistent fantasy about Western progress and ultimate preeminence.[62]

These examples of prosperous and long-lasting Eastern empires are as useful to Swift in developing his satiric response to the corrupting onslaught of progress as are the examples of public spirit from once-exemplary Rome, Athens, and Sparta. Porter, Markley, Annette Keogh, and other critics have unpacked Swift's allusions to early modern England's complex global milieu in useful and insightful ways. However, their foci on Swift's descriptions of *either* China *or* Japan minimizes how Swift inherits and reflects Temple's fascination with the global nature of modernity—that is, with the ways in which impulses of modernity repeat themselves, with difference, across centuries and around the world. As soon as we pin down Swift's ideal or model of virtue (whether to a lost agrarian moment or to Spartan temperance or to Chinese linguistic order), we lose the crucial cyclicality of the *Travels*, the fact that Gulliver maintains his identity and his sanity through constant movement and the accumulation of models of virtue that are themselves limited, derivative, and not quite real. As with each of the ancient models of virtue Gulliver explores in Glubbdubdrib, England's Eastern exemplars are limited in their usefulness. Analogies—whether between Swift's Houyhnhnms and the ancient Spartans or between the Houyhnhnms and thriving Eastern empires—create meaning by establishing similarity and difference. And it is, in the end, the subtle but real differences between past and present, East and West, that allow Swift to paint his portrait of "pure native virtues."

Indeed, each of Gulliver's examples from the past and the East foreground what England lacks or is *not;* in this regard, Swift's satire is easily recognizable. At the same time, however, these examples from other times and places do not, and cannot, represent the "true Spirit" of England: what virtue once was and what once again might be. After all, the nebulously ancient/Eastern Houyhnhnms have no learning to speak of but are simply *good*—they lack words to describe, let alone weapons to combat, the vices riddling England; having never been tested, their virtue cannot be proven (whereas the English, of course, had endured the refining violence of civil war and revolution). Meanwhile, Gulliver admires the Brobdingnags' wit and learning with a backhanded compliment: in contrast to a European obsession with the "Abstractions and Transcendentals" Swift himself mocked, the Brobdingnags' learning is "very defective, consisting only in Morality, History, Poetry and Mathematicks, wherein they must be allowed to excel" (*GT*, 113). And when Gulliver praises "this people" for having "the Art of Printing, as well as the Chinese, time out of mind," he adds that since they are "wholly secluded from the rest of the World" (as Far East Asia was and could well afford to be) they cannot help but evince a "certain *Narrowness of Thinking,* from which we and the politer Countries of *Europe* are wholly exempted" (112–13). Gulliver's praise for the "polite" is tongue-in-cheek, of course, a satiric jab at a middle-class euphemism for excessive consumption.[63] But the alternative is hardly a return to Western barbarity and ignorance. Swift uses fiction to imagine a movement through time and space that stops permanently at a moment when virtue—that quality of free and "Public Spirit" that is the pinnacle, impetus, and guarantee of all national virtues—truly thrived.

Insofar as Swift sees virtue as not just a political quality but also a distinctly Christian one, he can praise the remarkable virtue of Eastern empires while also holding out hope that England—and all of its Anglo-Irish heirs—will revitalize its "native Virtues" at some point in the future. Again, within the Protestant worldview, the notion of virtue extends beyond human excellence (both in terms of morals and of the material blessings that ostensibly accompany and reflect them) and chastity; it also signifies the operative and efficacious influence of a supernatural or divine power that enables and guarantees the virtue of chosen people. In a sermon entitled "On the Wisdom of This World,"

Swift demonstrates his adherence to this Protestant-political definition of virtue as he qualifies his praise for "the wisdom and virtue of the Gentile sages of those days, and likewise of those ancient philosophers who went before them."[64] Building upon his premise that the "unrevealed philosophy" of "heathen philosophers" falls short of divine revelation (31), he argues that the virtue of these philosophers, along with their admirable "sentiments of reason and justice" (34), must be attributed to their individual merits rather than to the influence of Christian "principles and doctrine" (39). Whereas some of his countrymen believe that "ancient philosophers rose to a greater pitch of wisdom and virtue . . . purely upon the strength of their own reason, and liberty of thinking," he contends, such "preference of heathen wisdom and virtue before that of the Christian is every way unjust, and grounded upon ignorance or mistake" (30–31). He admits that Christianity has been tainted and perverted over time by outside influences; however, he insists that it remains the only system of ideas that can unify reasonable people under an umbrella of proper government. It is only "by the assistance of God's grace" that principles "can influence our practice," he avers (39). After all, while "heathen philosophers" such as Socrates and Confucius may be renowned for their superior virtue, these wise men "were not agreed what this virtue was, or wherein it did consist" (32). In fact, "several among the best of them taught quite different things, placing happiness in health or good fortune, in riches or in honour, where all were agreed that virtue was not" (32). Because "they could not agree about their chief good," Swift contends, their claims about the links between happiness and virtue were "but vain babbling, and a mere sound of words" (32). The heirs to these pagan philosophers inherited such thinking, as virtue became a meaningless word rather than a sign of right principles worked out in practice. Some even went "so far as to call virtue its own reward," failing to recognize whence and from whom true virtue stems (32). Without the divine motivation and assistance "which Christian[s] only can boast of," Swift argues, virtue is impossible to recognize or understand, let alone attain (40). It is this same confusion or cultural amnesia that Gulliver suggests has taken root in England, where "the

Names of all [the old] Virtues are still retained" even as the practice of these virtues has shifted elsewhere (perhaps eastward) or disappeared entirely (*GT*, 247–48).

RECOVERING VIRTUE THROUGH REVOLUTION

Gulliver's task is to recoup virtue, not by returning to a lost past but by developing out of his disparate examples a sustainable model of virtue for his native land. Decades before Swift penned his *Travels*, Temple neutralized the sting of English weakness by situating the concept of national virtue within a cyclical theory of global history. Echoing the classical republican fear that prosperity leads to the downfall of empires, he predicts in *Of Heroic Virtue* that "the excellence of the Chinese wit and government [will render] them, by great ease, plenty, and luxury, in time effeminate."[65] The very excellence of the Chinese leads them first to prosperity and then to complacency, he suggests, for among them there is little of the vigilant patriotism that Swift works to cultivate in his readers. As it waits for its own age of prosperity—that which Pope suggests has been inaugurated by the Treaty of Utrecht—England has a chance to do things differently, fending off complacency so it can come into its own on the world stage. Indeed, Temple's belief in divinely orchestrated "revolutions of empire" partially mitigates the threat posed by the prosperous and still-dominant Eastern powers (*Heroic*, 449).

Gulliver's wish is to watch this global revolution occur. At one point in the *Travels*, while visiting one of the fictional "Eastern Countries," he comes across a strange breed of immortal beings called Struldbrugs. Of these creatures' fellow citizens, he exclaims, "Happy People who enjoy so many living Examples of antient Virtue!" (*GT*, 175–76). Believing that the Struldbrugs provide their community with "Examples, of the usefulness of Virtue in publick and private life," Gulliver fantasizes about what it would be like to live forever: to have "the pleasure of seeing the various Revolutions of States and Empire . . . the Discovery of many Countries yet unknown . . . barbarity over-running the politest Nations, and the most barbarous become civilized" (177–78). If only one could see global revolutions happening in real time, he believes, one might "remark the several Gradations by which Corruption steals into the World, and oppose it in every step" (178). Such a perspective on the world out of time is impossible, of course, and Gulliver is rudely brought back to reality when he is told that these immortals spend their years "impotent" and "melancholy and dejected," not contributing in any way to the common good (179–80).

This, of course, is Swift-the-conservative's greatest fear: that, seeing corruption, he and his countrymen will fail to stop it. Like Neville, however, he is more interested in reconciling England's foundational principles with its future fortunes than in turning back the hands of time. In response to what Swift and his contemporaries perceived as a moment of English moral crisis and Eastern strength, *Gulliver's Travels* holds out the possibility that global revolution will inevitably trouble but perhaps also revitalize Anglo-Irish virtue for the modern age. After all, if Swift longs for the order and stability exemplified by Eastern empires, he does not think that an isolated China will escape Sparta's fate any more than an overreaching England can escape that of Rome. He is aware that progress and decay go hand in hand and recognizes that universal human depravity renders "pure virtues" a fantasy regardless of national origin. If virtues can move, like commodities do, traffic may improve men as often as it corrupts them. While Swift wishes to halt cultural, political, and linguistic decline, he appears to admit that change is the only constant. Echoing Temple, he writes in *Contests and Dissentions* that "the Fate of Empire is grown a common place" and "all Forms of Government ... must be mortal like their Authors."[66] He continues, "We cannot prolong the Period of a Commonwealth beyond the Decree of Heaven ... any more than Human Life beyond the strength of the Seminal Virtue ... we may [only] watch and prevent Accidents" (48). Swift acknowledges that some do not share his views: "There is a set of sanguine Tempers," he writes, "who deride and ridicule ... all such apprehensions as these" simply because they believe "that the People of *England* are of a Genius and Temper, never to admit Slavery among them" (50). Yet such beliefs are based upon "short Views" rather than global perspective: "I think it a great Error to count upon the Genius of a Nation as a standing Argument in all Ages," he avers, "since there is hardly a spot of ground in *Europe*, where the Inhabitants have not frequently and entirely changed their Temper and Genius" (50). Variety and variance are a society's only givens. For this reason, the earnest patriot must plan and prepare for future action, not just reminisce about past ideals. In this regard, to contemplate the loss of England's "pure native virtues," as Gulliver does, is not only to call attention to cultural decay but also to propose a plan for renewal and regeneration of those virtues. The task of the virtuous patriot-citizen is to fight, with intention and vision, for the good of the nation; critique must always be followed with a plan of action, however unlikely it is that the plan will succeed.

In his preface to *The Idea of a Patriot King*, Bolingbroke echoes Swift in questioning what (and how long) it will take to revitalize his country's "pure native virtues":

> Will the British spirit, that spirit which has preserved liberty hitherto in one corner of the world at least, be so easily or so soon reinfused into the British nation? I think not. We have been long coming to this point of depravation: and the progress from confirmed habits of evil is much more slow than the progress to them. Virtue is not placed on a rugged mountain of difficult and dangerous access ... but she is seated, however, on an eminence.... To perform, therefore, so great a work, as to reinfuse the spirit of liberty, to reform the morals, and to raise the sentiments of a people, much time is required; and a work which requires so much time, may, too probably, be never completed. (220)

Bolingbroke, like Swift, sees virtue and liberty as inextricably linked: in order "to reform the morals" of a nation, one must first "reinfuse the spirit of liberty." For it is liberty that connotes the "British spirit," and it is "the British nation"—including, for Swift, England's Protestant heirs in Ireland—that has the clearest and most lasting claim to liberty among all the nations of the world. He is not optimistic that liberty will be restored, at least during his lifetime. Like Temple, Bolingbroke depicts "progress" not as a straightforward trajectory of improvement, but simply as movement itself, for better or for worse. Despite the time and labor required to reinvigorate it, and despite his uncertainty that liberty will be restored in his lifetime, he remains convinced that the "true Spirit of Liberty" is Britain's legacy, its raison d'être and guarantor of greatness.

Swift likewise sees liberty as a double-edged sword. Liberty is the core and essence of political virtue, he suggests, but it is also a dangerous quality. The unlimited ability to think, believe, and act freely, Swift writes, inevitably "produces," rather than precludes, "revolutions, or at least convulsions and disturbances, in a state."[67] Freedom foments—or at least raises the possibility of—cultural regression, political revolution, and social disorder. As Gulliver learns in the course of his travels, the desire for liberty is a universal trait. He sees in the land of the Brobdingnags, for example, through "conversation and reading their histories[, that] in the course of many ages, they have been troubled with the same disease to which the whole race of mankind is subject; the nobility often contending for power, the people for liberty, and the king for absolute dominion" (*GT*, 116). The pursuit of liberty is a risky endeavor; for those with "British spirit," however, it is a risk worth taking, a trait worth testing, and a virtue worth preserving precisely because it is theirs to preserve.

Two years after *Gulliver's Travels* was published, Swift returned to reimagine the murky possibilities of revolution. In his unfinished political allegory, *An Account of the Court and Empire of Japan* (penned in 1728 but published posthumously by a second cousin, Deane Swift), Swift uses Japan as a device to satirize the corruption surrounding George II's succession and Walpole's rise to power. What troubles him is not only the alienation of the Tory party and the celebration of corruption by Walpole and his cronies, but also the ramifications of a culture of bribery and debt for England's interests and reputation abroad. The new emperor calls together his counselors shortly after taking the throne and interrogates his prime minister Lelop-aw (i.e., Walpole) about the state of the empire. How is it, he asks, that the "empire of Japan" (i.e., England) has come to "so low a condition"—and "the debts of the empire [become] so prodigiously advanced"—"that the imperial envoys at foreign courts must be forced to purchase alliances, or prevent a war, by immense bribes given to the ministers of all the neighbouring princes?"[68] Lelop-aw defends his behavior by saying that it was designed to protect the empire from those who would usurp the throne and destroy the constitution (277). Exorbitant expenditures in the form of internal bribes and payments to foreign courts were necessary to keep the king and his family in power and to maintain power for "a majority of senators of *the true stamp,* as your majesty can desire" (279, emphasis added). Bribes are cheaper than war, he reasons, and without the "wholesome necessary expedient" of "this bribery and corruption, the wheels of government will not turn" (280). Since "it is well known we are a trading nation," he says, we must make sure these wheels are "greased at proper times" (280). He encourages the emperor to keep trusting his judgment and agenda, noting that "it is the laudable custom of all eastern princes, to leave the whole management of affairs, both civil and military to their visirs" (279). Through Lelop-aw, Swift again raises the question of what it means to be virtuous in such a climate, which requires a seemingly impossible balance of self-interest and sacrifice for the common good. The fictional emperor is "equally attentive and uneasy" at Lelop-aw's words, and he decides to wait for "some other counsellor [to] deliver his thoughts, either to confirm or object against what had been spoken by Lelop-Aw" (282). Swift leaves the satire unfinished, with the empire left paralyzed and deferring any decision for a different time.

The clash Swift illustrates between ideal and action, nostalgia and revolution, illumines England's history and imperial trajectory as much as it reflects Swift's own anxiety about living in a rapidly changing world. Indeed, the patriotic sentiment to which he subscribed was hugely influential on American revolutionaries even as it fizzled at home as the eighteenth century progressed. The Country Party proved largely reactionary, for while its members were quick to identify systemic flaws, they were unable to define and enact a compelling and viable solution for restoring public spirit. As Jonathan Lamb has argued, "The rhetoric of patriotism, always traversing the boundaries between historical and ideal referents, cannot provide an equivocal image of virtue or innocence."[69] It is nostalgia for habits of thought and action that grounds Swift's desire for a "pure native virtue" untainted by the world in which he must act. Yet, as Swift—a keen observer and critic of human nature—seems to understand, appeals to primitive values, lost references, or "pure native virtues" often take shape via derivation, accumulation, or imitation of examples from that world. The problems of frenzied consumption, ruthless conquest, and blind pursuit of technological progress are exercises in freedom that render liberty a chain. In one sense, then, *Gulliver's Travels* is a pessimistic coda to Henry Neville's vision—a tale of despicable Yahoos who are, like the "un-Englished" and "naked people" who eventually populate the Isle of Pines, degraded skeletons of Englishness.[70] But, as Swift knew all too well, it is far easier to expose and critique than to rebuild and conserve. He proves himself as visionary as Neville or Dryden in crafting a tale that works to reconcile foundational English virtues with the present realities of global modernity. In the end, the only brand of "made in England" virtue Swift can put forth is one forged through the very traffic he opposes. Gulliver's travels back in time and across the globe underscore a lack of virtue while keeping alive the potential that it might someday return.

For Swift and Bolingbroke, liberty is the prerogative of the male, and the problem of virtue is one of propagation and patrilineality. Swift, through Gulliver, emphasizes the commonplace belief that female "constancy and chastity" are requisite for national virtue and, as with all manifestations of virtue, have come under attack in the modern age (*GT,* 161). In virtuous Houyhnhnmland, after all, "the violation of marriage, or any other unchastity, was never heard of" (227). In turning to the work of three very different women writers—Mary Pix, Jemima Kindersley, and Charlotte Lennox—the next chapter interrogates two interlocking assumptions that undergird the political imaginations of Neville, Dryden, and Swift: first, that female chastity is the bedrock of national virtue, and, second, that chastity trumps liberty as the chief virtue and political power of the Englishwoman.

4

"HAPPY TO BE ENSLAVED"

Feminist Orientalism and the Constraints of Romance in Pix's *Ibrahim*, Kindersley's *Letters*, and Lennox's *Female Quixote*

A tradesman's credit and a virgin's virtue ought to be equally sacred from the tongues of men; and it is a very unhappy truth, that as times now go, they are neither of them regarded among us as they ought to be.
—Daniel Defoe, *The Complete English Tradesman* (1726)

The age of chivalry is gone ... and the glory of Europe is extinguished forever. Never, never more, shall we behold that generous loyalty to rank and sex, that proud submission, that dignified obedience, that subordination of heart, which kept alive, even in servitude itself, the spirit of an exalted freedom!
—Edmund Burke, *Reflections on the Revolution in France* (1790)

AT ITS 1696 DEBUT ON the London stage, Mary Pix's *Ibrahim, The Thirteenth Emperour of the Turks* transfixed spectators with its graphic depiction of rape. Targeted for ruin by her jealous rival, Sheker Para, the mufti's virtuous daughter Morena is ruthlessly violated by the emperor, Ibrahim. Dressed in white to signify her purity but driven to escape the "polluted cage" of her "soul," Morena poisons herself just before her lover, Amurat, top general of the Ottoman sultan's forces, has a chance to tell her that he loves her despite her sullied body.[1] "The / Spring, thy virgin mind was pure!" he cries, too late (5.40). Consumed with grief at Morena's death, Amurat kills himself, abdicating his command of the declining empire's army. As Jean Marsden has argued, Pix's tragedy—a commercial success—offered a sustained and sensationalized spectacle of a heroine's suffering structured around "the crucial contradiction of purity tainted."[2] Even as Morena must pay for her "pollution" with her life, she empowers the people to pursue Ibrahim's downfall precisely because she exhibits the irreparable results of his tyranny on her body. Like Lucretia, whose "great Example" of *"Roman* Courage" Morena explicitly invokes as one of the *"Roman* Ladies / Whose tracks of Virtue I with care, / Have followed," her sacrifice ensures her people's freedom from despotic rule not despite her ruin but because of it (5.38).[3]

Loosely based on Paul Rycaut's 1680 *History of the Turkish Empire,* as Pix claims in her preface, *Ibrahim* shares with Dryden's *Aureng-Zebe* an interest in dramatizing the power dynamics of an Eastern court in order to comment on the residual threat of absolutism at home; but Pix's provocative subject matter vividly showcases, too, how gendered assumptions trouble virtue discourse throughout the eighteenth century. If Aureng-Zebe's "captive queen" Indamora allowed Dryden to examine the complex interplay of morality and politics, as I argue in chapter 2, romanticized figures of besieged virginal virtue also gave women writers fodder for interrogating the role of chastity in upholding English liberty. While my previous chapters have focused their critical intensity on the work of a single author, this chapter traces a debate that resonates across decades and genres, about the value and limits of chastity as a form of political virtue. After setting up the contradiction of chastity, as Pix provocatively articulates it, I consider how two writers from later in the century—traveler and essayist Jemima Kindersley (1741–1809) and novelist Charlotte Lennox (1730–1804)—deploy similar strategies of feminist orientalism to critique their nation's gendered construct of political agency.

Drawing upon the sociopolitical stereotypes at her disposal, Pix makes her case for virtue through an Eastern heroine who exhibits

Western qualities: "A Free-born Maid" (4.31) who states that all her "ambition terminates in the contented paths / Of virtue" (3.20). While Morena's "free-born" status and identification with "the *Roman* Ladies" mark her as a worthy heroine for an English audience, her virtue is tested by the cruel whims of a ruthless Turkish tyrant, who flouts Islamic "holy Law" (3.19) and exhibits "pomp and show, instead of real greatness" (1.1). As Bernadette Andrea has argued, Pix's theatrical spectacle relies on a key assumption of "feminism orientalism"—namely, that "Western women . . . are the 'freest' women in the world as opposed to inherently oppressed Muslim women."[4] A century before Mary Wollstonecraft would refer to oppressive treatment of women as behavior that aligns with "the true style of Mahometanism" yet should be unknown to free and rational Englishwomen,[5] Andrea notes, Pix follows what was even in her time a "characteristic pattern of . . . displacement, followed by distancing, which enables self-definition."[6] Rather than indict the English patriarchy for its own "ruthlessness" and exploitative sexual double standards, Pix displaces systemic oppression onto the stock figures of a licentious Turkish tyrant and his hapless mistress.[7] Andrea contends that the meaning of Pix's tragedy depends upon its strategic opposition between East and West, insofar as Pix "proposes the courtly love ideal as intrinsic to western European culture and hence a foil for the supposed sexual tyranny of the East."[8] Indeed, as Ibrahim's court prepares virgins for his inspection, Sheker Para remarks to the chief eunuch, "How different, Achmet, is this from *the European stories; / I have read there, twenty Heroes for the Ladies / burn and die, here twenty Ladies for the Hero*" (1.4, emphasis added). Achmet replies, "It shows that Mankind maintains his Charter / Better here, yet loses sure the sweetness / Of Submissive Love"—a love, he implies, that flourishes best in a liberated Europe. According to Andrea, Pix uses this dramatic moment to posit "misogyny" as "essentially Islamic" and "oppos[e it] to supposedly more progressive western norms."[9] In other words, insofar as Morena is ruined thanks to the sexual double standards that her society not only tolerates but also encourages, she is a norm and not an exception. What Amurat's friend Solyman describes as "the Guard our Country lays on that fair charming Sex" is merely a cover under which those in power exploit the weak (2.6). In Morena's case, this "guard" destroys rather than protects, bringing about Amurat's ruin alongside that of his beloved.

In labeling *Ibrahim* the work of a "feminist orientalist," critics retroactively identify a political shortsightedness on Pix's part. Such a label, however, does not account for the more foundational problem of virtue Pix foregrounds in her play, in which the chaste yet ruined female body displays England's anxieties about enacting political virtue. Indeed, the play underscores a dilemma that would plague Englishwomen throughout the following century: that of how to *visibly prove* one's chastity. After all, while Daniel Defoe's ideal tradesman might prove his credit by flaunting his possessions, how does a woman prove her virginity (or her reputation for virginity, which Defoe calls the equivalent of a tradesman's credit) except by losing it? Meanwhile, how does a society educate innocent virgins to cultivate a virtue that both anticipates and is prepared to withstand repeated assault? Morena embodies for Pix's English spectators the paradoxical nature of virtue-as-chastity, demonstrating how a woman's virginal body serves both as a sign of her nation's moral excellence and as proof that virtue is a moving standard. Morena must die, in the end, because "female virtue, once tainted, cannot be allowed to live."[10] Marsden argues that turn-of-the-century tragedies like *Ibrahim* were supplanted by tamer, domestic accounts of virtue as the century progressed. "By the mid eighteenth century," she writes, "chastity on all social levels becomes an expected virtue."[11] And yet, I argue, folding "chastity" into a discourse of domestic virtue serves to emphasize, rather than erase, the epistemological problem of virtue—that is, the problem of how an Englishwoman can know herself to be virtuous when external signifiers of that virtue have been tainted or lost in the course of proving it true. Chastity remains tricky to define and prove in part because of the anxieties about national virtue that are embedded in Defoe's analogy between credit and virginity. Morena is driven to death not only because Pix's plot demands it, for political or marketing reasons, but also because, as a heroine in a modern, postromance world, she suffers from the same dilemma that Samuel Richardson's Clarissa encounters: she has no framework within which to reconcile the essential purity of her "virgin mind" with the violation of her body (whether anticipated or accomplished).[12] After all, as Margaret Anne Doody contends, "the story of the righteous virgin is a story we have been perpetually telling and trying to interpret."[13] On the Restoration stage or in the mid-century sentimental novel, barring providential protection or supernatural intervention, a woman's efforts to protect her virtue in the face of physical and psychological onslaught are often for naught. And yet, at the same time, both her virtue *and that onslaught* remain essential to displaying personal and national character. In other words, virtue is validated and proven true through its bearer's conscious acts of fortitude in the face of difficult tests and dangerous trials.

To call Pix a "feminist orientalist" assumes that we can read in *Ibrahim* a case for thinking of female virtue as signifying differently in Eastern reality than it does in the "European stories" Sheker Para evokes. Within the seraglio as Pix imagines it, Morena has no choice but to "burn and die"—to sacrifice her "Snowy vertue" and bear the penalty for that sacrifice—at the whim of a tyrannical "Hero" (4.29). Morena's virtue (or intact chastity) is both an ideal standard and an impossible one, insofar as it is doomed to ruin by the very test that proves it true. While "Manly Vertue" can manifest itself in visibly rewarded acts of "Courage" (1.2), the "Snowy vertue" of chastity apparently cannot translate into any act except sacrifice (4.29). With this contradiction in mind, however, Pix's analogy between Eastern realities and Western stories deserves closer attention. Sheker Para brings what she has "read there" in the old "European stories" into the present moment, interpreting this body of literary knowledge in such a way that obscures her villainous role in bringing about Morena's ruin. But, through Sheker Para's comparison, Pix complicates any neat opposition between East and West. She suggests that the ostensibly Eastern practice of sacrificing "twenty Ladies for the Hero" has little to do with the "ladies" and more to do with the elevation of villainous Ibrahim, rather than virtuous Amurat, to the position of national "Hero." In contrast to Sheker Para's claim, the truly heroic figure in Pix's play is Morena herself, one of the "twenty ladies" sacrificed to a despot's cruel rule. Morena remains essentially pure after her rape only through the generic demand of European stories, within which the rules of chivalric romance require that the hero sacrifice himself for the lady, rather than that the lady be sacrificed for the hero. Her violation means that the rules have been broken; there is no true "hero," and Amurat, recognizing his failure, must kill himself as well.

At the same time, these "European stories," in which, Achmet claims, men enjoy the "sweetness / of Submissive Love" (1.4), are hardly indicative of the "progressive western norms" to which Andrea refers. For one thing, the unnamed "Heroes" and "Ladies" of "European stories" are heroic only in the abstract—after all, where "*twenty* Heroes for the Ladies burn and die," there is no one hero who stands out above the crowd (4, emphasis added). Moreover, the "stories" to which Sheker Para alludes—romance narratives of a chivalrous hero and his chaste yet "submissive" heroine—were themselves the subject of debate in late-seventeenth-century England. In *Ibrahim,* Pix does not refer to a sultan/slave binary in order to compare Eastern and Western realities; rather, she builds on stereotypes about the East in order to revitalize ancient stories that elevate women to a position of sociopolitical agency. By invoking "European stories" of "Heroes" and "Ladies," of chivalric courage and heroic chastity, Sheker Para calls attention to the intertwining of East and West through the specific narrative form of romance. As a literary paradigm, feminist orientalism allows writers to select from the generic model of romance those themes and tropes that are useful for representing female agency while filtering out what is limiting or troubling for a particular audience. By comparing "European stories" to her own version of Eastern reality, Pix reaches back to a set of older narratives, and the places that give them meaning, to call attention to a domestic dilemma: expected to exalt chastity above all forms of virtue, freeborn Englishwomen find their natural liberty curtailed. Pix is neither the first nor the last of England's women writers to link tropes of the Orient and romance in order to participate in a long-standing feminist debate: What does it mean to be *free* as a woman, and to enact that freedom in the political sphere? Torn between seeing in the seraglio a space of freedom, where women are allowed to flourish, and a space of oppression, where women are veiled, repressed, and thus not really free, writers long after Pix continue to explore whether and how Eastern figures offer models of feminine political agency for Western imitation.

ORIENTING CHASTITY IN A POSTROMANCE WORLD

Shifting expectations for female virtue paralleled shifts in generic conventions during the seventeenth and eighteenth centuries. Critical accounts of realism's increasing hegemony in the realm of English prose fiction suggest that, by the end of the seventeenth century, romance encoded a bygone aristocratic social system that could not account for England's newly quantitative and middle-class measures of virtue.[14] Michael McKeon has argued that this generic shift—in which romance was increasingly figured "as a distinct generic, but also as a broadly epistemological, category whose meaning is overwhelmingly trivializing or pejorative"—was accompanied by a shift in social attitudes toward virtue that was marked by an "epidemic disenchantment with aristocratic ideology."[15] "Questions of virtue" were informed by an ideological dialectic between aristocratic, progressive, and conservative worldviews, he contends, in which nostalgia for the past clashed continually with a desire for progress.

Meanwhile, the tension between what McKeon calls aristocratic and progressive views of reality had distinctly gendered implications. With an eye for the "vital links that the heroic romance established between a gender (femininity) and a genre (the romance)," Ros Ballaster has traced English writers' reception and appropriation of French heroic romance—a form, she argues, that valorizes an aristocratic fiction of "heroinism, or female agency in the public sphere."[16] Later forms of romantic fiction came to emphasize the desiring and libidinous woman rather than an idealized, asexual one, she notes, ensuring that "death, ruin, and renunciation become the limited options of the romantic heroine."[17] With the rise of the sentimental novel and Richardson's virtuous heroines, there emerged a new dilemma for women writers. Ballaster contends that "the hegemony of the figure of the virtuous woman ... simultaneously provided the figure of the woman with a new cultural authority beyond the purely party political resistance she had represented in [earlier] works . . . and severely restricted the possibilities for the woman writer herself to undermine and manipulate fictions of gender identity as she had done earlier in the century."[18] According to Ballaster, alongside the glorifying of women within the private sphere came expectations that women would restrict their participation in political activity—including writing—outside of that sphere. In other words, "the dominance of a feminocentric idealization of woman as the signifier of moral purity and incorruptible truth from the 1740s onwards [following Richardson's 1740 publication of *Pamela*] had come to limit her possibilities for negotiation within the world of fiction."[19] Without legitimate outlets for expressing her political virtue, the chaste woman came to function "not just as the conduit but [also] as the repository of an honor that ha[d] been alienated from a corrupt male aristocracy."[20] Ultimately, if the image of the heroine shifts between the heroic romance and the domestic novel, her situation of constraint remains the same: she is exalted only to the extent that she is not free.

As David Hume explains in his *Treatise of Human Nature* (1739–40), this burden borne by eighteenth-century Englishwomen is essential to society's smooth functioning and the nation's well-being. Like the vaporous yet material force of credit, chastity is an invisible yet crucial component of national virtue. E. J. Clery has argued that civic humanism in England was a decidedly "gendered tradition," not only in its focus on masculine, patrician virtues but also in its "historical mode of thought," in which the narrative of "national character" was always one of decline into effeminacy.[21] Hume was an important contributor to an ongoing debate that saw "the overcoming of misogyny [as] a vital part of the moralizing of commerce."[22] Hume is fully aware that the emphasis on female virtue, in the form of the chaste female body, both reflects and reinforces a sexual double standard in England. In the *Treatise* he explores how the "notions" of "*modesty* and *chastity*"— terms denoting a "set of duties . . . which belong to the fair sex"—"arise from education, from the voluntary conventions of men, and from the interest of society," rather than having a clear "foundation in nature."[23] The "vast [and crucial] difference betwixt the education and duties of the two sexes," he writes, comes down to a "trivial and anatomical observation"—namely, that a woman can know that her children belong to her whereas a man can never be certain of his children's paternity (365). Given that the proper "end" of marriage is "the propagation of the species," Hume writes elsewhere, this uncertainty presents a social problem that requires an effective solution.[24] Since "men are induc'd to labour for the maintenance and education of their children, by the persuasion that they are really their own," society must find a way to guarantee the purity of women (*Treatise*, 365). The only proven deterrent to female infidelity, Hume suggests, is to "attach a peculiar degree of shame to infidelity [and to] bestow proportionable praises on their chastity" (365). He justifies the resulting double standard by emphasizing that chastity is an artificial virtue—that is, while not natural, it is nonetheless crucial to society. While it is "contrary to the interest of civil society, that men shou'd have an *entire* liberty of indulging their appetites," Hume contends, "this interest is weaker than in the case of the female sex" (366). As a result, it becomes necessary to cultivate in "the female sex a repugnance to all expressions, and postures, *and liberties,* that have an immediate relation to that enjoyment" (365, emphasis added). The requirement that women shun erotic "liberties" extends to those beyond childbearing age. Because men tend to associate "ideas of modesty and decency" with sexuality, Hume notes, society "extend[s] the notions of modesty over the whole sex, from their earliest infancy to their extremest old-age and infirmity" (366). Within Hume's system, Ann Levey writes, "it is the general functioning of a convention in which chastity and modesty are connected that provides the regularity that allows us to take modesty as a sign of chastity."[25]

According to Hume, this emphasis on female chastity as a guarantor of social stability is both a generally civilizing trait and a specifically European one. In a 1742 essay entitled "Of Polygamy and Divorces," Hume argues that "our present EUROPEAN practice with regard to marriage" is the only system suitable for civilized societies.[26] He examines two alternative case studies: the "voluntary divorces" (111) of the ancient Greeks and Romans and the Eastern practice of polygamy, both of which he sees as misguided attempts to ensure "the natural liberty of men"

(110). First of all, he writes, polygamy divides families and, by extension, empires. The "Asiatic manners are as destructive to friendship as [they are] to love," he claims, causing families "all over the east" to live "separate from [one] another, as if they were so many distinct kingdoms"; such jealous behavior leads to "another unavoidable consequence of these eastern institutions"—namely, "the bad education of children" (112). Most important, he asserts, the practice of polygamy negatively impacts a nation's women, and "the constraint in which it holds the fair-sex all over the east" should "render polygamy more odious" to freeborn English readers (113). Echoing orientalist stereotypes about oppressed Eastern women and their free Western counterparts, Hume asks his readers to imagine the astonishment of "an honest TURK, who should come from his seraglio, where every one trembles before him ... to see SYLVIA in her drawing-room, adored by all the beaus and pretty fellows"—in such an environment, "he would certainly take her for some mighty and despotic queen" (112). Hume makes a subtle jab here at the vanity of a Sylvia, of course, but he also evinces a degree of pride at the gendered role reversal that goes on in the English drawing room, that bastion of domestic sovereignty. "Barbarism," he concludes, "appears, from reason as well as experience, to be the inseparable concomitant of polygamy," whereas civility is achieved through procreative monogamy and sustained by chastity (113).[27] Hume echoes an anxiety that Shaftesbury articulates in *Characteristics of Men, Manners, Opinions, Times*, where he laments that England's "tender virgins"—"the fair sex of this island"—have been "so seduced" by "monstrous tales" and "Moorish fancy" that, like Shakespeare's Desdemona, they are in perpetual danger of "chang[ing] their natural inclination for fair, candid, and courteous knights into a passion for a mysterious race of black enchanters" and of "resign[ing] fathers, relations, countrymen and country itself to follow the fortunes of a hero of the black tribe."[28] Shaftesbury goes on to portray such seduction by "Moorish fancy" and Eastern wealth as a threat to England's national virtue: "So far are our modern moralists from condemning any unnatural vices or corrupt manners," he writes, "that they would have vice itself appear as natural as virtue," which "has the same fixed standard" across time.[29] While he denounces the "fancy" of orientalized romance for the threat it poses to the "fixed standard" of English virtue, he nonetheless reaches back to the very tropes of romance he dismisses, suggesting that it is the task of modern Britain's "candid, and courteous knights" to ensure that women maintain the sexual standards Hume sketches in such detail.

This reversion to older tropes of romantic constraint, by Shaftesbury and Hume, demonstrates how chivalry becomes shorthand for new hierarchies, in which the elevation of women remains contingent upon patriarchal expectations. Hume was wrong, of course, to imply that eighteenth-century Englishwomen were actually treated as (or mistaken for) queens. As Sarah Chapone's anonymously published 1735 pamphlet, *The Hardships of the English Laws in Relation to Wives,* makes clear, England was just as much a "Paradise of Men" as Hume supposes the realm of the "Grand Seignior in his Seraglio" to be.[30] Lady Mary Wortley Montagu makes a similar jab at the English patriarchy in her *Turkish Embassy Letters,* where she famously observes that the veiled Muslim women she meets in the Ottoman seraglio "have more liberty than we have."[31] Some critics have noted how this scene exemplifies the "contradictions of feminist orientalism," insofar as Montagu simultaneously envies and pities her Ottoman counterparts.[32] As Denys Van Renen argues, however, Montagu's attention to the seraglio as a model of "female subjectivity" shows her broader resistance to the "increasingly entrenched boundaries of national identity" structuring her own political milieu.[33] Daniel O'Quinn pushes this point about Montagu's political engagement further, arguing that her layered intertextual allusions let her articulate a "counter-epic" to the imperial imagination she and her contemporaries inherit from Virgil.[34] Although she cannot escape her complicity in Britain's imperial vision, O'Quinn argues, Montagu is aware that "hospitality and empire find themselves radically at odds" and feels a "melancholy loss of [the] cosmopolitan exchange" she so admires in the seraglio.[35] This sense of loss shapes Montagu's assessment of England's misplaced ideals of chivalry. In a reflection on French moralist Monsieur de la Rochefoucault's "maxim" about marriage, appended to her *Letters,* she lambasts "*our* antiknights-errant, who are ever in pursuit of adventures to reduce innocent virgins to distress, and to rob virtuous women of their honour; who regard beauty, youth, rank, nay *virtue itself,* as ... incentives" to their perverse game. She holds up "the Turkish manners" in comparison, asking, "What would these *moral people* think" of "our barbarous manners" and "our ridiculous customs, which form a confused medley of the rigid maxims of Christianity, with all the libertinism of the Spartans"?[36] In contrast to Hume's nostalgia, she links romance imagery to her observations of women's agency in and outside of the seraglio in order to question ideals of virtue that depend on chastely passive bodies.

The remainder of this chapter further teases out the discursive contradictions that emerge when writers invoke tropes of chivalric romance in order to work through perceived crises of national virtue, especially insofar as that virtue is said to be embodied by the chaste woman. Given British women's marginalized status in an increasingly (but not entirely) postromance milieu, the paradoxical image of the East as a source of wisdom *and* ignorance, wealth *and* ruin, virtue *and* heresy let writers hold in tension realistic and romantic ways of seeing the world and their places in it. As these women writers adapted the strategies of romance to represent their experiences and their sense of what virtue means, in a modern world, they found themselves invested in oriental spaces. In what McKeon calls its abstracted form, romance was often associated with antiquated modes of thinking that appeared antithetical to progress—the Gothic, the aristocratic, the oriental, and other "ways of thinking incompatible with [England's] own rational empiricism."[37] "Tropes of romance" persisted, Eugenia Zuroski writes, because they "represent[ed] the limits of [modern] order"; in this regard, romance came to signify an underside of modernity and all that had to be repressed in service of progress.[38] At the same time, the power of romance persisted partly because it affirmed a coherent structure for political agency that rooted England's national virtue in its valuation of the chaste female. Despite an antiempirical stigma, romance held out a certain promise of order—a set of social constraints, clearly defined roles, and recognizable hierarchies—that remained attractive precisely because these constraints seemed to ensure a level of gendered respect that many saw as being eroded by modern commercial priorities, the shadows of global revolutions, and other threats.

To emphasize how persistently this dual investment in Eastern spaces and romance tropes echoed throughout the eighteenth century, I turn to two other writers who draw on tropes of feminist orientalism to explore the concerns Pix raises in her play. Jemima Kindersley, a travel writer and essayist, follows Montagu in using firsthand observations of women's experiences abroad to comment on what she perceives to be a lack of opportunity and protection for women back home. Similarly, though in the realm of fiction, Charlotte Lennox's protagonist in *The Female Quixote* invokes legendary Eastern heroines in order to critique the constructed customs of chastity in which she is steeped. For both writers, feminist orientalism is not simply a mode of ethnographic judgment or a way to displace national anxieties. Insofar as it is intertwined with romance, it offers a framework for wrestling with oft-contradictory cultural codes of virtue, and for reaching back to antiquated gender relations in order to make sense of present expectations for women's participation in the public sphere. Both writers reconceive of the strictures of chastity as a vehicle for liberty and use the process of orienting virtue to imagine how confinement forestalls agency and ruin alike.

"HAPPY TO BE ENSLAVED": JEMIMA KINDERSLEY

Long after the ostensible discrediting of romance, Jemima Kindersley exploited its enduring potential, in conjunction with Eastern spaces, to help writers imagine forms of virtuous female agency. Kindersley, the wife of an artillery officer with Britain's EIC, traveled with her husband and baby son to India during "a turbulent, transformative period in Indian history and in Britain's relationship with the subcontinent," after British victories in battles at Plassey (in 1757) and Buxar (in 1764) had given the EIC control over new territories there.[39] She documented her experiences in *Letters from the Island of Teneriffe, Brazil, the Cape of Good Hope, and the East Indies,* which she began writing in 1764 and published in 1777, several years after returning to England. Montagu's *Turkish Embassy Letters*, which were posthumously published in 1763, had sparked a keen interest in women's travel writing, and Kindersley—who had opportunities to visit Allahabad and other cities where the EIC was just gaining access—found herself uniquely poised to describe the company's outposts and factories, along with customs of places in India that she knew most readers would never see for themselves.[40] In her position as an unofficial EIC ambassador, Kindersley often moves beyond describing cultural practices she observes to attempt an explanation of the origins and rationale behind them. For instance, like Dryden, whose dramatization of sati was considered in chapter 2, Kindersley calls attention to sati as "the most extraordinary and astonishing custom in the world"; she claims, however, that her focus is not on describing a "well-known" practice but on "endeavour[ing] to find out what could give rise . . . to such a barbarous exertion of virtue."[41] As we will see, her observations in India fuel her argument, in later writings, about the troubling expectations for women's chastity back home in England. Recognizing, as she puts it, that "we [English expatriates] always flatter ourselves with hopes of returning home again," she works to make her observations useful for her target readers (28).

In many of her *Letters*, Kindersley demonstrates genuine appreciation for the different cultures she encounters and a fascination with global differences in custom and law. She follows Enlightenment thinkers, especially Montesquieu, in linking this variance to climate and geography—observing, for instance, that Hindostan's heat breeds the political despotism that, in turn, encourages pervasive lethargy.[42] Elsewhere, however, she makes sweeping generalizations about the archaism and superstition that she suggests distinguish a stunted, stagnant East from a free, progressive West. Upon arriving in Pondicherry in June 1765, she records her first impressions of India: it is a "once fine place," she writes, that "fills my mind with a sort of pleasing melancholy . . . a kind of reverence and pity for ruined grandeur" (*Letters*, 75). She goes on to claim that "neither Mahomedans or *Hindoos* ever change their mode . . . therefore invention and improvement are no part of [Eastern] ideas" (240). With such a claim, she affirms both the broad conflation of distinct nations and peoples and the "ontological and epistemological distinction" between East and West that Edward Said called a trademark of orientalist thinking.[43] Eastern people are skilled at imitating quality products and ideas, Kindersley avers, but they lack the "ingenuity to make any alteration" to their situations (*Letters*, 244). "While all other nations, those in Europe particularly, have been making constant improvements and new discoveries," she writes, "they have contented themselves with that which has been handed down to them from their forefathers" (132–33). She goes on to offer a brief history of the Mughal Empire's decline, concluding that "it is not here we must look for learning and science," since "the wise men of the East have disappeared" (176).

Kindersley extends these observations to the "poor women" (226) that she meets when she is invited "into a great *Mussulman's Zanannah*," or harem (220).[44] "Many of the Eastern women have so much beauty," she notes, despite their "disagreeable complexions," uninhibited "wantonness," and "unchangeable" fashion, so that if only their features "were set off by a fine red and white complexion they would be incomparable" (*Letters*, 221–22). However, because they have been confined by jealous "Mahomedan" men in a notoriously "despotical state," she continues, these "Oriental ladies" can aspire neither to earthly fame nor to heavenly "felicity" (200).[45] Moreover, she observes, frequent childbearing and excessive exposure to the torrid climate "hastens their decline" (227). Kindersley offers a disclaimer that, since she has not experienced every microclimate, readers "are not to apply [her] accounts to all India" (247). Yet she concludes her travelogue with a blanket judgment: "I should think it necessary to make an apology for these observations if I did not look upon them as . . . instances of the universality and unchangeableness of . . . customs in the East" (266). By the end of her *Letters*, Kindersley's enlightened awareness of differences in custom is overshadowed by confidence in her own cultural superiority.

Kindersley's opposition of a stagnant East to a progressive West echoes the belief voiced by many of her contemporaries that progress in the form of "improvements" and "discoveries" is a requisite sign of national greatness in the modern age (132). For example, while describing the revolutionary events whereby the Mughal Empire was born, she goes on to underscore a "great analogy between the present and ancient manners in the east" (263). If we "judge of the future by the past" (208), as she assumes one inevitably does, we may see why, despite "the riches of the country[,] we must henceforth speak of it in its decline," recognizing that India has been "reduced to a dependence on the English" (151–52). Due to the "lofty and figurative style of the East," for example, the sort of religious and intellectual revolution that Martin Luther sparked in Europe could never take place in India (138). Kindersley assumes that, despite its natural deficiencies, England is providentially destined (and thus extraordinarily capable) to revise its own moral, economic, and historical shortcomings, whereas Eastern nations are confined and defined by theirs. She echoes her predecessors from a century earlier in positing a theory of history according to which the West will progress whereas the East will regress.

Apart from allowing writers to displace domestic anxieties, this kind of orientalist narrative was not particularly useful for thinking critically about the role of women in Britain's future. Felicity Nussbaum has argued that the act of travel gave writers like Kindersley an "opportunity to articulate alternative visions of modernity that fracture the inevitability of progress [and] of the native woman's certain trajectory towards European modernity."[46] Yet the problem of freedom—with its political and gendered implications—proved difficult for Kindersley to explain. If political liberty supposedly distinguished Britons from their ancient and contemporary exemplars alike, it was much more difficult for Englishwomen to practice this same virtue. This tension is at the heart of the literary obsession with the Eastern harem that Montagu illustrates; however, whereas Montagu emphasizes the seraglio's exemplary enabling of cross-cultural sociability, Kindersley focuses on the impact of confinement on gendered virtue. Kindersley writes of the "Oriental ladies" she meets that "confinement cannot be reckoned a misfortune to these women, as they have always been accustomed to it"; in fact, she writes, they would instantly "be degraded to a level with the lowest people were they to appear in public" (*Letters*, 224–25). In other words, she suggests, one's habits and nationality do (and ought to) affect whether a "confined" lifestyle is perceived as a negative experience or an enviable one.

Four years after her *Letters* were published, Kindersley published a translation of Antoine Léonard Thomas's *Essay on the Character, the Manners, and the Understanding of Women, in Different Ages;* in the editorial materials she included with this translated work, she complicates her earlier, more straightforwardly orientalist sentiments. Kindersley explains in her introduction to the translation that she had been working on her own collection of *Essays on the Female Mind* when she came across this essay by Thomas, a French poet and critic. Their "designs" and "opinions" were "nearly the same," she writes; however, because "his abilities [were] superior," she decided to translate his essay instead of finishing her own.[47] In his original essay, Thomas contrasts a free Europe to an oppressive East in order to develop a myth of ahistorical, domestic, and distinctly European virtue. "The same period in which [women's] empire in Europe commenced destined them forever to slavery in Asia," he claims.[48] He writes,

> If we look amongst the Orientals, we shall find another species of despotism and tyranny; amongst them, confinement, and the domestic servitude of women, is authorized by the manners, and consecrated by the laws. In Turkey, in Persia, in Hindostan, in Japan, and in the vast empire of China, one half of the human species is oppressed by the other. These excesses of oppression, take their rise from the excess of love itself: all Asia is covered with domestic prisons, where beauty in slavery attends the caprices of a master. (3–4)

Thomas links this institutionalized slavery to a harem dynamic that, he suggests, prevails not only in the Islamic Ottoman Empire but across "all Asia." He claims, "In these countries,... women are obliged to repay even their servitude with the most tender love, or, what is more frightful, with the resemblance of love which they do not *feel*.... All their education tends to their debasement [and] *their virtues are constrained*" (4, emphasis added). The effects of such servitude-sans-sentiment are as much physical as mental, he notes, echoing Kindersley's assessment of the women in the harem: "After an existence of a few years, their old-age is long and frightful" and sadly premature (5). Thomas does not pretend that European women are absolutely free; on the contrary, he writes, "upon three quarters of the globe, Nature has placed [women somewhere] between contempt and unhappiness" (6). "In more temperate countries," however, "where the climate gives less ardour to desires, and [gives] places more confidence in virtue," "women are not deprived of [their] liberty" even though "the severity of legislation has everywhere placed them in a state of dependence" (5). He goes on to trace how European women have diverged from the path of their more virtuous ancestors; yet, he adds, since *"our virtue* is proved by trials," it is not too late for them to recover this virtue (8, emphasis added). Like Kindersley, Thomas develops his argument by contrasting East and West, emphasizing cultural similarities and differences in order to find in the East a laudable model that can nonetheless be surpassed by those who have a genuine ability to "feel" rather than exhibit the mere "resemblance of love" (4).

Using the East as a foil, Thomas charts what he sees as the parallel trajectories of chivalry and romance in history. He contends that the gradual "extinction of chivalry in Europe" (158) from its medieval glory days to an eighteenth-century heyday of "false wit" (161) mirrors the decline of romance from a feminocentric vehicle for heroism to an empty word for "those qualities we have not merit enough to attain" (199). According to Thomas, romance in the modern era has become an empty form, a way to "talk . . . of pleasure, but . . . feel it not" (199). He concludes his essay with a nostalgic wish: "Could we but learn how much *virtue* . . . is superior to pleasure," he exclaims, "it is then that women would recover their empire; it is then that beauty, embellished by virtue, would command mankind, *happy to be enslaved,* and great in their weakness" (212, emphasis added). Linking female freedom to chastity, Thomas proposes that female virtue truly flourishes only in confinement. After all, he surmises, it is not only laws but also cultural expectations that keep European women dependent. They will never be "at perfect liberty" (206) as long as they must focus on pleasing others through perpetual "movement," "ostentation," and an obsession with frippery and fashion (213). If we would recover and practice Europe's virtue of yore, he suggests—that is, if we would enable the "virtuous enjoyment" that "render[s] life an enchanting dream" (213)—we must hearken back to a simpler past, drawing on forgotten cultural norms and reinvigorating older stories of romance within which women are empowered even as they are enslaved.

Kindersley appended two of her own, original essays to her translation of Thomas's work; in these essays, she applies his ideas to her own, English society without overtly disputing his Eurocentric and seemingly paradoxical claims that the Islamic East oppresses women and that European women would have greater "virtuous enjoyment" if likewise enslaved. While Thomas "considered the female character in different ages," she writes, her own essays "consider the character of women in different countries, of different religions, and under different forms of government, in the present age" (iv). "I do not flatter myself that my Essays will work a reformation in the morals and manners of the age," she adds, though she goes on to state that her goal in writing is to "inspir[e] [English] daughter[s] with those sentiments which are the basis of every virtuous and every noble action" (vi). She explicitly offers her comments as instructive for young girls who are learning the ways of virtue. In her first essay, Kindersley sets up her primary case study, in which she purports to contrast the "laws and manners" of "the Mahomedans in Asia" with those of "the people of Holland" (220). She concludes, rather surprisingly, that Eastern women, confined to the seraglio, have more "natural power over" men than do ostensibly liberated women in the West (221). The "Mahometan . . . confine[s] his wives [not from] contempt [but out of] violent fondness," she asserts, and it is precisely because "he guards their persons as his most valuable treasures" that his wives maintain their "natural power" (220). She compares this picture of mutual respect to the situation in Holland, where "the natural power of the women [is] small" (222). There, laws, rather than sentiment, protect women. Holland's liberating legal structure has a deleterious effect: while women are treated as equal partners, they are "valued [only] in proportion to [their] usefulness and oeconomy," rather than for their uniquely feminine beauty and virtues (224). Practically speaking, as a result, she sees Eastern society as more feminocentric than that of the West. For "in spite of the severity of the Mahomedan laws respecting women, and the lenity of the laws respecting them in Holland," she notes, numerous "Mahomedans... have given themselves up to the entire direction of their female favorites"; by contrast, "it does not appear that Dutch husbands give up their interest through the influence of their wives" (223). Without well-intentioned constraints, she concludes, women are unprotected from exploitation.

Kindersley's second essay is concerned entirely with the homegrown problem of abusive English husbands. Moving from considering ideals to examining practices of virtue, she remarks on how many Englishwomen "must practice virtues, which although not the most shining, are perhaps of all virtues the most difficult to persevere in" (229). When a husband—the one "who ought to be the guardian, the protector, the director, and comfort of both her and [their children]"—instead behaves with "folly and ignorance," is "sunk in debauchery," and "sets [her children] every example of vice," it is nearly impossible for a woman to practice expected graces (229–30). "Is woman capable of such greatness?" Kindersley asks. "Will a modish education inspire her with such virtue?" (231). All that a woman can do in such situations (which are, Kindersley notes, all too typical in England) is to "regar[d] her sufferings as trials of her virtue," sustaining herself with the "consciousness of having performed her duty" and the knowledge that "the tears of the virtuous are sweeter than the pleasures of vice" (231–32). This kind of virtue as domestic duty cannot be taught by "the dancing-master [or] the music-master" or learned "at the opera, at concerts, or the gaming-table" (231). Instead, it is a "fortitude" born out of and evidenced through a woman's "own reflections in retirement," practiced and proven through suffering (231). Kindersley concludes the collection of essays by claiming that this expression of female fortitude in the face of indifference and even abuse is the greatest virtue of all. She asks, "Where is the man who can pretend to boast of greater merit?" (232).

We can see some inconsistencies between Kindersley's Eurocentric *Letters* and her essays, in which she admires the result, if not the structure, of Eastern gender dynamics. But her writings are linked insofar as Kindersley recognizes romance to be a powerful form for communicating desire and loss (the very emotions India's landscape evokes in her) and revitalizing national virtues that have been devalued or forgotten in the lurch toward modernity. Echoing Swift and other patriotic predecessors, she contends that, regardless of gender, true liberty can never be synonymous with individual autonomy; instead, political liberty ensures one can act in a way that is driven and constrained by a broader commitment to communal health. Kindersley echoes Thomas in claiming that an intangible but valuable cultural quality has been lost in postromance England's treatment of women. But she pushes his argument further as she implies that it is the "despotical Mahometans," not the freeborn English, who practice this lost standard of treating women with deference and respect. In fact, rather than emphasize the mutual plight of women across the globe, she singles out non-European systems as more feminocentric, though not necessarily more equitable. In the essays' nostalgia for romance as in the *Letters'* "reverence for [the] ruined grandeur" of Mughal India, feminist orientalism provides a framework for grappling with, rather than displacing, the inconsistent standards for female virtue.

For Kindersley, as for Montagu, the seraglio illustrates a productive paradox: women find freedom in and through constraint. In its stereotyped form, as Pix's Morena demonstrates, the seraglio represents a dangerous model of patriarchal control: if the model does not function properly—if the cherished female has no guard or protection—then she will be violated. Reimagined through the lens of romance, however, the seraglio becomes a space where women flourish, individually and collectively, because they are valued and protected rather than used and exploited. In this sense, Kindersley links the East to antiquity, not to dismiss either but to imagine how women's virtue transcends newer notions of chastity as commodity. Her admiration for romance underscores a certain discomfort with Defoe's notion that "a tradesman's credit and a virgin's virtue ought to be equally sacred," even if she agrees with his assessment that "neither of [these are] regarded among us as they ought to be."[49] Something is lost when society defines virtue solely in quantitative terms, as the mercantile Dutch do, and by so doing invalidates the sacrifices it regularly demands of its women.

"THE EMPIRE OF LOVE": CHARLOTTE LENNOX

Kindersley's argument—which she articulates well after aristocratic-romantic ideals supposedly get displaced by modern England's commercial-empirical priorities—takes explicit form in the work of her contemporary Charlotte Lennox, whose *Female Quixote* similarly highlights contradictions of female virtue by troubling stereotypes of the orientalized romantic heroine. If Kindersley writes with the aim to "inspir[e]" young English "daughter[s]" to virtue, Lennox's 1752 novel displays this education in action. Her novel has generally been read as a parody of Miguel de Cervantes's *Don Quixote* and the voluminous French heroic romances that were popular in the preceding century. In it Lennox traces the reeducation and extrication of her heroine, Arabella, from a realm of illusion, in which she interprets every aspect and incident of her life according to "the Rules of Romance" (as spelled out by writers like Madeleine de Scudéry and La Calprenède), to a realm of reality, in which she marries her long-suffering cousin, Glanville, breaks her bondage to an idealized past, and conforms to social expectations of domestic virtue.[50] According to Arabella, the French romances (*Clelia* and *Artemenes, Cassandra* and *Cleopatra*) are "Books from which all useful Knowledge may be drawn" (48). In their "Heroines of Antiquity," including the orientalized *"Statira, Parisatis,* [and] *Mandana"* (44), she finds "the most shining Examples of Generosity, Courage, Virtue, and Love; which regulate our Actions, form our Manners, and inspire us" (48). "But for the inimitable Pen of the famous *Scudery*," she exclaims, society would have remained "ignorant of the Lives" of these "bravest Men, and most virtuous of Women" (62) in whose steps she believes it her "Duty to follow" (45). Focusing on the intersection of genre and gender in the novel, critics have argued that Arabella illustrates the difficulties women writers face while finding their voices in a patriarchal milieu.[51] As Felicity Nussbaum points out, Lennox is ambivalent toward romance insofar as she "mocks romance's self-delusion while employing its techniques."[52] Thanks to the patient tutelage of the Countess and the Doctor, Arabella learns that the rules of romance neither apply to nor can change the actual domestic realm in which women live. "Your Writers have instituted a World of their own," the Doctor tells her, and "nothing is more different from a human Being, than Heroes or Heroines" (*FQ*, 380). Duty trumps ideals in a postromance reality.

In some sense, Arabella's final conversion by the end of the novel is a triumph not only of realism over romance but also of Eurocentric values of progress and domesticity. According to Eugenia Zuroski, the novel also reflects a mid-century shift in England from cosmopolitan admiration for the East to nationalist denigration of it. She contends that *The Female Quixote* is "one of the earliest texts to render romance utterly foreign to the English sensibility by Orientalizing its characteristic tropes."[53] After all, the French romances that Arabella admires are largely set in exotic oriental locales, and "the greatest Princesses" she holds up as exemplary are nearly all, without exception, foreigners. At one point the skeptical and jealous Miss Glanville says to Arabella, regarding the latter's admiration for romantic heroines, "What signifies what Foreigners do? I shall never form my Conduct, upon the Example of Outlandish People; what is common enough in their Countries, would be very particular here" (*FQ*, 184). In the end, Zuroski asserts, "the Orient in whose image Arabella fashions herself—an amalgam of mythologized Eastern settings, including Persia, Scythia, Ethiopia, and Egypt—refers to nothing else but fictionality itself."[54] As Samara Anne Cahill contends, Arabella begins by expressing "a genuine interest in . . . the particularities of other cultures and other women" but, in the course of her education, ultimately "abandons [both] her romances and their valorization of transnational heroism."[55] By linking romance to the East, in the tradition of feminist orientalism, Lennox displaces a lack of actual (nonfictional) female agency onto the Eastern woman—in this case, not the real harem-bound women that Kindersley encounters but rather the time-bound women of the ancient Eastern past.

That most critics find the novel's ending unsatisfactory, however, troubles readings of the novel that affirm straightforward distinctions between romance and realism, East and West. One problem with taking at face value the novel's dismissal of romance, Margaret Anne Doody has argued, is that Lennox "leaves unsolved the problem of whether a woman ought or ought not to risk death in order to escape rape."[56] "After all," she writes, "considering the high value placed on physical virginity in well-born marriageable girls," a value that was "inculcated both by seventeenth-century romances and by eighteenth-century conduct books," "it is nonsense to tell a young woman that rape and abduction are only fictions."[57] The double bind of chastity and the instability of virtue drive Arabella to madness and render her conversion unconvincing. I argue that Lennox uses references to the East, in conjunction with romance, not to lambast fictionality as fruitless but to highlight the persistent contradictions plaguing female virtue in the modern age. Arabella is nostalgic for a world in which virtue makes sense because love follows strict rules, a world in which chastity is tested and proven by its conformity to standards. "The Empire of Love," she claims, "like the Empire of Honour," "is govern'd by Laws of its own" (*FQ*, 320). Her statement is not true, of course, and she is reminded repeatedly that neither of these empires, nor their rules, reigns in her world. She is nostalgic for the structure that Thomas and Kindersley describe, *even when that structure fails*—when women are ravished and must, therefore, die—because her delusion depends upon a belief that this structure works if and when men and women play their roles according to these rules. As Arabella embraces her veil and the isolation of the castle, and as she creates her own set of tests to prove her virtue true, we see her constructing a fantasy of confinement in which she validates her experiences by aligning them with those of past Eastern heroines and with the harem-bound women that she imagines still exist.

In order for Arabella's conversion to be complete, she must relearn what female virtue means; and yet in some sense it seems due to the instability of "virtue" itself that her conversion has proven unconvincing for Lennox's readers. Arabella frequently recites stories of heroines who perform feats of strength and courage to withstand assaults on their chastity and for whom death is preferable to ruin. "For instance," she recounts, there was "*Clelia*, who, to save her Honour . . . leap'd into the River *Tyber*," and there was "the incomparable *Candace*, who, to escape out of the Hands of her Ravisher ... committed herself to the Mercy of the Waves," and there was "*Mandana*, who, for the Sake of a *Cyrus*, refused the richest Crowns in the World, and braved the Terrors of Death to preserve herself for him" (277–78). By imitating their bravery—and, of course, by *not* "consum[ing] her Days in Dressing, Dancing, listening to Songs, and ranging the Walks with People as thoughtless as herself," as modern women do (279)—Arabella hopes to live a life worthy of a "History" of her own (121). Toward this end, she creates fictional situations in which her own virtue can be tested. For example, she orchestrates an "escape" from the castle in which she freely lives, allegedly to avoid being ravished and to prove true what she tells her servant Lucy: "My own Virtue shall support me" (93). Virtue, she suggests, is meaningless apart from the tests that prove it.[58]

The Countess and the Doctor, both of whom Arabella greatly respects, attempt to reshape her understanding of virtue by critiquing her use of language, her understanding of history, and her global sense of connection to the experiences of women in the past. Targeting Arabella's vocabulary, for example, the Countess instructs her to stop using the word "adventures" in a positive sense. "The Word Adventures carries in it so free and licentious a Sound in the Apprehensions of People at this Period of Time," she says, "that it can hardly with Propriety be apply'd to those few and natural Incidents which compose the History of a Woman of Honour" (327). In response to Arabella's request for information about the "history" of her own life, the Countess responds that "my Life ... differ[s] very little from those of other Women of the same Rank, who have a moderate Share of Sense, Prudence and Virtue" (327). A woman should aspire to conformity, not fame, she suggests—that is, she should aspire to a "moderate Share of ... virtue," rather than to the singular and remarkable Virtue of a heroine.

Next, the Countess and Doctor address Arabella's flawed notions of history, assuring her that the "misfortunes" (not to be confused with "adventures") that her legendary princesses endured are not at all like the situations English ladies now face. One of Arabella's fantasies involves captivity in the Ottoman Orient. During one conversation, she expresses her desire to see the "Valley of *Tempe,* so celebrated by all the Poets and Historians" and "which excited the Curiosity of all Travellers whatever" (260). Glanville questions why she would choose that location, asking, "What Chance, in the Name of Wonder, should take you into *Turky,* at so great a Distance from your own Country?" (260). His father, meanwhile, confused, conflates India with Ottoman Turkey, asking why Arabella "would [wish to] go into the *Great Mogul's* Country, where the People are all Pagans" (260). She responds that she would not go "unless... forcibly carried thither" (261), a possibility at which her uncle scoffs, saying, "It is not very likely you should be forcibly carried away into *Turky*" (261). In reply, Arabella asks a series of questions: "Do not the same Things happen now, that did formerly? And is any thing more common, then Ladies being carried, by their Ravishers, into Countries far distant from their own? May not the same Accidents happen to me, that have happened to so many illustrious Ladies before me? And may I not be carried into *Macedonia* by a Similitude of Destiny with that of a great many beautiful Princesses, who, though born in the most distant Quarters of the World, chanced to meet [each other]?" (261). Through these questions, Arabella shows that she imagines abduction (which she describes alternately as an "accident" and as an "adventure") to be a means for transcending her own time and place. This "Misfortune," as she has learned to call it, would have a happy effect beyond that of merely satisfying her curiosity (261). Her harem fantasy—one of social and intellectual, rather than sexual, pleasure—is that, by being "forcibly carried away into *Turky,*" she might find a community of like-minded women and participate in the mutual exchange of knowledge that she imagines goes on there. After all, she explains, in "antient Times, when Ladies of the highest Rank and sublimest Virtue, were often expos'd to a Variety of cruel Adventures[,] they imparted [these] in Confidence to each other, when Chance brought them together" (327). "It happened very luckily for" the ladies in her stories, she continues, "that they were brought into a Place where they found so many illustrious Companions in Misfortune, to whom they might freely communicate their Adventures, which otherwise might, haply, have been concealed" (261). The Countess responds by discounting Arabella's desire for community and discrediting her fantasy of how "cruel" confinement might enable serendipitous community.

Meanwhile, Arabella's well-meaning but misguided educators tell her that she cannot judge the present by an idealized past. The Countess says, "One cannot help rejoicing that we live in an Age in which the Customs, Manners, Habits, and Inclinations differ so widely from theirs, that 'tis impossible such Adventures should ever happen"; in fact, she continues, "not one of these Things [has] happen'd within the Compass of several thousand Years" (326). The Doctor adds to the Countess's admonitions, reminding Arabella that "we can judge of the Future only by the Past"—or, rather, that one can predict future obligations via one's interpretations of what happened in the past (373). Refuting each of Arabella's heroic examples, he insists that never "in the Records of the World appear[s] a single Instance of such hopeless Villany" as that experienced by Candace or Mandana (373). Arabella resists her interlocutors' notion of time. On one hand, she acts as if the worlds of past and present are one and the same. On the other hand, she is well aware of differences based on her own experience of the present. "The World is not more *virtuous* now than it was in [those] Days," she exclaims (45, emphasis added), and "the Difference [between past and present] is not in Favour of the present World" (380). Arabella sees in the antiquated world of romance certain structures and systems that worked to uphold the very virtue that seems lacking in her own place and time.

Arabella's response to the Countess regarding shifting definitions of chastity, in particular, demonstrate how she sees romance—in its orientalized and antiquated form—as applicable to the amoral present in which she lives. According to the Countess, "Custom . . . changes the very Nature of Things," so that "what was honourable a thousand Years ago, may probably be look'd upon as infamous now" (328). Underscoring, once again, Britain's crisis of morality, she explains that "what was Virtue in those Days, is Vice in ours," and yesteryear's heroism has become today's crime (329). Regarding female virtue, the Countess says, "A Lady in the heroic Age you speak of, would not be thought to possess any great Share of Merit, if she had not been many times carried away by one or other of her insolent Lovers"; by contrast, "a Beauty in this [day] could not pass thro' the Hands of several different Ravishers, without bringing an Imputation on her Chastity" (328). Arabella's earlier defense of Cleopatra illustrates the Countess's point. In response to Arabella's query as to whether her listeners are "acquainted with *Parthenissa,* or *Cleopatra* ... who were both, for some Months, in the Hands of their Ravishers," one of them responds by stating that Cleopatra "was never ravished, I am certain; for she was too willing. ... a Whore, was she not?" he adds (105). Sir Charles later echoes this assumption about Cleopatra's reputation, asking, "Why she was a Gypsey, was she not?" (207). Arabella is incensed at these insults to "that Queen ... whose Courage was equal to her Beauty, and [whose] Virtue surpassed by neither" (105). The exchange foregrounds an interpretive dilemma: How does one know whether Cleopatra was a whore, *and,* by extension, whether a person who behaves like her now is one as well? The answer to this question proves troubling for Arabella, as she must decide not only whether to keep following the examples of her romantic models but also how to interpret the moral examples of women around her. For example, when she hears one acquaintance's story of exploitation, Arabella likens the woman (Miss Grove) to Cleopatra and exonerates her for any indiscretions of which she is being accused. After all, she notes, Caesar "left that great Queen big with Child, and, never intending to perform his Promise, suffered her to be exposed to the Censures the World has so freely cast upon her" (77). Because Caesar violated the rules of romance, she suggests, Cleopatra—along with her successors in dalliance—must be forgiven. Arabella's friends, of course, who see the behavior of Cleopatra *and* of Miss Groves in an equally negative light, vehemently disagree and chastise her for her ignorance. If "chastity" at one time indicated a woman's ability to withstand great assault or temptation, however, Arabella's educators never fully clarify what it means in the present day. Underscoring the interpretive dilemma at play, Arabella resists the Countess's distinction between past and present definitions of virtue. She argues that "custom" alone "cannot possibly change the Nature of Virtue or Vice" (328). At this, the Countess reverses her earlier statement, admitting that "though the *Natures* of Virtue or Vice cannot be changed, ... yet they may be mistaken" or misinterpreted, because "different Principles, Customs, and Education, may probably change their Names, if not their Natures" over time (328, emphasis added). The Countess reinforces the notion that "virtue" is requisite for young Englishwomen without defining what that virtue looks like in its modern form.

The novel ends with Arabella's external reformation according to her elders' sage advice. Glanville's "happiness depended upon curing her of her romantic notions" (117) and, as Arabella well knows, when the heroine "at last condescends to reward [her hero] with her Hand... all her Adventures are at an End" (138). The novel concludes by pointing out a difference between Arabella's union with Glanville and that contracted between Miss Glanville and Sir George—while the latter "Pair were indeed only married in the common Acceptation of the Word; that is, they were privileged to join Fortunes, Equipages, Titles, and Expence... Mr. *Glanville* and *Arabella* were united, as well in these, as in every Virtue and laudable Affection of the Mind" (383). Virtue, in the end, comes in male and female varieties—not in the old romantic sense of chastity and honor but in the new sense of reasonable self-interest that Hume and others describe.

Yet Lennox's ending remains unconvincing for readers in part because Arabella herself is "not convinc'd" by the arguments that the Countess and Doctor level against romance (329). First, Arabella calls attention to the fact that her training in virtue is flawed and incomplete insofar as she is repeatedly told to ignore or isolate herself from difficulty rather than taught how to face and overcome it. According to the narrator, Arabella struggles to take her reformers' words to heart because "Heroism, romantick Heroism, was deeply rooted in her Heart... a Principle imbib'd from Education" (329). Her experience, too, illumines a contradiction at the heart of women's education in the ways of virtue. Women are taught to learn and not to learn; they are taught to remember and look with horror upon the examples of ruined predecessors while also disbelieving that such horrific events ever happened or could happen again. For all that her educators attempt to inculcate in her, Arabella does not receive any lessons in analogy—that is, in the skill of comparing what was happening *then* to what is happening *now*. As a result, she has no accurate framework for understanding and responding to the abuses and exploitations she and her companions do endure and may face in the future. Her most poignant defense of the truth of romance comes when she asks the Doctor, "What Pleasure or Advantage can arise from Facts that never happened? What examples can be afforded by the Patience of those who never suffered, or the Chastity of those who were never solicited?" (376). After all, she emphasizes, "the great End of History, is to shew how much human Nature can endure or perform" (376). But Arabella is given no examples, beyond Richardson's virtuous yet fatally ruined heroine, nor is she admired for her efforts to prove her own virtue true (377).

In addition to the framework they provide for analogizing past and present, Arabella surmises that the stories she lives by better reflect an Englishwoman's reality than her detractors would like to believe. For example, while eighteenth-century readers were familiar with "novels of single, respectable, unfortunate women undergoing ordeals and persecution such as *Pamela* and *Clarissa*," as Linda Colley writes, many were also aware that these stories were not merely fictional.[59] When Arabella asks the Doctor why she should "imagine that the Face of the Earth is alter'd since the Time of those Heroines, who experience'd so many Changes of uncouth Captivity," she highlights certain global realities (*FQ*, 373). For example, Colley's *Captives: Britain, Empire, and the World, 1600–1850* documents numerous tales by and about British captives abroad that together reveal a pervasive uncertainty, fear, and vulnerability regarding Britain's position in the world. From stories like that of Elizabeth Marsh, who was captured by Moroccan pirates in 1756, just a few years after Lennox published *Female Quixote;* to travelogues by writers such as Montagu (whose *Letters* Lennox would have read and which prefigured later accounts by Kindersley, Anna Maria Falconbridge, Lady Elizabeth Craven, and others); to earlier harem fantasies by writers like Penelope Aubin and Eliza Haywood, eighteenth-century readers were aware that "adventures" (or "misfortunes," or "accidents") in faraway lands were hardly a phenomenon relegated to the distant past.[60] As Khalid Bekkaoui has argued, "eighteenth-century fiction . . . [is] replete with allusions to white women who defect to the Moorish fold."[61] In this regard, Arabella's fantasies of "Turky" adventures call readers' attention to the parallels between her wish for adventure and the actual experiences of contemporary captives and travelers. Precisely because she frames her romantic fantasies in terms of global realities, the questions Arabella raises ring in readers' minds after the novel ends: If she *were* to travel the world, for example, what would become of her? Would the harem look like she envisions it, complete with a cosmopolitan community of fellow world-weary women? Left unanswered, these questions destabilize the model of domesticated virtue Lennox otherwise seems to offer.

LOVELY COUNTRY, LOVE OF COUNTRY: REFLECTIONS ON CHIVALRY

As the eighteenth century progressed, the question of whether an orientalized mode of romance served to enslave or empower Englishwomen in their pursuit of political virtue not only persisted but became more politically urgent. On one end of the political spectrum, at least, the notion that chivalric ideals served as a litmus test of national virtue remained potent. In 1766, James Fordyce grounded his *Sermons to Young Women* in a lament for lost virtue, contending that "the times in which we live are in no danger of adopting a[n antiquated] system of romantic virtue," given an unashamed embrace of global trade and "the wealth of the world."[62] Fordyce goes on to argue "that in so polite an age the elevations of love, the sanctity of truth, and the majesty of virtue, should pass for knight-errantry, cannot be surprising."[63] Whig statesman Edmund Burke echoes Fordyce, Kindersley, and Thomas in his 1790 *Reflections on the Revolution in France,* where he argues that chivalry functions as shorthand for the best of European values. He laments that "the age of chivalry is gone," and "that of sophisters, economists, and calculators has succeeded."[64] Gone is the "loyalty to rank and sex," he continues, "that proud submission, that dignified obedience, that subordination of the heart, which kept alive, even in servitude itself, the spirit of an exalted freedom!" (78). And yet, he writes, the "principle" of "ancient chivalry" is far from being outmoded and obsolete; "though varied in its appearance by the varying state of human affairs, [it has] subsisted and influenced through a long succession of generations, even to the time we live in" (78). This principle "has given its character to modern Europe," he continues, and "has distinguished [Europe]" both "from the states of Asia" and "from those states which flourished in the most brilliant periods of the antique world" (78). He deploys an organic metaphor to make his point, arguing that, unlike the French revolutionaries, who are "filled, like stuffed birds in a museum, with chaff and rags, and paltry, blurred shreds of paper about the rights of man . . . we [in England] have real hearts of flesh and blood beating in our bosoms" (89). To the extent that "we cherish and cultivate, those inbred sentiments" that make us great ("fear" of God, "awe" of kings, and "respect" for nobility), English men and women "still bear the stamp of our [fourteenth-century] forefathers" (89). Burke goes on to explain that it is *only* within the context of such traditional constraints that civilized society has flourished across time. What is the social contract, he asks, if not "a partnership in every virtue and in all perfection," a partnership "between those who are living, those who are dead, and those who are to be born" (101)? Chivalry's "pleasing illusions" undergird all of the "manners" and all of the "civilization" of modernity, he claims—for, without them, "a king is but a man, a queen is but a woman" (79–80). Moreover, and most important, without them, "a woman is but an animal," and "all homage paid to the sex" is to be "regarded as romance and folly" (79). Herein lies the travesty for Western civilization, Burke suggests, for "to make us love our country, our country ought to be lovely" (80). Without chivalry's gendered hierarchies—without embodied female chastity, as Hume describes it—the virtue that once distinguished England is no more.

    Burke reiterates a revealing doublespeak here, as he simultaneously praises chivalry's "pleasing illusions" (evoking romance hierarchies of gender and class) and equates "romance and folly." Mary Wollstonecraft was quick to refute this method of "gauging the quality of a civilization by the way that women were treated in it" and to offer a different approach to the relationship between public and private virtue than that voiced by Hume and Burke, Thomas and Kindersley.[65] She notes in

A Vindication of the Rights of Woman that men like Burke, nostalgic for romance's neatly gendered hierarchies, "conside[r] females rather as women than as human creatures" and that, when women are judged by the antiquated framework of romance, their "strength and usefulness are sacrificed to beauty."[66] Romance appears to elevate women while actually keeping them in a position of weakness, she contends, as "men of fancy... outwardly respect and inwardly despise the weak creatures whom they thus sport with" (129). Meanwhile, exalting a reputation for bodily chastity above "purity of mind" contributes to the fatally "grand ruin" of such unfortunate heroines as Lucretia, Morena, and Clarissa (125). Noting that "public spirit must be nurtured by [the] private virtue" of all citizens, male and female alike, Wollstonecraft sets out to redefine virtue as a universal quality marked by "soberness of mind," proper "exercise of duties," and the "pursuit of knowledge," rather than by the "artificial mode of behavior" that Hume identifies and many appear to endorse (135). Attacking the "false system of education" under which Englishwomen languish, Wollstonecraft goes on to posit her own pedagogical system for cultivating virtue (6).

Wollstonecraft's rebuttal of Burke showcases how Englishwomen had begun to articulate a new political imagination and identity, thanks to what Harriet Guest has described as an accumulation of "small changes" across the century that together made "different forms of patriotic consciousness available to women."[67] What we see in the discrepancy between ideals of feminine virtue, as voiced by Kindersley and Wollstonecraft, Arabella and her interlocutors, is a nuanced polyphony of "Enlightenment feminisms," and a range of competing beliefs about the efficacy of chivalric hierarchy to elevate the status of Englishwomen—all imagined and articulated against the backdrop of Eastern counterparts.[68] Wollstonecraft makes her case against aristocratic gender norms and sexist education with a rhetorical flourish that is often cited as an overt example of feminist orientalism: "Surely these weak beings are only fit for a seraglio!" (9).[69] Wollstonecraft's judgmental reference to an Eastern seraglio calls attention to the tensions that Pix's Morena, Lennox's Arabella, and Kindersley herself foreground. For in emphasizing "female rights" above all, Wollstonecraft discounts as "weak" and "degrading" and fit for "mere animals" a model of femininity that others find (with Burke) both natural and nourishing (6). Indeed, despite the Enlightenment cry that romance and its aristocratic trappings should be discarded as relics from a premodern past, romantic tropes persist because they encode certain ways of thinking and ordering the world that people cannot let go. Lennox's characters of the Doctor and Countess dismiss romance as illusion not only because they see it as antiquated but also because they recognize it as a timeless, transnational generic form that might threaten a brand of domestic, time-bound virtue that they see as essential to English character. Their negative depiction of romance clashes not only with that of the parodied Arabella but also with that of Pix and Kindersley and Thomas, for whom a nebulous memory of chivalrous romance signifies a type and degree of virtue that is essential to the Western concept of self. In different ways, these writers foreground the productive tensions between discrepant eighteenth-century ideas of how romantic ideals shore up national virtue. By fashioning a stereotyped Eastern treatment of women as a model for the modern West, they posit ways in which women may flourish even within oppressive political structures. True freedom, some suggest, lies in what Wollstonecraft calls a "purity of mind" (125)—an awareness that a woman remains virtuous despite the condition of her body if she performs her domestic duty to the country and suffers insult and injury, as Kindersley puts it, with dignity and grace. The seraglio, much like romance itself, may not offer truly liberated conditions of existence; however, both spaces represent what is, for some, a compelling ideal of mutual gendered respect. In imagining productive constraints, these writers resist Defoe's statement that chastity and credit "ought to be equally sacred,"[70] for they fear that when morality and self-interest become indistinguishable, "the glory of Europe is extinguished," perhaps never to return.[71] It is to this persistent, haunting fear—which resonated even and especially as "the glory of Europe" and Great Britain became more visibly secure—that the next and final chapter turns.

5

RASSELAS'S "CONSCIOUS VIRTUE"
Cosmopolitan Civics in Johnson and Ellis Cornelia Knight

It is therefore to be steadily inculcated that virtue is the highest proof of understanding, and the only solid basis of greatness.
—Samuel Johnson, *Rambler* no. 4 (1750)

To read virtue right, we must divest ourselves of all partialities and prejudices; and to divest oneself of all partialities and prejudices, is a task which perhaps has never been thoroughly accomplished by any man.
—Catharine Macaulay, *Letters on Education* (1790)

MIDWAY THROUGH SAMUEL JOHNSON'S PHILOSOPHICAL and pseudo-oriental tale, *The History of Rasselas, Prince of Abyssinia* (1759), Rasselas's sister Nekayah observes, "We do not always find visible happiness in proportion to visible virtue."[1] In fact, she continues, "all that virtue can afford is quietness of conscience [and] a steady prospect of a happier state" that "may enable us to endure calamity with patience." The siblings' conversation takes place at the end of their journey out of the idyllic "Happy Valley" in which they were raised, a place where "every art was practiced to make [them] pleased with their own condition" (75), and into the world seeking purpose, or "something to desire" (78). Rasselas gently rebukes his sister for her pessimism, suggesting that the "examples of national calamities and scenes of extensive misery" she cites "are found [only] in books rather than in the world" (115), and that "these bursts of universal distress are more dreaded than felt" (116). Quotidian life marches on "while courts are disturbed with intestine competitions, and ambassadors are negotiating in foreign countries"; each person "labor[s] for his own happiness" while "the necessaries of life are required and obtained, and the successive business of the seasons continues to make its wonted revolutions" (116). And yet, even if he believes that Nekayah's fear of "calamity" is largely fictitious or rooted in "foreign countries," rather than relevant to their own life journey, Rasselas cannot disagree with her point about the instability of "virtue" as a sign of happiness. At the end of their journey he, too, remains dissatisfied and unfulfilled, having seen that neither commercial "traffic" (100), nor philosophical wisdom, nor pastoral simplicity, nor political power, nor celibacy or marriage, nor devotion to science, nor monastic "mortification" (149), nor any other occupation or pastime can guarantee "visible happiness" (158). In fulfillment of Nekayah's observation, this lack of "visible happiness" prompts the travelers to redefine virtue from a visible external trait to an internal sense of perspective and purpose that lets them defer present satisfaction in favor of a "steady prospect of a happier state" (115). Virtue fills the gap where "happiness"—that elusive "something to desire"—cannot be found.

The tensions *Rasselas* foregrounds between reflection and action, as well as between universal ideals and local duties, are related to the broader anxieties I have traced thus far regarding the costs of pursuing "visible happiness" and rewards of profit at the expense of what Nekayah describes as internal "quietness of conscience." As I argue in this concluding chapter, Johnson's pseudo-oriental tale, together with Ellis Cornelia Knight's *Dinarbas*, a sequel to *Rasselas* that she published at the end of the century, offer a philosophical narrative that defines national virtue not as a set of specific or static qualities but as an unresolved dialectic between a deferred political ideal and the dutiful action of a properly educated citizen. Specifically, these texts reflect ongoing anxiety about a lack of virtuous political identity in Britain at a moment when the global balance of politico-economic power was visibly shifting in its favor. Once again, writers like Johnson and Knight use the rhetoric of virtue to parse civic commitments—both national and global—in the face of a lingering dilemma. If luxury inevitably begets lethargy and passivity, then the nature of virtuous political duty is hardly clear cut—for, as Neville and his fellow seventeenth-century republicans had recognized, the same acts that could render Britain's "virtuous" status visible to the world involve behaviors of consumption or conquest that threaten to undermine that status altogether.

"NEGLECTED VIRTUE CALLS": JOHNSON AND BROWN ON BRITAIN'S MORAL CRISIS

The rhetoric of civic "virtue" in the second half of the eighteenth century once again reflected Britain's global outlook at a moment of increasing material prosperity and perceived moral crisis. Published in 1759, a year when Britain enjoyed decisive military victories in the Seven Years' War and, in Frank McLynn's words, "became master of the world," Johnson's *Rasselas* echoes works by Swift and earlier republican thinkers in simultaneously praising progress and mourning a supposedly simpler, more virtuous time in Britain.[2] Johnson warns that power, prestige, and prosperity come at a cost. "The dangers gather as the treasures rise," he writes in *The Vanity of Human Wishes*.[3] "Britain's modish tribe" is increasingly "athirst for wealth, and burning to be great" (61, 74); "now no more we trace in every line / Heroic worth" (87–88), and "with distant voice *neglected virtue calls*" (333, emphasis added). Echoing long-standing debates about the tensions between individual consumption of luxury and what Joyce Appleby describes as the "highly artificial construct" of "classical citizenship," Johnson links Britain's lack of "heroic worth" to its burgeoning participation in global commerce, which, he fears, has introduced the foreign luxuries he sees invading and infecting the nation.[4] Reflecting his obsession with linguistic and constitutional purity, Johnson prefaces his *Dictionary of the English Language* (1755) by acknowledging that "commerce, however necessary, however lucrative, as it depraves the manners, corrupts the language."[5] Even as he attempts to stabilize language by pinning down the meanings of words,[6] Johnson acknowledges the myriad meanings of terms like "virtue." His *Dictionary* includes a total of ten denotations for "virtue," explaining that it signifies either "moral goodness" or "acting power"; either "a particular moral excellence" or "that which gives excellence"; either visible "valour" or "secret agency; efficacy, without visible or material action."[7] To define the term is to raise certain questions of cultural import: What does virtue look like? What if the material rewards of "excellence" appear identical to those forms of luxury whose consumption eroded the civic virtue of now-defunct empires? Moreover, whose efficacious labor guarantees virtue's value? And if there is a virtuous agent working "secretly" on Britain's behalf, how exactly does one know oneself—and the nation one represents—to be virtuous, after all?

John Brown, a contemporary of Johnson who was likewise alarmed at the effects of wealth on Britain's collective character, similarly waxes nostalgic for "the simplest and most virtuous Times" in his 1757 *Estimate of the Manners and Principles of the Times*.[8] "By a gradual and unperceived decline," Brown apocalyptically laments, "we seem gliding down to Ruin," disfigured by "malady" and "miscarriages" (144). "The Enemy is *within*," he insists, for our "public virtue" has disappeared (18). "There never was an Age or Nation that had not Virtues and Vices peculiar to itself," he admits, "and in some Respects, perhaps, there is no Time nor Country . . . in which a wise Man would so much to have lived, as in our own" (15). "Notwithstanding this," he goes on, "our Situation seems most dangerous: We are rolling to the Brink of a Precipice that must destroy us" (15). Picking up on the concerns of earlier English patriots, Brown points to the enervation of liberty, specifically, as both a particular example and potent catalyst of Britain's decline. "This great Spirit [of Liberty] hath produced more full and compleat Effects in our own Country, than in any known Nation that ever was upon Earth," he argues; for "whereas it hath been ingrafted by the Arts of Policy in other Countries, it shoots up here as from its natural Climate, Stock, and Soil" (18–19). While Britain's innate "Love of Liberty is not extinguished" completely, he writes, it "hath grown weak in *Deeds*" even as "it hath gained Strength in *Words*" (18). In this regression lies the problem: if England's legacy of liberty fails to produce action on individual and collective scales—that is, if it fails to uphold the "public spirit, or love of our country" (62) that works itself out in citizens' sacrificial "deeds" of "suffering for [their] country's welfare" (72)—then Britain's claim to a "peculiar" virtue vis-à-vis France or China or any other nation is empty rhetoric. After all, even the French, notoriously beleaguered as Britons believe they are by corruption and effeminacy, consistently act according to their own national ideals—thus, Brown admits, while they are "in Manners weak, [France is] strong in Principle: Contemptible in Private Life; [but] in public, Formidable" (141). Brown echoes Johnson's sentiment in "An Introduction to the Political State of Great Britain" (1756), where Johnson concludes, "We continue every day to show by new proofs, that no people can be great who have ceased to be virtuous."[9] Ever skeptical about Britain's imperial ambitions, Johnson traces the link between politics and commerce from Queen Elizabeth's day to the present, emphasizing that Britain is by no means the most virtuous of European competitors, especially insofar as Britain's traders, *unlike* the French, "hav[e] no other purpose in view than immediate profit."[10] Johnson, like Brown, sees Britain as lacking consistency between its principles and actions.

Brown, like Johnson, is pragmatically ambivalent in describing the role of global commerce in simultaneously enabling and threatening Britain's claim to greatness. Brown points to unprincipled and uncontrolled commerce as a cause of Britain's virtue crisis, asserting that, while the "benefits [of commerce] are generally acknowledged . . . the dangerous effects of its exorbitance or excess have not yet been sufficiently developed" (*Estimate*, 153). He writes that "the Spirit of Commerce, now predominant, begets a kind of *regulated Selfishness*" (22, emphasis added) that is dangerous because it encourages individual over collective interest; as he puts it, "a chain of self-interest is indeed no better than a Rope of Sand: There is no Cement nor Cohesion between the Parts" (111). At its worst, he suggests, trade cultivates a "dastard Spirit of Effeminacy" (91) according to which "every gaudy *Chinese* crudity . . . is adopted into fashionable use, and become[s] the standard of taste and elegance" (48). He fears that Britain is following in the footsteps of ancient Rome, insofar as "the honest Pride of *Virtue* is *no more;* or, where it happens to exist, is overwhelmed by inferior Vanities" (59). Brown goes on to argue that Britain's obsession with global commerce is particularly self-destructive, insofar as "Trade and Wealth . . . destroy the Principle of Public Spirit" by ensuring that "our Attention and Regard is turned on *others*" (174). Whether in a fully commercial state like Holland, or in a "mixed [commercial and landed] state" like Britain, the pursuit of wealth "as the *chief Good*" will not only "terminat[e] in selfish Regard" (174)—contributing to the "regulated Selfishness" he fears (22)—but also end up "creat[ing] a new Train of Wants, Fears, Hopes, and Wishes" (173). The problem with commerce, in Brown's view, is that it encourages a "Passion for Money" that, "being founded, not in Sense, but Imagination, admits of no Satiety" (155). He goes on to link such insatiable desires of individual citizens to the overall health of their nation, adding, "What is true, in this respect, of trading Men, is true of trading Nations" (155). While it is benign and productive in its early stages, "Commerce searches every Shore and Climate for its Supplies," voraciously encouraging higher degrees of acquisition and refinement, along with "new habits of higher Indulgence" (157). In other words, Brown sees commerce as a source of "national debility" precisely because it encourages an endless *desire* that defers all possibility of satiety. Rather than disavow such desire, Brown acknowledges that Britain depends upon it; indeed, he is skeptical that "lessening this exorbitant Trade and Wealth [can] bring back manners and principles, and restore the nation's strength" (216). One can learn from history but not reverse or reset its course; instead, he realizes, one must cultivate a new form of virtue that can withstand the particular assaults of global modernity.

By examining the necessary evils of commerce, Brown and Johnson theorize the problem Nekayah observes—namely, that there is a gap to be navigated between "visible happiness" (most often seen in the material prosperity commerce enables) and "visible virtue" (ostensibly seen in the "manners and principles" that have been lost in pursuing such prosperity). In response to this problem, Brown echoes Rasselas by proposing a return to "*Books*, where the Wisdom of Ages lies reposed," rather than thrusting "untutored Youths... into the World" (*Estimate*, 31). Johnson agrees, noting in the *Rambler* that what must "be steadily inculcated" is a belief that "virtue is the highest proof of understanding and the only solid basis of greatness."[11] People must be made to see that virtue is not an "angelical [quality] nor [one] above probability," Johnson writes, but rather a quality "that humanity can reach"—one "which, exercised in such trials as the various revolutions of things shall bring upon it, may, by conquering some calamities and enduring others, teach us what we may hope, and what we *can* perform."[12] For both Johnson and Brown, insofar as "virtue" refers to a "public spirit" that animates civic action by "teach[ing] us what we may hope," it must be framed as a perspective on struggle and suffering, rather than as a static set of standards. This perspective must account for the problem Brown articulates—namely, that the self-interested impulse that "destroy[s] the Principle of Public Spirit" is animated and fueled by "Attention and Regard [that] is turned on *others*," particularly those who produce or possess the commodities Britain desires (*Estimate*, 174).

"ALL JUDGMENT IS COMPARATIVE": DEFERRED DESIRE AND MORAL DUTY IN THE ORIENTAL TALE

Both Johnson and, as I examine later in this chapter, Ellis Cornelia Knight in her 1790 sequel to *Rasselas*, deploy the oriental tale as a narrative form capacious enough to accommodate troublingly insatiable British desire while also distinguishing between those who stagnate in this state of desire and those who learn to channel desire in appropriate ways that boost the visible (commercial) *and* invisible (moral) virtue of the nation. On one hand, Johnson and Brown point to France as their immediate gauge of British lack, reflecting what Gerald Newman has described as a tide of rising English nationalism during Johnson's lifetime. "Every nationalist movement," Newman argues, "involves a search for the 'essence and inner virtue of the community'—a quest, that is, for the National Identity" and "spirit of the people" that depends, in Britain's case, on defining itself against its long-time foreign rival of France.[13] And yet Brown's reference to a "gaudy Chinese crudity" and Johnson's choice to frame his philosophical ideas in the form of an oriental tale make clear that they are orienting their perspective on virtue not only in terms of Continental politics but also of Eastern commodities and the threat those commodities pose. According to Brown, the "gaudy Chinese crudity" threatens Britain's spirit at least in part because, unlike the French, Britons have *not* found a way to accommodate their desires with their principles. Both Chi-ming Yang and Eugenia Zuroski have argued that English representations of Chinese things had more to do with English self-identity than the actual value of the objects; in this sense, Zuroski contends, shifting attitudes toward commodities reflected internal shifts in English subjectivity, as an early eighteenth-century embrace of Chinese commodities morphed into a nationalist "disavowing" of cosmopolitan thinking in the latter half of the century.[14]

Running alongside such ambivalence toward Chinese objects, however, is a keen recognition—rather than disavowal—that unmitigated desire destabilizes national manners and is precipitating Britain's crisis of virtue. If, in Nekayah's words, "all that virtue can afford is . . . a steady prospect of a happier state," claims to virtue become a way of deferring visible manifestations or proof of virtue itself. Johnson and Knight deploy the generic form of the oriental tale as a way of teaching readers "what we may hope" when put through "such trials as the various revolutions of things shall bring upon" humanity. The oriental tale, reformulated by Western authors for Western readers, offers a moral staging ground at a comfortable remove from British politics: readers have space to learn their civics lessons from "books," and to contemplate what dutiful action entails without (yet) being forced to put it into practice. In this sense, the oriental tale offers a narrative space for deferral—it is, as Ros Ballaster argues, a "place not only where two spaces meet (western print culture re-narrates the oral fables of the East)[15] but also two temporalities: the ancient and the modern."[16] The oriental tale works on two planes at once, as any allegory does. But in the hands of English writers like Johnson, abstract spatiotemporal coordinates get translated into the comprehensible language of global trade. *The School of Virtue,* a collection of "novels, tales, fables, allegories, &c. &c. moral and entertaining" that was published anonymously in London in 1763, offers one example of what oriental fables were meant to teach Western readers. *The School of Virtue* contains a number of these fables, with titles such as "An Arabian Anecdote"; "A Remarkable Fable, Common in the Mouths of the Indian Mahometans"; "Providence Vindicated: An Eastern Tale"; and an "Extract from Churchill's Collection of Voyages" that describes a meeting between a king and a Brahman in India.[17] This last anecdote, about a magical cow of plenty, concludes with a moralizing application for English readers. "This Story, in the literal Meaning of it, is a senseless Account of some *Pagan* Idolatry amongst the *East-Indians,*" writes the anonymous compiler-editor; "taken in an allegorical Sense," however, it "is full of fine Morals, and capable of many instructive Applications."[18] He goes on to unpack the allegory, asking "readers" to "suppose that Trade was meant by this cow of plenty," and that "by the miserable, wretched Hut of the *Brahman,* may be understood any poor, barren Country, which by Trade is immediately rendered opulent and abounding in all Things," with "Plenty of Provisions . . . Necessities and Conveniences, or even . . . Luxury brought home to our own Doors" (122–23). He goes on to argue that wealth is "bestowed, by the King of the blessed Souls, as Reward for . . . Piety and Virtue" upon the country that values "Liberty," and that the "trade" which brings prosperity "cannot even exist where Fraud, Violence, Oppression, or Injustice reigns" (123). "Many other useful Allegories might be pointed out in this short Story," he concludes (124). The story, while "senseless" if read literally, becomes useful for teaching virtue when its allegory is explained in the language of Western reality; reified as "Trade," the Brahman's cow is rendered knowable within a European framework of prosperous commerce and just government. Running alongside admiration for the philosophical contemplation and personal reflection that the oriental tale makes possible is a recognition that the Western reader must *act* upon their reflections in the material world of "Trade" rather than leaving them to stagnate within the realm of the "allegorical." In this regard, the tale is not just a prop for affirming a providentialist British historiography; it also encodes some anxiety about what, precisely, such virtuous actions entail.

Srinivas Aravamudan has argued that the "Enlightenment orientalism" flourishing in England and France prior to the institutionalized orientalism of the nineteenth century entails "a universalism that is not about a separate sphere—whether geographical, ethnocultural, or religious."[19] Rather, Enlightenment thought involved many "spheres" informing and infiltrating and colliding with each other, as any belief in the universal was inevitably complicated by the messy material realm of human interaction. With this complexity in mind, Karen O'Brien reminds us that "cosmopolitan history" is a "rhetorical strategy... and a habit of thought" that "simultaneously encapsulates an attitude of detachment towards national prejudice... and an intellectual investment in the idea of a common European civilization."[20] In portraying this dual investment, both Johnson and Knight show that their Enlightenment orientalism has less to do with affirming Britain's virtuous reputation, and more to do with anxiously articulating what national virtue-as-duty looked like, as Britain grew in wealth and global power. A key component of their "rhetorical strategy," as O'Brien describes it, involved properly weighing and prioritizing the responsibilities of national and global citizenship. At one point Johnson's Imlac states to Rasselas that, "to judge rightly of the present we must oppose it to the past; for all judgment is comparative, and of the future nothing can be known" (*Rasselas*, 120). However, Imlac's recognition that "judgment is comparative" does not fully account for how the "bursts of universal distress" that Rasselas and Nekayah discuss reverberate beyond the borders of home (116). Their dialogue shows that "to judge rightly of the present" requires careful comparison not just between times but also between places.

Adam Smith, a contemporary of Johnson, offered a reasoned response to the problem Brown had described, of how commerce creates new and endless and insatiable *desire* that drives nations like Britain to "searc[h] every shore" in a futile effort at fulfillment.[21] Smith works to reconcile moral thinking with economic and political theory, recognizing that any framework for moral politics must account not only for foreign *things* but also for the self-interested *desire* for things. A key figure in giving voice to classical republican ideals of civic duty at a moment when, per Pocock, virtue was being redefined as "a 'sociological' rather than a 'civic' principle," Smith wrestles with the tensions of living as a citizen of the world while operating out of moral self-interest.[22] What does it look like, he asks, to live in virtuous relationships within concentric circles of influence? In other words, what are the *duties* of a global citizen, when "the mean principle of national prejudice is often founded upon the noble one of the love of our own country"?[23] Is it possible to frame self-interest as both rational *and* moral—as motivating, rather than competing with, sympathy for foreign others? Smith identifies a clear link between individual and national greatness, insofar as a society's "prosperity and glory seem to reflect some sort of honour upon ourselves" (268). Underscoring the role of the individual, he contends that virtuous citizens must understand their real but limited duty to others, within and beyond their immediate circle of influence; to do so, they must learn to properly read similarities and differences *between* members of the global community, thereby forming an appropriate discriminatory framework. This framework, in turn, lets them accommodate their desire for others' things in a way that coexists with civic virtue and bolsters the health of the nation.

In a move that should now be familiar to my readers, Smith's framework accounts for a particular country's *lack* of visible virtue in the present moment by positing that such visible virtue is merely *deferred* rather than permanently missing. One of the moral dilemmas for commercial countries, he recognizes, lies in distinguishing internal principles of virtue from visible manifestations of that virtue. In other words, because moral virtue is largely invisible in the global marketplace, it is difficult to objectively value and reward. What we see, instead, are socially endorsed and culturally variable—as well as variably *valued*—behaviors. Smith uses a providentialist logic to correct for this problem of virtue's invisibility. In general, he observes, "every virtue naturally meets with its proper reward," whether that be "wealth and external honours" or "the confidence, the esteem, and love of those we live with" (193–94). However, when we do not see the external rewards we expect, "we naturally appeal to heaven, and hope, that the great Author of our nature will ... complete the plan which he himself has thus taught us to begin; and ... in a life to come, render to every one according to the works which he has performed in this world" (196–97). For this reason, Smith writes, "we are led to the belief of a future state, not only by weaknesses, by the hopes and fears of human nature, but [also] by the love of virtue" (197). He concludes, "It is in this manner that religion enforces the natural sense of duty" (198). Key to Smith's defense of political virtue is this now-familiar logic of *deferring* virtue's providentially guaranteed rewards and *accepting* the inevitable anxiety that attends such deferral.

Within this framework of civic virtue, revised for realities of global commerce, Smith tackles the problem of cosmopolitan thinking—of how the natural phenomenon of national prejudice works in tension with a love of humankind. Insofar as it aims to cultivate civic virtue that can withstand dangerously enervating desires—and respond appropriately to those "bursts of universal distress" with which, Rasselas notes, the average citizen has a difficult time sympathizing—Smith's model of sympathetic interest assumes distinct geographical and cultural limits. For instance, Smith leaves China and Japan out of Britain's circle of responsibility, suggesting that, despite Britain's economic interests, these Far Eastern empires are *too different* to be folded into his model—so different, in fact, that "neither [the French] nor we bear any sort of envy to the prosperity of China or Japan" (270). In a brief anecdote about China, he sets out a hypothetical thought experiment: "Let us suppose that the great empire of China, with all its myriads of inhabitants, was suddenly swallowed up by an earthquake," he writes, "and let us consider how a man of humanity in Europe, who had no sort of connection with that part of the world, would be affected upon receiving intelligence of this dreadful calamity." In Smith's thought experiment, the "man of humanity" would, for two distinct reasons, "express very strongly his sorrow for the misfortune of that unhappy people"—first, because such news would awaken in him "melancholy reflections upon the precariousness of human life," and, second, because it would arouse his concern about "the effects which this disaster might produce upon the commerce of Europe." In the end, the distance between Europe and China renders misfortune only marginally relevant, for "we are always so much more deeply affected by whatever concerns ourselves than by whatever concerns other men." Moral virtue is limited to our circles of sympathy, Smith concludes, though, within those circles, "the wise and virtuous man is at all times willing that his own private interest should be sacrificed to the public interest of his own particular order or society" (277).

Smith's China example—and his broader call to contextualize others' suffering based on one's proximity and consequent duty to them—recalls the opening scene from *Rasselas*, where Rasselas redirects Nekayah's attention and concern to the quotidian realities of their own time and place, rather than the "national calamities" and "bursts of universal distress" and "competitions" of "foreign countries" that one reads about "in books" (*Rasselas*, 115–16). Other nations' "calamities," like their heroes, serve solely as interesting examples to understand (and adopt, or adapt, or reject) along the way of their own quest to practice virtue. Read within the framework of Smith's moral politics, *Rasselas* affirms that "doing one's duty" as a virtuous Briton requires learning how to read these models rightly, so as to properly balance one's responsibility to humankind with the particular interests of the nation.

RASSELAS'S "CONSCIOUS VIRTUE": KNIGHT'S ADAPTATION FOR THE AGE OF REVOLUTIONS

Ellis Cornelia Knight's 1790 *Dinarbas; a Tale: Being a Continuation of Rasselas, Prince of Abissinia* tries to resolve the tension between reflection and action by positing virtuous duty as an antidote to any angst posed by Britain's global dominance. Published at a moment when Newman and others suggest British cosmopolitan thinking was hardening into nationalism, Knight's tale nonetheless continues to portray English virtue as an unstable ideal. She opens her story by claiming to answer some of the questions Johnson raises—specifically, by showing where and how Rasselas and his fellow travelers can find the happiness they seek. She explains in her introduction that Johnson's portrait of the "evils attendant on humanity" is limited and misleading; her goal, by contrast, is to show "the fairer prospect" of life and, by so doing, to "afford [some] consolation or relief to the wretched traveller [who is] terrified and disheartened at the rugged paths of life."[24] Yet, while she appears to take the side of Johnson's Rasselas against that of Nekayah, Knight's version of the tale likewise defers real solutions for Britain's crisis of virtue.

Dinarbas picks up the story of Rasselas and his companions after their travels, as they return home to Abyssinia's Happy Valley. Unlike Johnson's "Conclusion, in which Nothing is Concluded" (153), and the hero is left visibly dissatisfied in his quest for "something to desire" (78), Knight offers a more neatly conclusive portrait of virtue as dutiful patriotism. Writing in the immediate wake of the French Revolution, Knight affirms Tory hierarchies by tracing Rasselas's internal progression from a youth driven by existential angst and wanderlust, to a dutiful son who is eager to learn, and finally to a purposeful reformer and powerful successor to his father's throne. Stephanie M. Hilger contends that Rasselas's belief "in the gradual reform of the corrupt, but potentially salvageable, system of his father's reign" both reflects and addresses late eighteenth-century Britons' anxieties about the legitimacy of monarchical power and the political future of the nation.[25] By exalting the mature citizen's self-regulation over the individual traveler's wanderings, Jessica Richard argues, Knight "disables the dangerous discourse of liberty ... and replaces it with the safe, less threatening rhetoric of duty and resignation."[26] And yet, if liberty is a "dangerous discourse," as Richard puts it, what happens in the intervening decades to the "love of liberty" that Johnson and Brown identify as the crux of Britain's "public spirit"? Keeping in mind that the freeborn Briton's sense of civic "duty" always entails recognizing and upholding Britain's unique, original liberties, I argue that what we see in Knight's tale at the end of the century is a reformulated invocation of national "spirit" for a new moment of crisis—in other words, her portrait of civic duty retains what Gerald Newman calls the "old and familiar phenomenon" of patriotism.[27] Knight dramatizes the same gap Johnson identifies between "visible happiness" and "visible virtue," and, in the process, also portrays a deferral of British virtue.

In contrast to Johnson, Knight argues that neither happiness nor virtue is elusive; rather, true happiness is the reward of virtue, which takes the form of dutiful action. At one point Elphenor the Priest admonishes Nekayah to "remember that all happiness in this world is transitory, *except virtue*" (*Dinarbas*, 193, emphasis added). While reason merely "instructs without improving," says Imlac (110), virtue is a deeply rooted force of preservation (182). Elphenor's reminders that "virtue is wholly in our own power" (139) and that "the exercise of active virtue" tempers "mental afflictions" (146) buoy the Abyssinians' spirits when they languish in captivity and solitude, suffer unjust accusations, or mourn the loss of loved ones. Rasselas, in particular, as the future leader of his people, is "supported by the sentiment of conscious virtue" and by his awareness that "all his sufferings" are catalysts "to great actions, or painful sacrifices" in service of a greater good (160). As the rightful heir to his father's throne, Rasselas perceives that he has a greater capacity for virtue than most and thus has a greater responsibility to set aside self-interest for the common good. He realizes that, while all men, even his traitorous brother Sarza, are capable of experiencing "momentary ray[s] of virtue," most lack that resolve and "firmness without which virtue is useless" (156). His father reminds him in his dying moments that "we, in particular, are placed in a sphere, in which it is our duty to direct, like [a] pilot" (181). As he accepts his role as a "particular" individual in a social hierarchy, Rasselas takes responsibility to teach and train his people, "treat[ing] with tenderness the man whom weakness... has caused to deviate from the path of virtue" (125). He gives "thanks to Heaven for having inspired [him] with [the] active desire of knowledge" that has equipped him for the throne (209).

As in *Rasselas*, Knight's politicized version of Johnson's philosophical tale defines virtuous duty in terms of global networks. At one point, Imlac, a native Egyptian, tells Amalphis, one of the Abyssinian governors, "Whatever regard I have for my own country, my way of life has made me consider myself as a citizen of the universe... my mind, busied with intellectual enjoyments, has been equally uninterested in the shock of great empires and the petty pursuits of domestic life" (112). Imlac exclaims that "the world is my school," and that "in the labyrinths of science" there is no distinction of nation (112). In some sense, Imlac's sentiments here differ from those voiced by Johnson's character, who represents Europe as intellectually superior to Eastern nations. In Johnson's version, Imlac recounts an opportunity he had to "convers[e] with great numbers of the northern and western nations of Europe; the nations which are now in possession of all power and all knowledge; whose armies are irresistible and whose fleets command the remotest parts of the globe" (*Rasselas*, 91). Pointing to "the unsearchable will of the Supreme Being," he tells Rasselas that the Europeans "are more powerful... than we... because they are wiser; [and] knowledge will always predominate over ignorance" (91). By contrast, as Hilger argues, Knight "does not paint Britain as a model for other countries"; instead, she "returns to an idealized past" to find exemplary models of political society for Britain to emulate.[28] In fact, Knight expresses deep cynicism about the state of affairs in her home country. Upon returning to England from a lengthy stint abroad in France and Italy (1775–99), she writes in her *Autobiography* that she "had been accustomed to see foreign nations look to England as the most flourishing and potent of countries, and to regard it as the laurel-crowned island, the safeguard of Europe."[29] Yet "now that I was arrived in this highly favoured land, I heard nothing but complaints," she continues, and "it was in vain that I tried to feel at home in my own country... what surprised me most of all," she muses, "was the general cry of poverty, distress, and embarrassment."[30] What is clear from Knight's own experience and perception is that, despite Britain's growing reputation abroad, its citizens do not exude happiness as visible *evidence* of internal virtue.

What Hilger calls Knight's nostalgia for an "idealized past" is inextricably linked to the global realities of that past. Johnson and Brown (like Swift, Neville, and others before them) evoked ostensibly simpler and more virtuous times in England in part because, despite mid-century Britain's military victories, the outcome of imperial glory was still far from certain. As Rajani Sudan has argued, for instance, Johnson's Imlac does not reiterate assumptions about European hegemony but instead expresses anxiety that "progressive values claimed as products of the European Enlightenment [in the mid-eighteenth century] have genealogies and origins elsewhere."[31] Contrary to Imlac's wistful boast, Europe's "armies" and "fleets" did not yet "command the remotest parts of the globe" in 1759, and many of the scientific technologies and inventions in which Europeans took pride were borrowed or derived from empires they desperately wished to rule or engage.[32] Meanwhile, "swept under the auspices of the 'unsearchable will'" are "numerous and conflicting economic, political, and historical problems with 'Asiatic' trade that often troubled aesthetic accounts of British national integrity."[33] In other words, to return to the statement by Nekayah at the start of this chapter, English virtue was not yet "visible"; instead, virtue claims could only signify a *potential* "prospect of a happier state" in which internal and external qualities might once again align.

Knight writes at a different moment in Britain's imperial trajectory, and yet, for Knight's Rasselas, the journey to personal maturity remains ineluctably linked to the future of his nation within a broader world. For instance, after he identifies "the necessity of learning" as a top priority for governance (*Dinarbas*, 194), Rasselas sets about correcting and improving what he sees as the nation's "faulty or neglected education" system (198). "The Abissinians in general want neither acuteness nor application," he notes, "but their studies have been hitherto wrong directed" (194). Their "famous libraries," for instance, while extensive and magnificent, are "chiefly composed" of antiquated materials, including "manuscripts, which have no other merit than the claim of dubious antiquity; treatises on mystical devotion, or judicial astrology, and *annals of nations,* from whom we can gain little instruction, *because they were not further advanced than ourselves*" (194, emphasis added). Like the oriental tale—which becomes pedagogically useful only when approached analogically and abstracted from European science—treatises and stories from "nations . . . not further advanced than ourselves" have limited value. In lieu of these antiquated forms of knowledge, Rasselas wishes to "promote in [his] dominions the study of the sciences," much as England prioritized through its Royal Society

(195). Imlac agrees to some extent, admitting that his own discipline of "astronomy, though one of the noblest of studies," hardly "deserves the immediate attention of a monarch, who has to form an infant nation" (195). "More essential" to the nation, he admits, "are the mechanics, hydraulics, and in short every thing that contributes to ... the construction of machines, to spare labour, and to improve agriculture" (195). Technological progress—rooted, as Sudan makes clear, in "Asiatic" techne—should be the ruler's top priority.

Whereas Imlac agrees with Rasselas regarding the importance of scientific and mechanical learning, he corrects his protégé's view of history. Acknowledging that "no instruction equals that obtained by the perusal of history," the young emperor nonetheless thinks that most people (nonrulers) have no need to spend time learning about the "annals of nations ... not further advanced than ourselves" (*Dinarbas*, 194–95). After all, Rasselas asks Imlac, "are not most men devoted to pass their lives in one spot; and is not the history of their own country, if they mean to be useful to it, the only one necessary for them?" (195). Imlac argues, in response, that history *matters*—and the histories of *others* matter—because people "cannot learn how to act in the various circumstances of life, without considering various examples" from across time and space (195). Besides, he asks, "how can we find all these [examples] in the limited boundaries of one country? ... Though we would not be Romans at Constantinople, or Abissinians at Venice, we may, even from conditions directly opposite to our own, gain instruction and improvement" (195). The dialogue between Imlac and Rasselas highlights the importance of using global history to educate people as useful citizens of "an infant nation" (195). By suggesting that cosmopolitan civics lessons are crucial for developing an informed citizenry, Knight's Imlac offers a corrective to Johnson and an expansion of Smith's circles of sympathy.

And yet, despite her skepticism about Britain's present fortunes and moral vision, Knight's view of the past—like that of Johnson's Rasselas—is filtered through a Eurocentric lens. At one point her Rasselas asks Dinarbas to recount his "travels in the dominions of the sultan," noting that, while he has "always considered our total ignorance of other countries as one of the greatest misfortunes that attends our government," most of his own knowledge comes from "books" and not experience (173–74). The experienced world traveler obliges, painting a picture of cultural difference between East (their native Abyssinia and its neighboring nations) and West (ancient Greece, Rome, and their successors). Neither "the Abissinian, scorched on the burning sands that surround him," nor "the Scythian, sliding over frozen rivers . . . can have but a very imperfect idea of the variegated landscape that attracts the eyes of the fortunate inhabitant of Greece," Dinarbas avers (174). In fact, he continues, "our [Islamic] spires, our turrets, and our many-coloured roofs, are become odious to my eyes, since I have beheld simplicity and elegance on the desolate shores of Greece," for "it has ever been the irremediable error of weak minds and degenerate nations, to substitute ornament for proportion . . . and heterogeneous variety for harmony and grace" (176). Moving from aesthetic to historical judgment, Dinarbas goes on to imply that the Greeks' commitment to "harmony and grace" in architecture and art have prepared them, and their successors, to rule the world. He tells Rasselas:

> Such, in the view of moral or political greatness, if we examine history, was the conduct of the illustrious men of ancient Greece and Rome: their enterprises were vast, and their minds capacious; they formed a comprehensive plan, and acted up to it. . . . Alexander had conceived his scheme for the conquest of the east, before he left his native Macedon; nor did Caesar take the command in Gaul, without a previous design of becoming the first in the republic. I am not surprised at the policy of our courts, which usually excludes their subjects from all communication with the knowledge of Europe: in order to confine us to narrow views, to indolent magnificence, and, if I may so express it, to living by the day: this is the surest foundation for despotism. (176–77)

What seems striking about Dinarbas's argument, with Knight's readers in mind, is how *vague* the proposed action seems to be. It is neither the "enterprises" themselves nor the details of a "comprehensive plan" that matter; rather, Knight lauds simply the rejection of "narrow views" and the torpor of "living by the day." She underscores that virtue is a mindset of action, rather than a particular action itself. And herein lies a problem for her reader. As noted earlier, Knight herself was quicker to notice Britain's visible "poverty, distress, and embarrassment" than its famed potential to achieve glorious "escapades"; meanwhile, her predecessor, Johnson, sharply criticized the imperial ambitions of his homeland at the very moment of its becoming "master of the world."[34] In both versions of Rasselas's journey, then, the vague rhetoric of national virtue highlights not only Britain's ongoing lack of visible happiness but also the problem of proving whatever virtue one possesses or hopes to possess. After all, what, exactly, does "moral or political *greatness*" look like, if not conquest and riches? What specific actions make virtue real?

Like Johnson, decades earlier, Knight uses her tale to "orient virtue," so to speak: even as she critiques both European and Eastern forms of "despotism," she distinguishes between Eastern stagnation and Western potential—the latter, she suggests, are on a guaranteed track to achieve virtuous political action *in the future*. Dinarbas is quick to point out the difference between Western heirs to Grecian greatness and the "narrow views" of "our" Eastern courts, ostensibly a consequence of being removed from "the knowledge of Europe." In light of this judgment, Imlac's observation "that revolutions are frequent in eastern monarchies"—a comment that links "eastern monarchies" to revolutionary France—refers not to a prospect of future greatness-through-revolution but instead reinforces assumptions of Eastern instability and a tendency to decay (*Dinarbas*, 165). By contrast, Knight suggests, Rasselas's steadiness of purpose, design, and authority in recreating Abyssinia anew has been inherited, unbroken, from ancient Greek and Roman conquerors to a Britain beginning to flex its conquering arm in India. Herein lies a lesson for British readers wrestling with what Knight sees as the terrifying implications and crippling effects of a revolution that does not seek to understand and build on an inherited legacy of past greatness.

All men are not created equal, Knight's Amalphis points out, and "none should act the first parts on the great theatre of the world, but those who have talents to fill the character" (200). Individual virtue might contribute to the greatness of a state, but it is nations that interact—and jostle for positions—on the global stage. As the Ottoman Sultan tells Dinarbas, "Truth, honour, and integrity ought not only in individuals, but [also] in governments, to be the great ruling principles of action" (206). In highlighting the link (and gap) between internal principle and external action, the Sultan calls attention to how little has changed, in terms of the basis and state of virtue, since Johnson and Brown voiced their mid-century concerns. As monarch, for instance, Knight's Rasselas is highly ambivalent about trade; echoing Johnson and Brown, he sees commerce as detrimental to individual virtue but essential for proving—that is, making "visible"—the greatness of ambitious nations. Though "every ingot, stored by commerce in the treasury of a monarch, has cost him the virtue and principles of a subject," he declares, and "though I love virtue too well not to wish that I could be persuaded of its general influence in every station of life," yet "I cannot abolish" luxury or "its dependant, commerce," on which Abyssinia depends (205). The "virtue" that Rasselas loves "too well" turns out to be a nebulous ideal that, in reality, clashes with actions that support Abyssinia's great reputation. Even as he names the gap between "virtue" and "commerce," Rasselas works to cover over the lack of virtue caused by needed trade. At the conclusion of Knight's tale, Rasselas proudly states, regarding his nation's changing fortunes, "Much is to be suffered in our journey through life; but *conscious virtue,* active fortitude, the balm of sympathy, and submission to the *Divine Will,* can support us through the painful trial. . . . Let us now return to the busy scene of action where we are called, and endeavor, by the exercise of our several duties, to *deserve* a continuation of *the blessings which Providence has granted,* and on the use of which depends all our present, all our future felicity" (210, emphasis added). He goes on to underscore a teleological belief: though at one point in the past "our prospects were far different," he says, "it is true that we have been singularly favoured by Providence" (210). Once again, the rhetoric of virtue—with its tripartite definitions of human excellence, cultural purity, and the promise of providential help—reflects persistent tensions between local and global interests at the end of the eighteenth century. Like Neville's *Isle of Pines,* Dryden's

Aureng-Zebe, or Swift's *Gulliver*, Knight's *Dinarbas* is a parable about the difficulty of maintaining civic virtue while pursuing grandezza through commerce, consumption, and conquest. It is a tale of imagined integrity across time that nonetheless acknowledges the reiterated, revolutionary crises of "virtue" sparked by actual interactions between global powers.

Johnson and Knight underscore how "virtue" signifies both an unattainable ideal and a required action, insofar as virtue claims reflect little more than a desire to name the qualities that make Britain great while recognizing how these qualities are simultaneously threatened and upheld by a network of global interests. The power of oriental "fancy" lies in its ability to account for such deferred desire and thereby to keep that desire alive. As Nekayah tells Rasselas in Johnson's version of the tale, "Those conditions, which flatter hope and attract desire, are so constituted, that, as we approach one, we recede from another" (*Rasselas*, 58). Knight's Imlac echoes this sentiment, reminding Rasselas as they wend their way home that "our condition in this world is too distant from perfection to give us hopes of enjoying any one advantage in the supreme degree" (*Dinarbas*, 110). If, in the end, these characters define virtue as an ideal of visible happiness, bolstered by moral strength—an ideal that is preserved within the narrative space of the oriental tale—they also highlight, rather than erase, the material networks of *action* that, at any moment, might destabilize Britain's teleological story of the virtuous self.

MACAULAY'S CONCLUSIONS: ON "ACCIDENTS" OF HISTORY AND "READ[ING] VIRTUE RIGHT"

As these tales suggest, orienting virtue is a self-conscious act of deferral, a way of making sense of the gap Nekayah identifies between "visible happiness" and "visible virtue" (*Rasselas*, 158). In the decade leading up to Knight's publication of *Dinarbas*, Great Britain's reputation for virtue remained elusive—as Christopher Bayly describes it, "the 1770s and 1780s were a British recessional," as Britain lost its empire in America, faced crises in India, and stoked its rivalry with France, to the point that, "whatever the underlying strength of the commercial economy, many Britons felt that their great days were over."[35] According to Jeremy Black, "a sense that Britain was weak and weakening was not new," and this elegiac feeling, reiterated with each political crisis, was reinforced by the "unpredictability of international developments" at the end of the century.[36] "By 1815," Bayly notes, "the nation could celebrate an astonishing, indeed providential, recovery of fortunes" thanks to naval might and commercial successes.[37] But even such celebration, and the rising nationalism Newman and others document, remains rooted in a sense of lack—a nostalgic recognition of gaps between Britain's present and past, alongside anxious acknowledgment that any story of national virtue is always in progress and always contingent upon the virtue trajectories of others. I conclude my discussion of the eighteenth-century chapter of this story by turning to the work of Whig historian Catharine Macaulay, who reiterates not only the lasting legacy of English virtue—rooted in the exceptional liberties ensured by England's Protestant commitments—but also the ongoing threats to realizing that virtue within a constantly shifting global network.[38]

"Much has been said of the progress of modern civilization," writes Macaulay in her 1790 *Letters on Education*, "but it certainly has so little tended to bring us back to classic simplicity, that we are every day departing more and more from it."[39] In fact, Macaulay imaginatively prophesies, "if after ages should produce societies refined to an exalted pitch of humanity, with what surprise and detestation will they regard their ancestors of the eighteenth century" (269). As a reform-minded pedagogue and a historian known for her adherence to republican principles, Macaulay echoes the eulogy for English virtue—lost despite or because of a drive to progress through trade, science, and conquest—that was voiced by earlier conservation-minded thinkers from Neville to Johnson.[40] She asserts:

> It is true that most of the European states have at this day an *apparent* superiority in government, in arts, and in arms, to the inhabitants of Asia and Africa. But if we reflect on the rise and fall of nations, we shall find, that *accident alone*, without the assistance

of internal excellence, has produced this superiority, and that it has appeared and disappeared in the same society, as accident was favourable or unfavourable to its existence. It is to the inhabitants of Asia that we owe the rudiments both of the sciences and the arts; and the savage barbarism which is now displayed on the sultry shores of Africa, has at some period or another been exceeded in every country of Europe. (257–58, emphasis added)

A century after Temple published *Of Heroic Virtue,* Macaulay echoes his provocative questions about whether Europe's "first flights" of "heroic virtue" were indeed its "highest," and whether the inevitable "revolutions of empires" yet to come will affirm or undermine its own claims to excellence.[41] She recognizes the same troubling truth that Temple articulated: global history does not follow a guaranteed linear trajectory, and it is just as much the "accidents" of history, as it is calculated individual actions, that shape its course. Despite all that has changed in Britain's fortunes, over the course of the century, the possibility of revolution—not just within nations but also between them, in directions hardly certain and not necessarily favorable to the West—sets the hope of future greatness alongside the specter of future decay.

Echoing a long-standing concern, Macaulay frames the problems she sees in "modern civilization" in terms of a national crisis of virtue shaped by global cultural shifts. According to Macaulay, before people can *be* virtuous, they must learn "to read virtue right," by understanding and balancing their desires and duties as members of both national and global communities (127). Unfortunately, Macaulay argues, lingering traces of "partialities and prejudices" hinder Britons' progress in this project (127). She points to failures in the educational system as one cause of their deplorable atrophy of virtue, explaining that "ignorance is a soil in which no uniform virtue can take root and flourish" (484). Macaulay holds out hope that a reformed system of national education might reinvigorate virtue by sparking both cosmopolitan sentiment and renewed patriotism; she believes that education will help people put off "those prejudices, which national prosperity or individual greatness, engrafts on human selfishness" (268, 257). According to Macaulay, the task of such reform depends upon a rational government that, "by a proper use of [such] sources" as "laws, example, precept, and custom," can bring about "that improvement on which true civilization depends" (276). By "direct[ing] the course of [the] impression[s]" that comprise human understanding in its most rational and fully developed state, "proper" education can "put into motion" those "passions which belong to humanity" yet now "lie latent" and untapped (276).

In one sense, Macaulay pushes against Smith, Burke, and others who argue that prejudice is a useful tool for shoring up virtue; ultimately, however, Macaulay recognizes that eradicating prejudice, while a noble goal, is not entirely possible.[42] Like Temple, earlier, Macaulay's call for cosmopolitan values is tinged by her own ambivalence about European Enlightenment—namely, her assumptions about the "superiority" of "European states," coupled with anxiety about the origins, and thus the future, of their alleged excellence (257). Macaulay is unapologetic for such inconsistency in part because she recognizes that the "task" of "divest[ing] oneself of all partialities" is an arduous, ongoing process that "has never been thoroughly accomplished by any man" (128); indeed, such "divest[ing]" cannot be completed in the span of a lifetime or a generation of a nation. Macaulay recognizes, too, that global history is uncertain, even "accidental," and that culturally specific forces such as "laws, example, precept, and custom" can only go so far to stave off a return to (or exacerbation of) barbarity. In response to others' superior virtues—visible predominately in the past, to some diminished extent in the present, and, quite possibly, surpassing Britain's again in the future—Macaulay describes education not just as a corrective measure but as another strategy of deferral, an effort to frame continued lack of virtue in terms of future possibility. She lauds an ongoing work, rather than a particular end result.

At the same time, Macaulay's virtue claims buffer the uncertainty of such deferral. In Macaulay's words, the "superiority" that Europe now enjoys *may* be purely accidental; however, she takes comfort in the fact that virtue signifies an invisibly efficacious legacy of Protestant blessing as much as it signals evident excellence and rewards thereof. Macaulay qualifies her point about historical accident by asserting a link between human merit, wealth, and a Creator who controls, or at least mitigates, the effects of chance. "Virtue," she writes, "by a wise disposition of things, *will be found* to be in union with a reasonable enjoyment" (268, emphasis added). Whereas in her earlier statement on the "apparent superiority" of European government and culture she seems to discount the role of "internal excellence," she writes here that "the nature of merit, when considered in [man's] relation to the Creator, takes its rise from that degree of . . . excellence, which enables him to partake of *those blessings that attend his progress in virtue* through every stage of his existence" (473, emphasis added). In other words, merit or excellence—along with the attendant "blessings"—is determined by one's "relation to the Creator." But Macaulay goes on to account for an apparent *lack* of "blessings" as a test of virtue that ought to be expected. "If [man] be placed on this terrestrial globe as in a school," she writes, that is, "if he is surrounded with difficulties, dangers, and hostile powers, for the purposes of enlarging his experience, and inducing a trial of that virtue which his reason enables him to acquire, we shall have cause to admire the wisdom and the goodness of God" (472–73). If crisis forges character and moves people toward perfection, virtue indicates the progress, potential, and possibility enabled by such trial, rather than an objective state or static quality "acquire[d]." In a productive paradox, the trials that call virtue into question also provide the tests without which virtue can never be proven true. The usefulness of this paradox hinges upon virtue as a term that signifies human action along with the supernatural power that transcends such action and determines the trajectory of history itself.

In different ways, Johnson's and Knight's versions of Rasselas's story illustrate the dilemma Macaulay describes, about the necessary challenge of educating global citizens in national virtue. "Conscious virtue," as Knight's Rasselas puts it, plays out on the material stage of world affairs, not in the realm of abstract ideals (*Dinarbas*, 210). Since the same educational system must train citizens of a nation and citizens of a world, those wishing to "read virtue right" must learn, as Rasselas does, to sift through examples from elsewhere (at a convenient distance from the turbulent reality of global affairs). Within the discourse of global history from a Eurocentric perspective, the past and future are ineluctably linked, whereas the present is a moment of perpetual crisis—held in a sort of suspension, the present is contingent upon the past while in no way determining the future. In this discursive space of deferral, British writers and readers find a powerfully enabling myth of integrity that can acknowledge a lack of civic virtue while reiterating the efficacious legacy of England's virtuous spirit across time. They also find there a call to action, a reminder that virtue is not only the divinely endowed propensity or ability to act but also the acts that may someday prove virtue true. As Johnson and Knight suggest, it is by learning to see themselves as part of history, and by acting within it, that British men and women might make this narrative come true—so that their virtue is no longer "transitory" but indeed functions as a "solid basis of greatness."[43]

AFTERWORD
A Kantian Legacy of Cosmopolitan Virtue Signaling

I HAVE ARGUED THROUGHOUT *ORIENTING VIRTUE* that England's literary claims to civic virtue are rooted not only in an old story about the freeborn Briton's exceptional legacy of liberty but also in anxious moments of recognizing how this legacy has been threatened and to some extent forfeited by the very pursuit of commerce that made Britain visible on the world stage. The story of English virtue in the long eighteenth century is a story of deferral, insofar as it must account for present crises of civic virtue and what these crises signal for Britain's future fortunes amid the "accidental" shifts of global history. Despite clear messaging about how other nations' virtues are relegated to the past, the possibility that Britain will follow suit and experience its own reversal is never far from mind. As a result, the story is one that writers tell with an eye to the outside world: they reiterate claims to their unique legacy of political virtue while representing that virtue in terms of Eastern trade routes, political exemplars, and generic modes. Such representation aims to uphold Britain's present viability in the global marketplace of things and ideas while also differentiating *their* nation as the one with a promising future. In the century of political redefinition that followed the traumatic upheaval of England's Civil Wars, claiming national virtue was not just a matter of pinpointing specific qualities or characteristics that defined the "spirit" or "character" of a nation. Instead, it required maintaining this tale of unbroken potential across a century of crises—of telling and retelling England's story of virtuous identity even and especially in moments when it appeared untrue.

If this story is rooted in England's unique legacy of liberty, its storytellers keep it alive by tapping into what Karen O'Brien describes as a broader "strategy" of cosmopolitan virtue signaling.[1] In an article on "The New Cosmopolitanism and the Eighteenth Century," Mary Helen McMurran unpacks the debate between those who laud cosmopolitanism's "sober virtues" of "justice and equality" and those who see the term as a flimsy rhetorical disguise for darker, decidedly self-interested agendas.[2] While more recent debate reaches back to Enlightenment sources, McMurran argues that eighteenth-century cosmopolitanism in the decades before Kant was in fact "an unwieldy set of notions" and "counter-currents" regarding what it means to fulfill one's duty as a citizen of a nation *and* a citizen of the world.[3] McMurran offers an apt reminder that the eighteenth-century figure of the "cosmopolite" "developed as a creature of rhetoric" that signified a vaguely disinterested universality rather than a clear ethical position on citizenship.[4] The rhetorical strategies of "cosmopolitan" engagement that McMurran and O'Brien describe work in conjunction with "virtue": together, these discourses frame a dual commitment to patriotic duty and economic interest in a world where virtue *claims* cost little but where *being virtuous* requires situationally appropriate responses to each crisis at hand.

In his *Idea for a Universal History with a Cosmopolitan Aim,* which was first published in 1784 and translated into English in 1798, Immanuel Kant proposes a framework within which European citizens can articulate claims to patriotic virtue while also acknowledging their own nation's unstable position in global history.[5] According to Kant, people need a narrative that can supplement those histories that are "written merely *empirically*" by accounting for present uncertainty and the apparent accidents that drive the trajectory of global affairs.[6] In keeping with his premise that the end of history is a completely rational and fully actualized human race, Kant contends that one can sketch out a "universal world history" that begins with the ancient Greek and Roman civilizations, extends through the barbarian conquests, and ends in "the present time" (21).[7] If one "adds to this *episodically* the political history of other nations," he continues, "or the knowledge about them that has gradually reached us through these same enlightened nations—then one will discover a regular course of improvement of state constitutions in our part of the world (which will probably someday give laws to all the others)" (21). Part of Europe's present problem, Kant suggests, is that citizens lack any real understanding of what virtue means, beyond the cultural trappings of law and custom. "We are *cultivated* in a high degree by art and science," he explains, and "we are *civilized* ... by all sorts of social decorum and propriety. But very much is still lacking before we can be held to be already *moralized*" (18). Our limited notion of morality, he adds, "which comes down only to a *resemblance* of morals in love of honor and in external propriety, constitutes only being civilized," not in having attained an objectively virtuous state (18, emphasis added). Moreover, in pursuing the insatiable desires of the civilized—the "vain and violent aims of expansion"—most citizens have lost sight of what virtue really is, for "everything good that is not grafted onto a morally good disposition, is nothing but mere semblance and glittering misery" (19). To the extent that people conflate morals and markets, in other words, they will inevitably misunderstand how real virtue transcends the things and traits it resembles and how moral good promotes human actualization across time. In this regard, Kant argues, revolutions can be productive events, for it is "through each revolution" that "germ[s] of enlightenment" pave the way "for a following stage of improvement" (22). The seemingly unfair but "necessary" byproduct of this dialectic is that some people (or entire groups or generations of people) exist only to "prepare the steps" for others in the future (13).[8] In the end, Kant argues, it is "nature—or better ... *providence*" (22) that drives the course of history and, "as by a guiding thread" (10), works all things together for good, determining who will achieve the pinnacle of rational enlightenment and who, by contrast, will be included in the annals of history as mere stepping stones to the development of the "master" race (15).

By illustrating a key Enlightenment tension—that virtue is both an unattainable ideal (the highest stage of the human condition) and a required action (the systematic proof of one's reason-based worth)—Kant provides a philosophical rationale for the rhetoric of virtue that I have traced in this study. I have argued that what stabilizes English "virtue" claims in moments of perceived moral and material crisis across the long eighteenth century is, to some degree, the term's very polyvalence. Virtue does not simply signify the actions of human excellence (leading to visible economic prosperity or a sacrificially civic-minded citizenry) and chaste bodies (a physical purity that analogously ensures cultural purity); it also signifies a supernatural efficacy that allows believers to frame moments of crisis through a lens of exceptionalism. Where excellence is lacking or where chastity is, in Moll Flanders's words, a mere "dress," writers describe deferred dreams of grandezza and narratives of possibility and potential progress.[9] If there is a consistent meaning running through and informing virtue's varied manifestations, then, it is a belief in national "integrity," defined as a "soundness of moral principle" that can explain present lack in terms of myths of the past and visions of the future.[10] The belief in a "guiding thread," as Kant puts it (10), or the promise of providential efficacy, more broadly, lends a comforting sense of purpose to the vicissitudes of global history. It is this belief that undergirds eighteenth-century Britons' claims to represent a virtuous nation, despite troubling evidence to the contrary. Within the framework of this story—one of past heroics and future potential—ongoing politico-economic crises can serve to forge moral character and move people toward embodying a more perfect union of national ideals.

In the end, virtue serves as an ideal that transcends specific human behaviors, which are always culture-contingent and subject to complex and unpredictable global dynamics. In this sense, I have argued, even when signaling a proto-Kantian ethic—a "wholehearted commitment and effective capacity to fulfill our moral duties out of respect for the moral law," those "objective, unconditional, and necessary principles of reason"—eighteenth-century Britons were constantly "orienting" themselves, or determining their bearings, both in terms of place (by comparing their own achievements to those of other empires, both European and Asian), and in terms of time (by comparing their present situation to their own and others' storied pasts).[11] To understand their nation's role in global history, writers worked to explain, defend, or imagine the attributes that made England unique and irreplaceable on the world stage. As we have seen, Sir William Temple in 1690 and

Catharine Macaulay in 1790 are similarly burdened and excited by the weight of the past and a sense of possibility. The revolutions of history may or may not go in the West's favor, they realize; in Macaulay's words, the "superiority" that Europe now enjoys *may* be purely accidental. But in view of the *longue durée* of human morality, so to speak, these writers take comfort in the fact that virtue can signify invisible efficacy as much as it signals evident excellence. In this regard, to live self-consciously in modernity is to wrestle with one's evolving place in the folds of time, to paraphrase Geraldine Heng.[12] It is to wrestle not only with changing social, religious, political, and economic structures that are outside of one's control but also with a duty to act—and train the next generation to act—in ways that define and shape what modernity means and will look like in the future.

Eighteenth-century discourses of political virtue continue to shape ongoing politico-economic debates about the West's role in modeling and policing a sustainable global ethic. As the pendulum of Western sentiment shifts away from globalization and toward nationalism, once again, Brexit-era Britons and their American successors to the pursuit of virtuous liberty lament the loss of civic and civil discourse. At the same time, we collectively seek to find and embrace a "middle way" between indulging the desire to "[search] every Shore and Climate for ... Supplies," as John Brown disparagingly (even despairingly) put it, and resisting the costly erosion of national restraint.[13] Meanwhile, as some American economists have been quick to point out, if indeed "China's Century" has begun, then "the West's ... economic pre-eminence, and the habits of thought and action that flowed from it, can no longer be taken for granted."[14] Western unease about the relationship between morals and markets reiterates—at a new moment of political crisis centered on questions of freedom and global constraints—eighteenth-century England's desire to define those "habits of thought and action" that made it great and would make it great again. Like Swift's Gulliver, who laments the disappearance of England's "pure native virtues," qualities supposedly untainted by the world through which he travels and in which he must act, we are nostalgic for what is past even as we embrace what we understand to be progress.[15] We respond to politico-economic crises now as then, by turns reacting with paralysis or plans, waxing nostalgic or visionary, advocating cosmopolitan connection or nationalist isolation. Our political commitments and moral ideals are ineluctably linked to anxieties about the manufacturing origins of fast fashion and the dubious supply chains of our electronic devices; about rhetoric of borders closed against people in need or the invisible enemy of a deadly virus; about whether and how to repatriate citizens who left home to join terrorist organizations abroad—about traffic, in other words, of things and ideas, and about our seeming lack of control over whether that traffic is truly symbiotic. The West's crisis of virtue persists; its story of virtue is still being told.

NOTES

INTRODUCTION

1. Kaul, *British Literature and Postcolonial Studies*, 3.
2. Dryden, dedication to *Annus Mirabilis*, n.p.
3. Dryden.
4. Dryden, *Annus Mirabilis*, lines 1205 and 1185–88. Text references are to this edition.
5. Kaul, *Poems of Nation*, 78.
6. Kumar, *Making of English National Identity*, 7–8.
7. Kumar, 156.
8. Kumar, 17.
9. Baucom, *Out of Place*, 38.
10. MacIntyre, *After Virtue*, 52.
11. Aristotle, *Nicomachean Ethics*, 29.
12. Snow, "Neo-Aristotelian Virtue Ethics," 321.
13. Becker, "Stoic Virtue," 132.
14. Becker, 146.
15. Swanton, "Virtue in Hume and Nietzsche," 242, 249.
16. Hutcheson, *Our Ideas of Beauty and Virtue*, 139.
17. Mandeville, *Fable of the Bees*, 76. Text references are to this edition.
18. Wilson and Denis, "Kant and Hume on Morality," section 2.
19. MacIntyre, *After Virtue*, 50.
20. MacIntyre, 53–54.
21. On how "the complexity of a culture" emerges in its "social definitions" and in "the dynamic interrelations" of "dominant, residual, and emergent" cultural elements, see Williams, *Marxism and Literature*, 121ff.
22. Shaftesbury, *Inquiry concerning Virtue*, 34.

23. On seventeenth- and eighteenth-century discourses of self-interest, see Force, *Self-Interest before Adam Smith*; and Myers, *Modern Economic Man*.
24. On the distinction between "aristocratic" and "progressive" ideologies of virtue, see McKeon, *Origins of the English Novel*, chapter 4. According to McKeon, aristocratic ideology assumes that "the social order is not circumstantial and arbitrary, but corresponds to and expresses an analogous, intrinsic moral order" (131); by contrast, the progressive ideology emerging in early modernity assumes "the discord of internals and externals, of virtue, status, wealth, and power" (150).
25. Pocock, *Virtue, Commerce, and History*, 50.
26. Pocock, 49.
27. Gibbon, *History of the Decline and Fall of the Roman Empire*, 573.
28. Montagu, *Nonsense of Common-Sense*, 13.
29. Ward, *London Spy*, 71.
30. See Fraser, *Story of Britain*, 388. On eighteenth-century British debates about luxury commodities from the East, see Berg, *Luxury and Pleasure*, part I.
31. MacLean and Matar, *Britain and the Islamic World*, 214.
32. Pomeranz, *Great Divergence*, 5. Pomeranz distinguishes his argument from that of world systems theorists, who tend to emphasize the "fall of Asia" and rely on "an oversimplified contrast between an ecologically played-out China, Japan, and/or India, and a Europe with plenty of room left to grow" (12). See Abu-Lughod, *Before European Hegemony*; Chaudhuri, *Asia before Europe*; and Wallerstein, *Modern World System*. See also Frank, *ReOrient*; and "Assessing Kenneth Pomeranz's *The Great Divergence*," special issue of *Historically Speaking* 12, no. 4 (2011), edited by Peter Coclanis, devoted to qualifying and expanding upon Pomeranz's thesis.
33. Parker, *Global Interactions*, 3.
34. Pomeranz, *Great Divergence*, 23.
35. Defoe, *New Voyage round the World*, 40.
36. Defoe, *True-Born Englishman*, 196.
37. *Oxford English Dictionary*, 2nd ed., *OED* Online, s.v. "virtue."
38. See the *Oxford English Dictionary*, s.v. "virtù"; and Pocock, *Machiavellian Moment*, especially chapter 14. The *OED* defines Machiavellian "virtù" as "the strength of character necessary for political or military success; forceful vitality; ruthless determination." Chapter 2 examines this concept in more detail.
39. See Clery, *Feminization Debate*, 1–12.
40. Brown, *Fables of Modernity*, 112.
41. Markley, *Far East and the English Imagination*, 225. For Defoe, Markley

argues, credit "assumes two dialectically related and often gendered forms." On one hand, "credit is feminized either as a market for the luxury and complacence that enervate the nation or as the spectre of promises unfulfilled and expectations shattered." On the other hand, "credit is masculinized either as the immutable measure of all transactions, the guarantor of the integrity of the symbolic order—theological, political, and economic—represented by 'the Constitution' or as the marker of diligence, exchange, and mercantile energy" (226). On Defoe's masculinization of credit, see also Gregg, *Defoe's Writing and Manliness*, chapter 1.

42. Defoe, *Complete English Tradesman*, chapter 15, para. 8.
43. Defoe, *Essay upon Publick Credit*, 9–10.
44. McKeon, *Origins of the English Novel*, 158.
45. McRae, *God Speed the Plough*, 21.
46. McRae, 161, 215. On postlapsarian accounts of the natural world, see also Harrison, *Fall of Man*.
47. McRae, 78, 161.
48. Sidney, *Discourses concerning Government*, 166.
49. See Charles Taylor, *Sources of the Self*, chapter 16.
50. Perkins, "Leibniz's Praise of Chinese Morality," 450–51.
51. Perkins, 457. Perkins notes that "the praise of Chinese virtue was used against Christianity soon after Leibniz" (463).
52. Steele, *Christian Hero*, 15. Text references are to this edition.
53. *OED*, "virtue." Markley points out in *Far East and the English Imagination* that "stock" had both quantitative and qualitative meanings as a measure of goods and a measure of value: "as early as the sixteenth century, 'stock' became not merely an inventory of existing commodities but a representation of potential wealth, of returns yet to be realized" (222).
54. Defoe, *Moll Flanders*, 1–2. Text references are to this edition.
55. *Oxford English Dictionary*, 2nd ed., *OED* Online., s.v. "character."
56. Evans, *Colonial Virtue*, 123. Evans traces the "geographical, semantic, and ideological mobility" of temperance, specifically, as it migrates from classical and humanistic discourses into the politico-economic vocabulary of European colonialism.
57. Andrea and McJannet, introduction to *Early Modern England and Islamic Worlds*, 6.
58. As Carey and Festa make clear in their introduction to *The Postcolonial Enlightenment*, the Enlightenment is a global phenomenon marked by intellectual "tensions and disparities" rather than a "unified [European] construct" (4–5).
59. Said, *Orientalism*, 59, 1.

60. Aravamudan, *Enlightenment Orientalism*, 3. See also Ballaster, *Fabulous Orients*.
61. Aravamudan, 8.
62. Yang, *Performing China*, 25.
63. Yang, 25–26. Yang focuses on the literal staging of virtue during the Restoration and beyond, highlighting theatrical spectacles of Chinese heroism that demonstrate the "performativity, or constructedness, of British ideas of virtue" (10).
64. Porter, *Ideographia*, 2–3. See also Porter, *Chinese Taste*; and Markley, "China and the English Enlightenment."
65. Porter, 10.
66. Zuroski, *Taste for China*, 20.
67. Zuroski, 7, 49, 35, 151.
68. Zuroski, 18, 14, 151.
69. On how newly "individual, self-regulating moral virtue ... offers the key to understanding Occidentalist subjectivity" during the later Romantic period, see Makdisi, *Making England Western*, 136.
70. Porter, *Ideographia*, 7.
71. Yang, "Eighteenth-Century Easts and Wests," 96.
72. Yang, *Performing China*, 15–16. Zuroski similarly argues that China "refers metonymically to an emergent notion of the global" (7); Garcia contends that Islam provided English deists a "renovated constitutional idiom for reclaiming political subjectivity and national identity" (11).
73. Kaul, *British Literature and Postcolonial Studies*, 8.
74. Galland, preface to *Remarkable Sayings*, iv.
75. Schmidgen, *Exquisite Mixture*, 150.
76. Schmidgen, 151.
77. *Oxford English Dictionary*, 2nd ed., *OED* Online, s.v. "integrity." The word also denotes "the condition of having no part or element taken away or wanting," "the condition of not being marred or violated," and the "soundness of moral principle."
78. Yang, *Performing China*, 7.
79. Nussbaum, *Global Eighteenth Century*, 11. In considering English virtue as a global phenomenon, I am mindful of Sanjay Krishnan's reminder in *Reading the Global* that "the global" is always a particular perspective, not a comprehensive critical lens (3–4).
80. Schleifer, *Analogical Thinking*, 15. Schliefer proposes that analogy permeates Renaissance theology but disappears in the Enlightenment, only to reemerge in the twentieth century. Rajani Sudan argues in *Alchemy of Empire*, by contrast, that analogy provided a useful epistemological framework

throughout early modernity, particularly for European travelers who sought to understand unfamiliar cultures, practices, and landscapes by comparing them to their own (21–22).
81. Schleifer, *Analogical Thinking*, 192, 24.
82. Locke, *Essay concerning Human Understanding*, 4.16.12, 565. Text references are to this edition.
83. Zuroski, *Taste for China*, 35.
84. Batchelor, *London*, 26.
85. Batchelor, 237.
86. Geraldine Heng, "Early Globalities," 237. For a different perspective, see Chakrabarty, *Provincializing Europe*, who uses case studies from colonial and postcolonial India to examine modern "historicism" as a "'first in Europe, then elsewhere' structure of global historical time" (7). As a Western mode of thought, Chakrabarty explains, historicism insists "that in order to understand the nature of anything in this world we must see it [first] as a historically developing entity ... as some kind of unity at least in potential—and, second, as something that develops over time" (23).
87. Neville, *Plato Redivivus*, 108.
88. Swift, *Gulliver's Travels*, 164–65. Text references are to this edition.
89. Swift, letter to Charles Ford (14 August 1725), in *Correspondence*, no. 662, 586.
90. Andrea, *Women and Islam*, 78.
91. Hume, *Treatise of Human Nature*, 3.2.12, 364–66.
92. Brown, *Manners and Principles*, advertisement and part 3.5.
93. Hegel, *Philosophy of History*, 77.

1. "OUR LUSTS GAVE US LIBERTY"

1. Milton, *Areopagitica*, 743. Text references are to this edition.
2. As a dissenter, Milton emphasized liberty's distinctly religious dimension, claiming it ensured freedom of conscience and of speech. On religion and republicanism, see Coffey, who argues in "Quentin Skinner and the Religious Dimension of Early Modern Political Thought" that "parliamentarians worried about ecclesiastical as much as civil slavery" and about Christian liberty of conscience as much as political freedom (64).
3. Young, *Political Essays*, 50. Text references are to this edition.
4. Greene, *Exclusionary Empire*, 1.
5. Fortescue, *De Laudibus Legum Angliæ*, 29, 34.
6. Greene, *Exclusionary Empire*, 2. On Coke's contribution to the formation of a distinctly English identity, see Helgerson, *Forms of Nationhood*, chapter 2.

7. Greene, *Exclusionary Empire*, 2.
8. England's "mixed" constitution, according to seventeenth-century political theorists, was a unique combination of three types of government: monarchy, aristocracy, and democracy.
9. Neville, *Plato Redivivus*, 88, 108.
10. Harrington, *Commonwealth of Oceana*, 45.
11. Hill, *Puritanism and Revolution*, 64–65.
12. Hill, 69.
13. Hill, 70.
14. Toland, "Life of James Harrington," xvii. On the republican connotations of "commonwealthmen," see Robbins, *Eighteenth-Century Commonwealthman*.
15. Hobbes, *Leviathan*, 263. On similarities between Hobbes's and Milton's notions of dissent and tolerance, see Warren, "Milton, Hobbes, and Dissent."
16. See Kennedy, *Diggers, Levellers, and Agrarian Capitalism*.
17. Davenant, *Ways and Means*, 140. See Armitage, *Ideological Origins*; and Greene, *Evaluating Empire*, chapter 1.
18. Hill, *Puritanism and Revolution*, 74.
19. Sidney, *Discourses concerning Government*, 12.
20. Locke, *Two Treatises of Government*, 101.
21. Locke, 102.
22. See Stillman and the 2006 issue of *Utopian Studies* devoted to *Isle*'s publication and interpretive history.
23. Loveman, *Reading Fictions*, 69.
24. Neville, *Isle of Pines*, 198, 194. Text references are to this edition.
25. Scott, *Commonwealth Principles*, 6. See also Mahlberg, *Henry Neville and English Republican Culture*.
26. Scott, *Commonwealth Principles*, 23.
27. Harrington, *Commonwealth of Oceana*, 11, 4–5.
28. Scott, *Commonwealth Principles*, 164. Sparta's "anti-commercial ethics . . . praised rurality, austerity, and frugality as the basis for republican virtue" (94).
29. Visconsi, *Lines of Equity*, argues that *Isle* is an "ironical" text (118) that demonstrates how patriarchalism precludes the "executive acts of equity and mercy" essential to a mixed constitution (130). See also Carey, "Henry Neville's *The Isle of Pines*"; Mahlberg, *Henry Neville and English Republican Culture*; and Wiseman, "Porno-Political Rhetoric and Political Theory."
30. Neville, *Plato Redivivus*, 101.
31. Pincus, "Neither Machiavellian Moment," 711.
32. Scott, *Commonwealth Principles*, 228.

33. See Pocock, *Machiavellian Moment*, chapter 12.
34. Sullivan, *Liberal Republicanism in England*, 175.
35. Armitage, "Empire and Liberty," 39.
36. Quoted in Burton, *Diary*, 3:387–88.
37. Armitage, "Empire and Liberty," 40.
38. Scott, *Commonwealth Principles*, 95.
39. See Skinner, *Liberty before Liberalism*; and Scott, *Commonwealth Principles*, chapter 7. See also Skinner, "Third Concept of Liberty"; and Wootton, introduction to *Republicanism, Liberty, and Commercial Society*.
40. Amussen, *Caribbean Exchanges*, 18–19.
41. Amussen, 19.
42. Amussen, 108. See also Hall, *Things of Darkness*.
43. Beach, "Profound Pessimism about the Empire."
44. By contrast, Beach argues that Neville articulates a "profound vision of English weakness and degeneration" (21). On how the Dutch Republic became "the prototype for a new kind of mercantile state," see Ormrod, *Rise of Commercial Empires*, 33.
45. Markley, *Far East and the English Imagination*, 30.
46. Israel, "Emerging Empire," 423.
47. See Colley, *Captives*.
48. Frank, *ReOrient*, 126. See Burton's *Diary* (21 February 1658–59) for the transcript of a parliamentary discussion in which Neville engaged concerning the importance of commanding the "eastern seas" (3:382).
49. Markley, *Far East and the English Imagination*, 4.
50. Sudan, "Mud, Mortar, and Other Technologies," 149.
51. Marshall, "English in Asia to 1700," 269.
52. Bialuschewski, "Pirates, Slavers."
53. Lovejoy, *Transformations in Slavery*, 60–61.
54. Allen, "European Slave Trading," 40.
55. Allen, 43.
56. David Eltis estimates that the English transported 91 enslaved people from Southeast Africa to the Americas during 1662–70, 309 during 1671–80, and a high of 5,392 during 1681–90 (*Rise of African Slavery*, 166).
57. Revisionist historians offer several reasons for this inattention, including the low numbers of slaves trafficked in the Indian Ocean as compared to the Atlantic, perceptions of Islamic slavery as benign, and a lack of archival material on European participation (other than Dutch) in Indian Ocean slavery. At the same time, they resist the impulse to discount the significance of the slave trade and the suffering of enslaved peoples in the Indian Ocean region. See Allen, "European Slave Trading"; Bialuschewski, "Pirates, Slavers";

Hunwick and Troutt Powell, *African Diaspora*; Lovejoy, *Transformations in Slavery*; Manning, *Slavery and African Life*; Segal, *Islam's Black Slaves*; Toledano, *Slavery and Abolition*; and Vink, "World's Oldest Trade."

58. For example, Bialuschewski contends, since the Indian Ocean was outside the jurisdiction of the EIC's charter and the Royal African Company's west coast monopoly, it offered a profitable "legal loophole" to "venturesome entrepreneurs" seeking cheaper sources of slave labor ("Pirates, Slavers," 404).
59. Allen, "European Slave Trading," 66.
60. Segal, *Islam's Black Slaves*, 104.
61. Markley, *Far East and the English Imagination*, 4.
62. Amussen, *Caribbean Exchanges*, 110.
63. Amussen, 138–39.
64. Vink, "World's Oldest Trade," 152. I am grateful to Steven Weisenburger for his insights in our conversation about Philippa's racialized role in *Isle*.
65. "Except a corn of wheat fall into the ground and die, it abideth alone: but if it die, it bringeth forth much fruit" (John 12:24).
66. Visconsi, *Lines of Equity*, 127, 131. Denbo, "Generating Regenerated Generations," likewise argues that issues of race pale next to Neville's primary "problem of order and authority" (149).
67. See Carey, "Henry Neville's *The Isle of Pines*"; and Wiseman, "Porno-Political Rhetoric and Political Theory." On sexual promiscuity as a trope for antidemocratic anxieties and, later, for the degradation to which absolute sovereignty would lead a nation, see also Mowry, *Bawdy Politic*; and Weil, *Political Passions*.
68. Mahlberg, *Henry Neville and English Republican Culture*, 121.
69. Sullivan, *Liberal Republicanism in England*, 73.
70. Boesky, *Founding Fictions*, chapter 5.
71. After all, in Neville's story, Philippa initially gives birth to "a fine white girl" whose racial difference from Pine's other children is insidiously illegible (*Isle*, 198). In *Shades of Difference*, Iyengar argues that while the English did not decisively connect blackness and slavery until late in the seventeenth century, earlier texts document "an emergent myth linking dark skin and other physical features to an inherited destiny to slave labor on the one hand and to species difference on the other" (10–11).
72. Denbo asserts, "In a society in which no work is necessary to survive, slavery is unnecessary" ("Generating Regenerated Generations," 152). On women's status in and perspectives on early modern republicanism, see the essays in van Gelderen and Skinner, *Republicanism*, 2:2.
73. Amussen, *Caribbean Exchanges*, 134, 144.

74. Visconsi, *Lines of Equity*, 123. Such originary fantasies grounded the work of divine right political theorists.
75. Armitage, "Empire and Liberty," 32.
76. By the mid-seventeenth century, argues Pincus in *Protestantism and Patriotism*, the English had seen enough "Dutch treachery, pride, and self-interest" (61) to doubt their rivals' faithful adherence to shared Protestant and republican principles; many feared, too, that the Dutch were "imitating" the Spanish in their "commercial policies" as in "perfidy," "inhumanity," and overweening political aspirations (263). If Neville himself was somewhat unconventional in his religious convictions (he was accused, then acquitted, of atheism in 1659 and was known for his anticlericalism and toleration of Catholics), he was nonetheless invested in upholding "the purity of Christian religion" so as to ensure "good and orderly government" (Neville, *Plato Redivivus*, 115). For further discussion of Neville's religious ideas, see Mahlberg, *Henry Neville and English Republican Culture*.
77. Neville, *Plato Redivivus*, 111; *Isle*, 194.
78. Skinner, *Liberty before Liberalism*, 64.
79. Neville, *Plato Redivivus*, 88.
80. Armitage, "Empire and Liberty," 43.
81. Toland, "Life of James Harrington," ii.

2. "STRIKING SAIL" IN SATIRE

1. John Dryden, "Epistle Dedicatory," to *Aureng-Zebe*, n.p. Dryden's dedication is addressed to John, Earl of Mulgrave. Text references are to the Kessinger edition of *Aureng-Zebe* (hereafter cited in the text as *AZ*), act and page numbers.
2. Markley, *Far East and the English Imagination*, chapter 3.
3. On this tradition, see Orr, *Empire on the English Stage*.
4. When referring to Dryden's character, I use his (and Bernier's) altered spelling of the historical Aurangzeb's name.
5. Subrahmanyam, *Courtly Encounters*, introduction.
6. Braverman, *Plots and Counterplots*, 132.
7. Link, introduction to *Aureng-Zebe*, xvii.
8. Link.
9. Alssid, "Design of Dryden's *Aureng-Zebe*," 469.
10. Hughes, *Dryden's Heroic Plays*, 10. Kramer also unpacks Dryden's careful appropriating of French models, noting in *Imperial Dryden* that "to honor the present, one had to emulate the French style (but never admit it); to

honor the past, one had to extol the tradition of the great English poets (but never imitate them)" (143).
11. Hughes, *Dryden's Heroic Plays*, 9, 127.
12. Hughes, 141.
13. Hughes, 15.
14. Kirsch, *Dryden's Heroic Drama*, 62.
15. Kirsch, 121.
16. Kirsch, 124–25.
17. Levine, *Between the Ancients and Moderns*, 55.
18. Levine.
19. Dryden eulogized Oliver Cromwell in his *Heroic Stanzas*, for example, just one year before his *Astraea Redux* (1660) celebrated "the happy restoration and return of his sacred majesty Charles the Second." Moreover, while raised a Puritan, he later converted to Roman Catholicism, perhaps out of loyalty to James II. He was on the anti-exclusionist side of the Exclusion Crisis.
20. Levine, *Between the Ancients and Moderns*, 38.
21. Levine, 80. Levine argues that Dryden enacts his love of liberty by wrestling with the strictures of rhyme and heroic verse, seeking a middle ground between classical rules and modern flexibility and attempting to modify French conventions for distinctly English tastes.
22. Haley, *Dryden and the Problem of Freedom*, 21.
23. Haley, 108.
24. Haley, 111.
25. Haley, 47, 117.
26. Machiavelli, *Prince*, 14. Text references are to this edition.
27. The play and dedication reference "Fate" fifty-eight times, "Fortune" thirty-seven times, and "Heaven" fifty times.
28. Rajan, *Under Western Eyes*, 75. According to the *OED*, sati—or "virtuous wife," in Sanskrit—is the feminine form of *sat*, which signifies what is good, wise, and honest. The historical Aurangzeb halted the Hindu custom of sati in 1663. *Oxford English Dictionary*, 2nd ed., *OED* Online, s.v. "sati."
29. Orr, *Empire on the English Stage*, 146.
30. Vance, "Beneath the Physical Beauty," 167.
31. These lines complicate neat allegorical readings about England's entry into India.
32. Haley, *Dryden and the Problem of Freedom*, 125.
33. Haley, 127.
34. Haley, 125.
35. Choudhury notes, too, that "after the restoration, London was decidedly

bi-cultural—deeply English in spirit and decidedly French in tone" (*Interculturalism and Resistance*, 24).
36. Maurer, "Fathers, Sons, and Lovers," 153.
37. Bhattacharya, "Ethnopolitical Dynamics," 168–69.
38. Haley, *Dryden and the Problem of Freedom*, 17–18.
39. Ballaster, *Fabulous Orients*, 283.
40. Rajan, *Under Western Eyes*, 71.
41. Choudhury, *Interculturalism and Resistance*, 201.
42. Choudhury, 139.
43. Kramer, *Imperial Dryden*, 64–65.
44. Kramer, 67.
45. Kramer, 66.
46. P. W. Thomas, *Sir John Berkenhead, 1617–1679: A Royalist Career in Politics and Polemics* (Oxford: Clarendon, 1969), 97, quoted in Winn, *John Dryden and His World*, 56.
47. Gunn, *First Globalization*, 167, 145.
48. For a useful synopsis of recent historiographical research on the complexity of "Mughal polity well into the mid-eighteenth century," see Wilson, "Early Colonial India," 957.
49. Truschke, *Aurangzeb*, 72.
50. Richards, *Mughal Empire*, 172, 204.
51. Craft, "Dryden's Transformation," 51.
52. Bernier, *History of the Late Revolution*, 23. Text references are to this edition.
53. Both Bernier and his translator lump together the English and Dutch.
54. Craft explains the motivation behind Dryden's careful revision of Aurangzeb's character for English theatergoers: "Dryden's flattering and essentially false depiction of Aurangzeb's filial loyalty to his king and father creates a shared patriarchal royalist value system between India and England that could help to maintain cordial trade relations between these two countries in the event that Fazelkan chose to mention the play to the reigning emperor" ("Dryden's Transformation," 53).
55. Marshall, "English in Asia to 1700," 274.
56. Marshall, 279.
57. Orr, *Empire on the English Stage*, 43.
58. Marshall, "English in Asia to 1700," 280.
59. Marshall.
60. Alam, *Languages of Political Islam*, 1.
61. Alam, 24.
62. Drawing on Subrahmanyam's work in *Courtly Encounters*, Schleck and

Şahin argue that "commensurability may be defined as the wish for and ability to communicate across cultural boundaries, under the impact of several motivations that range from political idealism to sheer individual pragmatism" ("Courtly Connections," 81).

63. On this "well-known literary tradition in both Europe and the Middle East," see Darling, "Mirrors for Princes," 223. See also Muzaffar and Subrahmanyam, who explain that "an extensive body of 'advice literature' already existed in Mughal India, to which [Aurangzeb's grandfather] Jahangir had access.... The Mughals had a deep familiarity with a whole range of such materials," which emphasized "justice and social balance, to be ensured through appropriate regulations" ("Mediterranean Exemplars," 112).
64. Haslam, *No Virtue Like Necessity*, 20.
65. Haslam, 26.
66. Haslam, 58, 50.
67. On the circulation, reception, and adaptation of Machiavelli's work in the Islamic world, see Biasiori and Marcocci's collection on *Machiavelli, Islam and the East*; see also Meserve, *Empires of Islam*, 9.
68. Şahin, "Tale of Two Chancellors," 161.
69. Darling, "Political Change and Political Discourse," 522–23.
70. Marcocci, "Machiavelli, the Iberian Explorations," 147.
71. Bernier, *History of the Late Revolution*, 336.
72. Temple, *Of Heroic Virtue*, 373. Text references are to this edition.
73. Batchelor, *London*, 218.
74. Batchelor, 197–98.
75. Haslam, *No Virtue Like Necessity*, 68.
76. Temple, "On Popular Discontents," 65. Text references are to this edition. Plato first develops the "ship of state" metaphor in book 6 of *The Republic*.
77. As Britain's naval power increased in the seventeenth century, jurists debated the merits of open versus closed seas in terms of national sovereignty. In response to skirmishes with rivals over Eastern trade routes, Dutchman Hugo Grotius posited in his 1609 *Mare Liberum* that the sea was a free space, belonging to no state or people. England's John Selden argued the opposite in his 1635 *Mare Clausum*, claiming English sovereignty over English waters. Grotius's ideas ultimately prevailed, and freedom of the seas proved essential in Europe's quest to moderate monopolies and maximize trade routes. However, debates about who had sovereignty over which seas (and what that sovereignty entailed) continued into the eighteenth century. On Britain's "blue water policies" and ambition for an "oceanic empire" in the late seventeenth century, see Orr, *Empire on the English Stage*, 251.
78. Dryden, *Essay of Dramatick Poesie*, para. 1.

3. RECOVERING THE "TRUE SPIRIT OF LIBERTY"

1. Swift, *Gulliver's Travels*, 164. Text references are to this edition (hereafter cited in the text as *GT*).
2. Kelly, "Era of Liberty," 88.
3. McKeon, *Origins of the English Novel*, 351.
4. Reid, *Concept of Liberty*, 17.
5. Reid, 11.
6. Pope, *Windsor Forest*, lines 91–92. Text references are to this edition.
7. On Swift's participation in the Utrecht peace negotiations and apparent acceptance of the transatlantic slave trade, see Griffin, *Swift and Pope*; and Richardson, *Slavery and Augustan Literature*. Both Swift and Pope were stockholders in the South Sea Company, Griffin notes; however, unlike Pope, whose work exhibits his "discomfort with the institution" of slavery, "Swift seems in his early political writings to regard the slave trade neutrally, as a valuable part of England's foreign trade" (91).
8. Lamb, *Preserving the Self*, 66. On the event and effects of the crash, see Lamb, 62–66.
9. Pocock, *Virtue, Commerce, and History*, 175–76.
10. Pocock.
11. Lamb, *Preserving the Self*, 201. Robbins explains that Commonwealth doctrine was "an amalgam of theories drawn from several periods" (*Eighteenth-Century Commonwealthman*, 3).
12. Bolingbroke, *Dissertation upon Parties*, 118.
13. Bolingbroke, *Idea of a Patriot King*, 274. Text references are to this edition.
14. Joseph Addison, *Cato, A Tragedy* (London, 1712); John Trenchard and Thomas Gordon, *Cato's Letters: Essays on Liberty, Civil and Religious* (London, 1723).
15. Swift, "Thoughts on Religion," 56.
16. Mahoney, "Jonathan Swift," 272.
17. Connolly, "Swift and the Irish Past," 257–58.
18. Connolly, 257.
19. On the contents of Swift's library, see Connolly, "Swift and the Irish Past," 256–57; Robbins, *Eighteenth-Century Commonwealthman*, 148; and Passman and Vieken, *Library and Reading*. See Swift's *Drapier's Letters*, letter 6, for his references to Sidney, Locke, and Molyneux.
20. Robbins, *Eighteenth-Century Commonwealthman*, 148–49.
21. Armitage, "Empire and Liberty," 43.
22. Swift, *Drapier's Letters*, letter 4, 85–86.
23. Swift, "On Doing Good," 44.

24. Swift, 43.
25. On how "Swift exposes the human/horse relationship as hypocritical, incoherent, and contradictory," see Alkemeyer, "Natural History of the Houyhnhmns" (24). See also Nash, *Wild Enlightenment*, chapter 4.
26. For instance, McKeon refers to Houyhnhnmland as a "conservative utopia" (*Origins of the English Novel*, 348), whereas Knowles argues that Houyhnhnm "integrity is nominal only, an artificial fabrication, like their utopia, and meant to be seen as such" (*Politics of Satire*, 135).
27. On the debate between "hard" and "soft" critics of this scene, see Clifford, "Gulliver's Fourth Voyage," 45. "Hard" critics find *Travels* a fundamentally negative text: Swift's equine Houyhnhnms are unattainable ideals, his description of the Yahoos is shocking, and Gulliver's expulsion from Houyhnhnmland appears a genuine tragedy. "Soft" critics, by contrast, read *Travels* as a comic tale rather than a tragedy; for them, the Houyhnhnms are part of Swift's joke, and it is Gulliver's kindly rescuer, the Portuguese Captain Mendez, who embodies Swift's "ideal of human excellence" in his compromising balance between extremes.
28. Boyle (Earl of Orrery), "Letter XV," 121. Text references are to this edition.
29. Mackie, "Swift and the Progress of Desire," 174, 191.
30. Swift, letters to Alexander Pope (29 September 1725, no. 673, 606), and Charles Ford (14 August 1725, no. 662, 586), in *Correspondence of Jonathan Swift*.
31. Weinbrot has argued that "to call the eighteenth century an 'Augustan age' ... is to misrepresent British history," given that neoclassical republicans and staunch royalists alike were well versed in and opposed to any repetition of Caesar Augustus's tyrannies (*Augustus Caesar*, 52–53).
32. Swift, *Contests and Dissentions*, 23.
33. Elagabalus was a third-century Roman emperor notorious for his gluttony and lust.
34. In one notable way, the Houyhnhnms are unlike the stereotypical Spartans. Gulliver observes that they "appear not to be so well prepared for War, a Science to which they are perfect Strangers" (*GT*, 247). By contrast, the Spartan state was a well-oiled war machine, with each citizen performing their duty toward that end. In this regard, the primary goal of the Spartan state is rendered both inconceivable and worthless in Houyhnhnmland. Given Gulliver's antipathy to violent conquest, which he articulates in the final chapter of the *Travels*, the Houyhnhnms' lack of preparation for war underscores rather than undermines their generally virtuous character.
35. The Yahoos' enslavement is justified, Gulliver notes, because their "capacities never [reach] higher than to draw or carry Burthens" (*GT*, 224). On

parallels between Swift's Yahoos and the Spartan Helots, see Rawson, *God, Gulliver, and Genocide,* chapter 4.
36. Plutarch, *Lives,* 1:291.
37. Drummond, *Review of the Governments,* 187.
38. Higgins, "Swift and Sparta," 513.
39. Bygrave, *Uses of Education,* 15, 123. Bygrave argues that debates about Sparta's example informed English models of education in the second half of the eighteenth century.
40. Bygrave, 123.
41. Bygrave, 125.
42. Bygrave, 130.
43. Mandeville, *Fable of the Bees,* 254.
44. Bygrave, *Uses of Education,* 144.
45. Higgins, "Swift and Sparta," 527.
46. Plutarch, *Lives,* 1:297.
47. Pocock, *Virtue, Commerce, and History,* 176, emphasis added.
48. Temple, *Essays,* 3. Text references are to this edition. Temple was revitalizing an earlier French debate on this topic; see DeJean, *Ancients against Moderns;* and Levine, *Battle of the Books.*
49. Swift, *Tale of a Tub,* 273.
50. On one such idea, which Temple identifies as "the transmigration of souls," see Yang, *Performing China,* chapter 3.
51. See Kelly, *Swift and the English Language.*
52. Swift, *Proposal for Correcting,* 18. Text references are to this edition.
53. Porter, *Ideographia,* 9–10. "To have no need for rules," Webb believed, "is, presumably, to exist in a state prior to transgression, whether linguistic or moral" (quoted in Porter, 45); on Webb, see also Ramsey, "China and the Ideal of Order." By contrast, Boyle, in *Swift as Nemesis,* argues that Swift echoes Temple's enthusiastic praise of the Chinese only to undercut it. He writes that "Swift saw in Temple's lucid summary of the features of the utopian China, a narcissistic reading of travel" (67) and a "delusional idealization of China" (70). Swift parodies all forms of modern optimism, Boyle argues, even those which appear genuinely cosmopolitan; in this regard, Swift ridicules Gulliver even and especially in the character's admiration for China (76).
54. Porter, *Ideographia,* 16.
55. Bolingbroke, *Idea of a Patriot King,* 225.
56. Markley, *Far East and the English Imagination,* 242, 247. After its defeat and humiliation fifty years earlier, the English East India Company (EIC) could only fantasize about reopening trade with Japan (246).

57. Markley, 243.
58. Gunn, *First Globalization*, 55.
59. Purchas, *Purchas His Pilgrimes*, part 1, book 3, chapter 1.
60. Quoted in Markley, *Far East and the English Imagination*, 243. Markley cites here the translator's dedication to Engelbert Kaempfer's *The History of Japan*, trans. J. G. Scheucher (London, 1727).
61. On Swift's complex attitude toward mercantilism, especially as it pertained to England's oppressive regulation of Ireland's economy, see Hinnant, "Swift and Mercantilism."
62. Markley concludes, in light of this global imbalance, that Swift is primarily interested in Japan as a "satiric foil for his anti-Dutch agitprop" (*Far East and the English Imagination*, 265). In this way, Swift echoes Neville's earlier triangulation of English, Dutch, and East Asian interests and demonstrates how the Anglo-Dutch relationship has become increasingly antagonistic since the 1660s. Keogh argues, similarly, that "the Japanese are largely shadowy background figures in this brief episode where the primary targets for satire are the Dutch, who place avarice for Japanese wealth above Christian fidelity"; in response to Japanese strength, she argues, writers linked "Japanese culture to either biblical narrative or ancient classical writers" so as to "imagin[e] ideal[s] of a world that is connected by universal understanding" ("Oriental Translations," 178–79).
63. See Langford, *Polite and Commercial People*, chapter 3.
64. Swift, "On the Wisdom of This World," 28. Text references are to this edition.
65. Temple, *Heroic Virtue*, 333.
66. Swift, *Contests and Dissentions*, 48. Text references are to this edition.
67. Swift, "Thoughts on Religion," 56.
68. Swift, *Account of the Court*, 276. Text references are to this edition.
69. Lamb, *Preserving the Self*, 236.
70. Neville, *Isle of Pines*, 111.

4. "HAPPY TO BE ENSLAVED"

1. Mary Pix, *Ibrahim*, 5.38. Text references are to this edition.
2. On Pix's reputation as a "Female Wit" who, despite her success as a playwright, has been dismissed by some feminist critics, see Marsden, "Mary Pix's *Ibrahim*," 42. Marsden argues in *Fatal Desire* that "she-tragedy" plays, in which "women are presented to the audience's gaze, established as desirable, and then driven into prolonged and fatal suffering," use spectacle to

represent national "honor and integrity" at a moment when "the sweeping oaths and pledges of honor prominent in an earlier generation of heroic drama had lost their validity" (61).

3. On how Lucretia's story of rape and suicide reverberated for millennia in republican myth-making and debates about civic identity, see Matthes, *Rape of Lucretia*.
4. Andrea, "Islam, Women, and Western Responses," 274. Zonana coined the term "feminist orientalism" to refer to a discursive practice of "displac[ing] the source of patriarchal oppression onto an 'Oriental,' 'Mahometan' society, [thereby] enabling British readers to contemplate local problems without questioning their own self-definition as Westerners and Christians" ("Sultan and the Slave," 593).
5. Wollstonecraft, *Vindication*, 6.
6. Andrea, *Women and Islam*, 89.
7. Stone has argued that the period in England from about 1680 to 1710 was marked by "an abnormally cynical, mercenary, and predatory ruthlessness about human relationships" (*Broken Lives*, 27).
8. Andrea, *Women and Islam*, 89.
9. Andrea, 103. Ballaster similarly argues that Pix's "oriental setting serves as a 'veil' or 'cover' for the performance of a verbal agency which is ultimately returned to the Occident" (*Fabulous Orients*, 89). In this regard, "the oriental woman . . . figures not only the enclosing and constraining power of despotism but also resistance to it" (22). As I argue here, however, some English writers express nuanced nostalgia for this very "constraining power."
10. Marsden, "Mary Pix's *Ibrahim*," 42. If Pix wrestled with such expectations, some of her male contemporaries treated chaste femininity as a joke. According to Gill, certain Restoration dramatists, including William Congreve and William Wycherley, exploited the unstable link between virtue and a reputation for virtue: "The playwrights' call for naïve female readers of their satiric sketches seems more than a bit disingenuous" (*Interpreting Ladies*, 2). In fact, any reader who understood their comedic sexual innuendo instantly proved herself unvirtuous: in their hands, "knowledge, especially sexual knowledge, is a gendered acquisition: only men are properly in possession of it" (1).
11. Marsden, *Fatal Desire*, 7.
12. After assaulting Clarissa and witnessing her body begin to waste away, Lovelace insists that no "lady in the world, can be more virtuous than Miss Harlowe is to this hour, as to her own mind" (Richardson, *Clarissa*, 1095). On how *Clarissa* demonstrates "competing ideologies" of virtue, see Lee, "Commodification of Virtue," 39.

13. Doody, *True Story of the Novel*, 10. This mind-body problem troubles Armstrong's important argument that domestic literature written by and for women "shifted the entire struggle for political power from the level of physical force to the level of language" (*Desire and Domestic Fiction*, 98). In her review of Armstrong's work, May notes that to focus on discursive empowerment to the exclusion of bodies (that is, to elide the real possibility that Pamela could be raped) is both unrealistic and problematic ("Strong-Arming of Desire").

14. On England's narrative shift from romance to realism, see Doody, *True Story of the Novel*; and McKeon, *Origins of the English Novel*; as well as Davis, *Factual Fictions*; Mayer, *History and the Early English Novel*; and Watt, *Rise of the Novel*.

15. McKeon, *Origins of the English Novel*, 27, 171. DiPiero similarly contends that "the stories of aristocratic virtue and its seemingly natural ascendancy... bolstered the morale of the financially faltering aristocracy by characterizing true nobility not as an economic status, but as a moral one" (*Dangerous Truths*, 64); see also DiPiero, "Unreadable Novels," 132.

16. Ballaster, *Seductive Forms*, 43, 49.

17. Ballaster, 56.

18. Ballaster, 206.

19. Ballaster, 210.

20. McKeon, *Origins of the English Novel*, 158.

21. Clery, *Feminization Debate*, 6–7.

22. Clery, 178.

23. Hume, *Treatise of Human Nature*, 3.2.12, 364. Text references are to this edition, book, part, and section. Hume sees these particular (and particularly female) virtues as "conspicuous instances" of the truth of his general ethical system (364).

24. Hume, "Of Polygamy," 110.

25. Levey, "Under Constraint," 221. Philosophers disagree on whether Hume is being prescriptive or descriptive. For example, while Levey sees Hume as upholding the artificial ideal of female chastity, Baier calls Hume's essay "remarkable for its devastating clarity [and] exposure of [this] double standard," particularly insofar as Hume pinpoints how the purity of high-ranking women depends upon the impurity of their lower-class counterparts ("Good Men's Women," 9).

26. Hume, "Of Polygamy," 116. Text references are to this edition.

27. On eighteenth-century debates about polygamy in England, see Nussbaum, *Torrid Zones*, chapter 3. Nussbaum argues, "England's toying with and ultimate rejection of polygamy near the end of the... century was part of

a nation's defining itself both as distinct from and morally superior to the polygamous Other" (83).
28. Shaftesbury, *Characteristics*, 155–56.
29. Shaftesbury, 157.
30. Chapone, *Hardships of the English Laws*, 54, 11.
31. Montagu, *Turkish Embassy Letters*, 71. On Montagu's defense of "Turkish women's socioeconomic freedom under Islamic law," see also Garcia, *Islam and the English Enlightenment*, 26, and chapter 2. On women's property rights in early modern Egypt and Turkey, see Ahmed, *Women and Gender in Islam*, part 2.
32. Andrea, "Islam, Women, and Western Responses," 286. For example, see readings of Montagu by Heffernan, "Feminism against the East/West Divide"; Lowe, *Critical Terrains*; Melman, *Women's Orients*; and Yeğenoğlu *Colonial Fantasies*.
33. Van Renen, "Montagu's Letters," 5.
34. O'Quinn, *Engaging the Ottoman Empire*, 210.
35. O'Quinn, 207, 209.
36. Montagu, "Concerning Monsieur de la Rochefoucault's Maxim—," 260–62, emphasis added.
37. Zuroski, *Taste for China*, 189. "Orientalism in eighteenth-century English culture was a counterintuitive rejection of a deeply rooted aristocratic paradigm," Zuroski contends, in which beauty (of women or objects) is ineluctably linked to "network[s] of noble privilege" (188, 163).
38. Zuroski, 203. See also Botting, *Gothic* and *Gothic Romanced*.
39. Thompson, introduction to *Women's Travel Writings in India*, 6.
40. Thompson, 8–9.
41. Kindersley, *Letters*, 124–25. Text references are to this edition.
42. Montesquieu, *Spirit of Laws*, chapter 17.
43. Said, *Orientalism*, 2.
44. *Oxford English Dictionary*, 2nd ed., *OED* Online, s.v. "zenana." The term is used "in Islamic South Asia and Iran" to refer to "that part of a dwelling-house in which the women of a family are secluded; a harem."
45. Cahill accounts for similarly dismissive claims about Islam's exclusion of women's souls from heaven by describing what she calls a trope of "misogynistic mortalism" (*Intelligent Souls*, 2).
46. Nussbaum, "British Women Write the East," 125.
47. Kindersley, introduction and essays, iii. Text references are to this edition.
48. Thomas, *Essay on the Character*, 65. Text references are to this edition.
49. Defoe, *Complete English Tradesman*, chapter 15, para. 8.

50. Lennox, *Female Quixote*, 184, 115. Text references are to this edition (hereafter cited in text as *FQ*).
51. See Langbauer, *Women and Romance*, chapter 3. Langbauer argues that "Lennox's novel both exposes and acts out the association between women and romance" at an "historical moment in England that critics associate with the rise of the novel" (62).
52. Nussbaum, *Torrid Zones*, 14–15. Nussbaum argues that Lennox "trivializes the issues of empire by confining them to an imaginative and antiquated space" (126).
53. Zuroski, *Taste for China*, 197.
54. Zuroski, 198. Zuroski situates Lennox along a broader chronological trajectory that moves from Enlightenment cosmopolitanism to empire-minded orientalism by the end of the eighteenth century.
55. Cahill, *Intelligent Souls*, 163.
56. Doody, introduction to *Female Quixote*, xxxi.
57. Doody, xxx–xxxi.
58. Underscoring the aristocratic biases of heroic romance, Arabella claims that Lucy, by contrast, is a "Weak-souled Wench" who is "unfit . . . for Accidents like these" (93).
59. Colley, "Narrative of Elizabeth Marsh," 142.
60. Montagu and Lennox were acquaintances but not especially friendly ones. On their relationship, see Lowenthal, *Montagu*, 161.
61. Bekkaoui, "White Women and Moorish Fancy," 154. In Penelope Aubin's *Count de Vinevil* (1721) and *The Noble Slaves* (1722), Eliza Haywood's *The Fruitless Enquiry* (1727), and, later, Hannah Cowley's *A Day in Turkey* (1792), Bekkaoui suggests, the East is portrayed as an exotic "land of opportunities" in which European women can achieve sexual, financial, and social freedom from the rigid structures that circumscribed female mobility and treatment in the West (162). See also Bannet, *Transatlantic Stories*, chapter 2.
62. Fordyce, *Sermons*, 1:127.
63. Fordyce, 129.
64. Burke, *Reflections on the Revolution*, 78. Text references are to this edition.
65. Colley, *Britons*, 253. Colley describes an "important paradox in the position of women in Britain and elsewhere during the half-century or so after the American Revolution" (248), as they "refrained, at least in theory, from invading the public sphere, the realm of action, on the understanding that their moral influence would be respected and recognised" (263).
66. Wollstonecraft, *Vindication*, 6. Text references are to this edition.
67. Guest, *Small Change*, 15–16.

68. See Bannet, *Domestic Revolution*.
69. Sudan uses the example of Wollstonecraft, a spokesperson for England's late eighteenth-century cult of domesticity and motherhood, to contend that "the whole model of imperial power rested on the fantasy of domestic cultural coherence" (*Fair Exotics*, 107). For a different perspective, see Cahill, who argues that Wollstonecraft's "rejection of Islam did not entail an assertion that the 'West' was innately superior to the 'East'" because her rhetorical position required that she eschew "cultural essentialism" in any form ("Powers of the Soul," 23).
70. Defoe, *Complete English Tradesman*, chapter 15, para. 8.
71. Burke, *Reflections on the Revolution*, 78.

5. RASSELAS'S "CONSCIOUS VIRTUE"

1. Johnson, *Rasselas*, 115. Text references are to this edition.
2. McLynn, *1759*.
3. Johnson, *Vanity of Human Wishes*, line 28. Text references are to this edition.
4. Appleby, "Consumption," 167.
5. Johnson, *Preface to a Dictionary*, 294.
6. On Johnson's project to stabilize the English language, see Sudan, "Lost in Lexicography."
7. Johnson, *Dictionary*, s.v. "Virtue."
8. Brown, *Manners and Principles*, 108. Text references are to this edition.
9. Johnson, "Political State of Great Britain," 182.
10. Johnson, 62.
11. Johnson, *Rambler* no. 4, 1750, 158–59.
12. Johnson.
13. Newman, *Rise of English Nationalism*, 123, 114.
14. Yang, *Performing China*, 8; Zuroski, *Taste for China*, 14.
15. The relationship between Western print and Eastern orality (or scribal culture, as in India) was even more determinate than Ballaster suggests. Through the mechanism of the printing press, European writers appropriated oral fables *for* print culture, altering their meaning through acts of translation and transcription; see Ogborn, *Indian Ink*.
16. Ballaster, *Fabulous Orients*, 7. Ballaster draws on Mikhail Bakhtin's concept of the chronotope, or "space-time metaphor." For an early study of the oriental tale's link to romance and British romanticism, see also Conant, *Oriental Tale in England*.

17. The *Monthly Review* described the collection, for which no editor was listed, as "a compilation of various pieces, from various Writers; some moral, and some immoral; some tolerably entertaining, and some very dull" (399).
18. *School of Virtue*, 122. Text references are to this edition.
19. Aravamudan, *Enlightenment Orientalism*, 203.
20. O'Brien, *Narratives of Enlightenment*, 2.
21. Brown, *Manners and Principles*, 157.
22. Forman-Barzilai, *Adam Smith*, 202.
23. Smith, *Moral Sentiments*, 269. Text references are to this edition.
24. Knight, *Dinarbas*, 105–6. Text references are to this edition.
25. Hilger, "Strategies of Response," 73.
26. Richard, "Women Writers and *Rasselas*," 338.
27. Newman, *Rise of English Nationalism*, 54–55.
28. Hilger, "Strategies of Response," 76–77.
29. Knight, *Autobiography*, 1:160–61. Knight goes on to explain: "The people of England had been very desirous to have peace, but they soon perceived how little they had gained by it" (166). She includes a footnote describing England's excessive rainfall, spoiled crops, and high wheat prices during 1800, a "year of scarcity."
30. Knight, 166.
31. Sudan, "Mud, Mortar, and Other Technologies," 148.
32. Johnson, *Rasselas*, 91.
33. Sudan, *Alchemy of Empire*, 31.
34. Knight, *Autobiography*, 1:166.
35. Bayly, *Imperial Meridian*, 2. Bayly offers a comparative perspective on the pervasive sense of crisis during an Age of Revolutions that impacted all of Eurasia.
36. Black, *British Foreign Policy*, 16, 7.
37. Bayly, *Imperial Meridian*, 3.
38. On Macaulay's distinctly Protestant historiography, see Littlefield, "Protestantism and Liberty." On Macaulay's gendered revision of republicanism, see Hicks, "Catharine Macaulay's Civil War."
39. Macaulay Graham, *Letters on Education*, 268. Text references are to this edition.
40. See Hill, *Republican Virago*.
41. Temple, *Heroic Virtue*, 458, 449.
42. By contrast, Burke suggests that "old prejudices" are useful correctives to unbridled rationalism, particularly in moments of national crisis. He writes, in the same year as Macaulay, "Prejudice is of ready application in the

emergency; it previously engages the mind in a steady course of wisdom and virtue, and does not leave the man hesitating in the moment of decision.... Prejudice renders a man's virtue his habit; and not a series of unconnected acts" (*Reflections on the Revolution*, 90).

43. Knight, *Dinarbas*, 193; Johnson, *Rambler*.

AFTERWORD

1. O'Brien, *Narratives of Enlightenment*, 2.
2. McMurran, "New Cosmopolitanism," 22.
3. McMurran, 21, 32.
4. McMurran, 22.
5. On the compatibility of republican patriotism and cosmopolitanism in Kant's moral philosophy, see Kleingeld, *Kant and Cosmopolitanism*, chapter 1.
6. Kant, *Idea for a Universal History*, 22. Text references are to this edition.
7. Kant is interested in explaining the "history of humankind" (22), by which he means the development of the human race rather than of individual actors "on the great stage of the world" (10).
8. On the implications of Kant's philosophy for Eurocentric notions of race and empire, see Park, *Africa, Asia, and the History of Philosophy*, especially chapters 4 and 5; and Mensch, *Kant's Organicism*, especially chapter 5. See also Kleingeld and McMurran, who aptly caution readers against reading into Kant's moral philosophy racist ideas that he develops elsewhere. Kleingeld, *Kant and Cosmopolitanism*, argues that Kant had radically revised his racist views by the mid-1790s (chapter 4); McMurran sees arguments about the inherent imperialism of eighteenth-century "cosmopolitanism" as "fail[ing] to account for the complexity of [Kant's] anti-imperial political theory of cosmopolitan right" ("New Cosmopolitanism," 25).
9. Defoe, *Moll Flanders*, 1–2.
10. *Oxford English Dictionary*, 2nd ed., *OED* Online, s.v. "integrity."
11. Cureton and Hill, "Kant on Virtue," 263.
12. Heng, "Early Globalities."
13. Brown, *Manners and Principles*, 157.
14. "China's Century Starts Now," Bloomberg View, 30 April 2014, http://www.bloombergview.com/articles/2014-04-30/china-s-century-starts-now. See also Shenkar, *Chinese Century*; and Brahm, *China's Century*.
15. Swift, *Gulliver's Travels*, 172.

BIBLIOGRAPHY

PRIMARY SOURCES

Addison, Joseph. *Spectator* no. 69 (19 May 1711). In *The Commerce of Everyday Life: Selections from the Tatler and the Spectator*, edited by Erin Mackie, 203–6. Boston: Bedford/St. Martin's, 1998.

Aristotle. *The Nicomachean Ethics*. Edited by Lesley Brown. Translated by David Ross. Oxford: Oxford University Press, 2009.

Bernier, François. *The History of the Late Revolution of the Empire of the Great Mogul*. Translated by Henry Oldenburg. London: Summachar [1661, 1671], 1830.

Bolingbroke, Viscount Henry St. John. *A Dissertation upon Parties*. 1733–34. In *Bolingbroke: Political Writings*, edited by David Armitage, 1–191. Cambridge: Cambridge University Press, 1997.

———. *The Idea of a Patriot King*. In *Bolingbroke: Political Writings*, edited by David Armitage, 217–94. Cambridge: Cambridge University Press, 1997.

Boyle, John, Earl of Orrery. *Remarks on the Life and Writings of Dr. Jonathan Swift, in a Series of Letters . . .* 3rd ed. London: A. Millar, 1752.

Brown, John. *An Estimate of the Manners and Principles of the Times*. 2nd ed. London: L. Davis & C. Reymers, 1757. Eighteenth Century Collections Online Text Creation Partnership, University of Michigan, Ann Arbor.

Burke, Edmund. *Reflections on the Revolution in France*. 1790. Edited by Iain Hampsher-Monk. Cambridge: Cambridge University Press, 2014.

Burton, Thomas. *The Diary of Thomas Burton, Esq., Member in the Parliaments of Oliver and Richard Cromwell from 1656–9*. 4 vols. Edited by John Towill Rutt. London: H. Colburn, 1828.

Chapone, Sarah. *The Hardships of the English Laws in Relation to Wives, with an Explanation of the Original Curse of Subjection Passed upon the Women . . .* London: W. Bowyer, 1735. Gale Eighteenth Century Collections Online Print Editions.

Cooper, Anthony Ashley, Third Earl of Shaftesbury. *Characteristics of Men, Manners, Opinions, Times*. 1714. 2nd ed. Edited by Lawrence E. Klein. Cambridge: Cambridge University Press, 2000.

———. *An Inquiry concerning Virtue, in Two Discourses*. 1699. Introduced by Joseph Filonowicz. Delmar, NY: Scholars' Facsimiles and Reprints, 1991.

Davenant, Charles. *An Essay upon Ways and Means of Supplying the War*. London: Jacob Tonson, 1695. Early English Books Online.

Defoe, Daniel. *The Complete English Tradesman*. 1726. Project Gutenberg.

———. *An Essay upon Publick Credit: Being An Enquiry How the Publick Credit Comes to Depend upon the Change of the Ministry*... London, 1710. Eighteenth Century Collections Online.

———. *Moll Flanders*. 1722. Edited by G. A. Starr. New York: Oxford University Press, 1971.

———. *A New Voyage round the World*. 1725. Edited by John McVeagh. London: Pickering & Chatto, 2009.

———. *The True-Born Englishman*. In *A True Collection of the Writings of the Author of the True Born English-man, Corrected by Himself*. 1703. In *The Earlier Life and the Chief Earlier Works of Daniel Defoe*, edited by Henry Morley, 175–218. New York: Burt Franklin, [1889] 1970.

Drummond, William. *A Review of the Governments of Sparta and Athens*. London: W. Bulmer, 1794. Eighteenth Century Collections Online.

Dryden, John. *Annus Mirabilis*. 1667. In *John Dryden*, edited by Keith Walker, 23–70. Oxford: Oxford University Press, 1987.

———. *Aureng-Zebe: A Tragedy*. In *The Dramatic Works of John Dryden*. Vol. 4. London, 1717. LaVergne, TN: Kessinger, 2009.

———. Dedication to *Annus Mirabilis*. In *The Poems of John Dryden*, 18. Edited by John Sargeaunt. New York: Oxford University Press, 1913.

———. *An Essay of Dramatick Poesie*. In *The Works of John Dryden*, vol. 17, edited by Samuel Holt Monk, A. E. Wallace Maurer, Vinton A. Dearing, R. V. LeClercq, and Maximillian E. Novak, 3–81. Berkeley: University of California Press, 1971.

Fordyce, James. *Sermons to Young Women, in Two Volumes*. Vol. 1. 1767. London: n.p., 1775. Eighteenth Century Collections Online.

Fortescue, Sir John. *De Laudibus Legum Angliæ*. London: E. & R. Nutt, and R. Gosling, 1737. Eighteenth Century Collections Online.

Galland, Antoine. *The Remarkable Sayings, Apothegms and Maxims of the Eastern Nations Abstracted and Translated Out of Their Books Written in the Arabian, Persian, and Turkish Language, with Remarks*. London: Richard Baldwin, 1695. Early English Books Online Text Creation Partnership, University of Michigan, Ann Arbor.

Gibbon, Edward. *History of the Decline and Fall of the Roman Empire*. 1781. Vol. 3. London: Electric Book Company, 2000.

Harrington, James. *The Commonwealth of Oceana*. 1656. Edited by J. G. A. Pocock. Cambridge: Cambridge University Press, 1992.

Hegel, G. W. F. *Lectures on the Philosophy of History*. Translated by J. Sibree. London: George Bell & Sons, 1902.

Hobbes, Thomas. *Leviathan, or the Matter, Forme, and Power of a Commonwealth Ecclesiastical and Civill*. Edited by C. B. Macpherson. London: Penguin, 1985.

Hume, David. "Of Polygamy and Divorces." In *Essays and Treatises on Several Subjects*, 110–16. London: A. Millar, 1758. Eighteenth Century Collections Online.

———. *A Treatise of Human Nature*. 1739. In *A Critical Edition, Volume I: Texts*, edited by David Fate Norton and Mary J. Norton. Oxford: Clarendon, 2007.

Hutcheson, Francis. *An Inquiry into the Original of Our Ideas of Beauty and Virtue in Two Treatises*. 1726. Edited by Wolfgang Leidhold. Indianapolis: Liberty Fund, 2004.

Johnson, Samuel. *The History of Rasselas, Prince of Abyssinia*. 1759. In *Samuel Johnson: Selected Poetry and Prose*, edited by Frank Brady and W. K. Wimsatt, 73–153. Berkeley: University of California Press, 1977.

———. "An Introduction to the Political State of Great Britain, Written in the Year 1756." In *The Works of Samuel Johnson, LL.D.: Together with His Life and Notes on His Lives of the Poets*, vol. 10, edited by Sir John Hawkins, 158–82. London: n.p., 1787.

———. "Preface to a Dictionary of the English Language." 1755. In Brady and Wimsatt, *Selected Poetry and Prose*, 277–98.

———. *Rambler* no. 4, 31 March 1750. In Brady and Wimsatt, *Selected Poetry and Prose*, 155–58.

———. *The Vanity of Human Wishes*. 1749. In Brady and Wimsatt, *Selected Poetry and Prose*, 57–67.

———. "Virtue." In *A Dictionary of the English Language*. 1755, 1773. Edited by Beth Rapp Young, Jack Lynch, William Dorner, Amy Larner Giroux, Carmen Faye Mathes, and Abigail Moreshead. Johnson's Dictionary Online. 2021. Accessed 22 March 2022. https://johnsonsdictionaryonline.com/1755/virtue_ns.

Kant, Immanuel. *Idea for a Universal History with a Cosmopolitan Aim*. Translated by Allen Wood. In *Kant's Idea for a Universal History with a Cosmopolitan Aim: A Critical Guide*, edited by Amélie Oksenberg Rorty and James Schmidt, 9–23. Cambridge: Cambridge University Press, 2009. 9–23.

Kindersley, Jemima. *Letters from the Island of Teneriffe, Brazil, the Cape of Good Hope, and the East Indies*. London: J. Nourse, 1777. Gale Eighteenth Century Collections Online Print Editions.

———. Introduction and essays to accompany *An Essay on the Character, the Manners, and the Understanding of Women, in Different Ages*, by Antoine Léonard Thomas. London: J. Dodsley, 1781. Eighteenth Century Collections Online.

Knight, Ellis Cornelia. *Autobiography of Miss Cornelia Knight*. 3rd ed. London: W.H. Allen, 1861. Project Gutenberg.

———. *Dinarbas; a Tale: Being a Continuation of Rasselas, Prince of Abissinia*. 1792. 2nd ed. Edited by Lynne Meloccaro. London: J. M. Dent, 1994.

Lennox, Charlotte. *The Female Quixote*. 1752. Edited by Margaret Dalziel. Oxford: Oxford University Press, 2008.

Locke, John. *An Essay concerning Human Understanding*. 1693. Amherst, NY: Prometheus, 1995.

———. *Two Treatises of Government, and a Letter concerning Toleration*. Edited by Ian Shapiro. New Haven, CT: Yale University Press, 2003.

Macaulay Graham, Catharine. *Letters on Education, with Observations on Religious and Metaphysical Subjects*. 1790. Edited by Gina Luria. New York: Garland, 1974.

Machiavelli, Niccolò. *The Prince*. 1513. New York: Dover, [1910] 1992.

Mandeville, Bernard. *The Fable of the Bees: or, Private Vices, Publick Benefits*. 1714. Edited by Phillip Harth. London: Penguin, 1970.

Milton, John. *Areopagitica*. 1644. In *John Milton: Complete Poems and Major Prose*, edited by Merritt Y. Hughes, 716–49. Indianapolis: Hackett, 2003.

Montagu, Lady Mary Wortley. "Concerning Monsieur de la Rochefoucault's Maxim—'That marriage is sometimes "convenient but never delightful."'" In *Letters of the Right Honourable Lady Mary Wortley Montagu, Written during Her Travels in Europe, Asia, and Africa...*, 252–62. London: M. Cooper, 1775.

———. *The Nonsense of Common-Sense, 1737–1738*. Edited by Robert Halsband. Evanston, IL: Northwestern University, 1947.

———. *The Turkish Embassy Letters*. 1763. Edited by Malcolm Jack. London: Virago, 1994.

Montesquieu, Charles-Louis de Secondat, Baron de. *The Spirit of the Laws*. 1750. Translated by Thomas Nugent. London: J. Nourse, 1750. Eighteenth Century Collections Online.

Neville, Henry. *The Isle of Pines*. 1668. In *Three Early Modern Utopias*, edited by Susan Bruce, 187–212. New York: Oxford University Press, 1999.

———. *Plato Redivivus: or, A Dialogue Concerning Government*. 1681. In *Two English Republican Tracts*, edited by Caroline Robbins, 61–200. Cambridge: Cambridge University Press, 1969.

Parker, Henry. *Of a Free Trade...* London: Fr. Neile, 1648. Early English Books Online Text Creation Partnership, University of Michigan, Ann Arbor.

Pix, Mary. *Ibrahim, The Thirteenth Emperour of the Turks, a Tragedy*. London: John Harding & Richard Wilkin, 1696. Early English Books Online Text Creation Partnership, University of Michigan, Ann Arbor.

Plutarch. *Plutarch's Parallel Lives*. Vol. 1. Edited by T. E. Page and W. H. D. Rouse. Translated by Bernadotte Perrin. London: Heinemann, 1914.

Pope, Alexander. *Windsor Forest*. In *Selected Poetry*, edited by Pat Rogers, 20–31. Oxford: Oxford University Press, 1994.

Purchas, Samuel. *Purchas His Pilgrimes*. London: William Stansby, 1625. Early English Books Online Text Creation Partnership, University of Michigan, Ann Arbor.

Richardson, Samuel. *Clarissa, or The History of a Young Lady*. 1748. Edited by Angus Ross. London: Penguin, 1985.

The School of Virtue. Consisting of Novels, Tales, Fables, Allegories, &c. &c. Moral and Entertaining: In Prose and Verse. London: n.p., 1763. Reviewed in the *Monthly Review, Or, Literary Journal, 1752–1825*, no. 31 (1764): 399.

Sidney, Algernon. *Discourses concerning Government*. London: n.p., 1698.

Smith, Adam. *The Theory of Moral Sentiments*. 1759. Edited by Knud Haakonssen. Cambridge: Cambridge University Press, 2002.

Steele, Richard. *The Christian Hero: An Argument Proving That No Principles But Those of Religion Are Sufficient to Make a Great Man*. 1701. Edited by Rae Blanchard. London: Oxford University Press, 1932.

Swift, Jonathan. *An Account of the Court and Empire of Japan*. In *The Works of the Rev. Jonathan Swift, D. D.*, vol. 6, arranged by Thomas Sheridan, 269–82. London: J. Johnson et al., 1808.

———. *The Correspondence of Jonathan Swift, D. D., in Four Volumes, Vol. II (Letters Nos. 301–700, 1714–26)*. Edited by David Woolley. Frankfurt: Peter Lang, 2001.

———. *A Discourse of the Contests and Dissentions between the Nobles and the Commons in Athens and Rome*. London: John Nutt, 1701. Eighteenth Century Collections Online.

———. *The Drapier's Letters*. In *The Works of the Rev. Jonathan Swift, D. D.*, vol. 8, arranged by Thomas Sheridan, n.p. London: J. Johnson, 1808.

———. *Gulliver's Travels*. 1726. Edited by Albert J. Rivero. New York: Norton, 2002.

———. *A Proposal for Correcting, Improving, and Ascertaining the English Tongue*. London: Benj. Tooke, 1712. Eighteenth Century Collections Online.

———. Sermons ("On Doing Good," "Thoughts on Religion," and "On the Wisdom of This World"). In *The Works of Jonathan Swift*, vol. 8, 2nd ed., edited by Sir Walter Scott, 41–52, 53–56, 28–41. London: Bickers & Son, 1883.

———. *A Tale of a Tub, Written for the Universal Improvement of Mankind. To Which Is Added, an Account of a Battel between the Antient and Modern Books*. London: John Nutt, 1704. Eighteenth Century Collections Online.

Temple, Sir William. *Essays on Ancient and Modern Learning and on Poetry.* Edited by J. E. Spingarn. Oxford: Clarendon, 1909.

———. *Of Heroic Virtue.* In *The Works of Sir William Temple Bart*, vol. 3, 304–93. London: n.p., 1757.

———. "Of Popular Discontents." In *The Works of Sir William Temple Bart*, vol. 3, 32–66. London: n.p., 1757.

Thomas, Antoine Léonard. *An Essay on the Character, the Manners, and the Understanding of Women, in Different Ages.* Introduced and translated by Mrs. Kindersley. London: n.p., 1781. Eighteenth Century Collections Online.

Toland, John. "The Life of James Harrington." In *The Oceana of James Harrington and His Other Works*, xiii–li. London: n.p., 1700. Early English Books Online Text Creation Partnership, University of Michigan, Ann Arbor.

Ward, Edward. *The London Spy.* London: J. How, 1703. Eighteenth Century Collections Online.

Wollstonecraft, Mary. *A Vindication of the Rights of Woman.* 1792. Mineola, NY: Dover, 1996.

Young, Arthur. *Political Essays concerning the Present State of the British Empire.* London: W. Strahan & T. Cadell, 1772. Eighteenth Century Collections Online.

SECONDARY SOURCES

Abu-Lughod, Janet L. *Before European Hegemony: The World System A.D. 1250–1350.* New York: Oxford University Press, 1989.

Ahmed, Leila. *Women and Gender in Islam.* New Haven, CT: Yale University Press, 1992.

Alam, Muzaffar. *The Languages of Political Islam: India, 1200–1800.* Chicago: University of Chicago Press, 2004.

Alam, Muzaffar, and Sanjay Subrahmanyam. "Mediterranean Exemplars: Jesuit Political Lessons for a Mughal Emperor." In Biasiori and Marcocci, *Machiavelli, Islam and the East*, 105–29.

Alkemeyer, Bryan. "The Natural History of the Houyhnhmns: Noble Horses in *Gulliver's Travels.*" *Eighteenth Century: Theory and Interpretation* 57, no. 1 (2016): 23–37.

Allen, Richard B. "Satisfying the 'want for laboring people': European Slave Trading in the Indian Ocean, 1500–1850." *Journal of World History* 21, no. 1 (2010): 45–73.

Alssid, Michael W. "The Design of Dryden's *Aureng-Zebe.*" *Journal of English and Germanic Philology* 64, no. 3 (1965): 452–69.

Amussen, Susan Dwyer. *Caribbean Exchanges: Slavery and the Transformation of English Society, 1640–1700.* Chapel Hill: University of North Carolina Press, 2007.

Andrea, Bernadette. "Islam, Women, and Western Responses: The Contemporary Relevance of Early Modern Investigations." *Women's Studies* 38, no. 3 (2009): 273–92.

———. *Women and Islam in Early Modern English Literature*. Cambridge: Cambridge University Press, 2007.

Andrea, Bernadette, and Linda McJannet. "Introduction." In *Early Modern England and Islamic Worlds*, edited by Andrea and McJannet, 1–19. New York: Palgrave Macmillan, 2011.

Appleby, Joyce. "Consumption in Early Modern Social Thought." In *Consumption and the World of Goods*, edited by John Brewer and Roy Porter, 162–173. New York: Routledge, 1993.

Aravamudan, Srinivas. *Enlightenment Orientalism: Resisting the Rise of the Novel*. Chicago: University of Chicago Press, 2012.

Armitage, David. "Empire and Liberty: A Republican Dilemma." In *Republicanism: A Shared European Heritage*, vol. 2, edited by Martin van Gelderen and Quentin Skinner, 29–46. Cambridge: Cambridge University Press, 2002.

———. *The Ideological Origins of the British Empire*. Cambridge: Cambridge University Press, 2000.

Armstrong, Nancy. *Desire and Domestic Fiction: A Political History of the Novel*. New York: Oxford University Press, 1987.

Baier, Annette. "Good Men's Women: Hume on Chastity and Trust." *Hume Studies* 5, no. 1 (1979): 1–19.

Ballaster, Ros. *Fabulous Orients: Fictions of the East in England, 1662–1785*. New York: Oxford University Press, 2005.

———. *Seductive Forms: Women's Amatory Fiction from 1684 to 1740*. New York: Oxford University Press, 1992.

Bannet, Eve Tavor. *The Domestic Revolution: Enlightenment Feminisms and the Novel*. Baltimore, MD: Johns Hopkins University Press, 2000.

———. *Transatlantic Stories and the History of Reading, 1720–1810*. Cambridge: Cambridge University Press, 1992.

Batchelor, Robert K. *London: The Selden Map and the Making of a Global City, 1549–1689*. Chicago: University of Chicago Press, 2014.

Baucom, Ian. *Out of Place: Englishness, Empire, and the Locations of Identity*. Princeton, NJ: Princeton University Press, 1999.

Bayly, C. A. *Imperial Meridian: The British Empire and the World, 1780–1830*. London: Pearson Longman, 1989.

Beach, Adam. "A Profound Pessimism about the Empire: *The Isle of Pines*, English Degeneracy, and Dutch Supremacy." *Eighteenth Century: Theory and Interpretation* 41, no. 1 (2000): 21–36.

Becker, Lawrence C. "Stoic Virtue." In Snow, *Oxford Handbook of Virtue*, 130–53.

Bekkaoui, Khalid. "White Women and Moorish Fancy in Eighteenth-Century Literature." In *The Arabian Nights in Historical Context: Between East and West,* edited by Felicity Nussbaum and Saree Makdisi, 153–66. New York: Oxford University Press, 2008.

Berg, Maxine. *Luxury and Pleasure in Eighteenth-Century Britain.* Oxford: Oxford University Press, 2005.

Bhattacharya, Nandini. "Ethnopolitical Dynamics and the Language of Gendering in Dryden's *Aureng-Zebe.*" *Cultural Critique* no. 25 (1993): 153–76.

Bialuschewski, Arne. "Pirates, Slavers, and the Indigenous Population in Madagascar, c. 1690–1715." *International Journal of African Historical Studies* 38, no. 3 (2005): 401–25.

Biasiori, Lucio, and Giuseppe Marcocci, eds. *Machiavelli, Islam and the East: Reorienting the Foundations of Modern Political Thought.* London: Palgrave Macmillan, 2018.

Black, Jeremy. *British Foreign Policy in an Age of Revolutions, 1783–1793.* Cambridge: Cambridge University Press, 1994.

Boesky, Amy. *Founding Fictions: Utopias in Early Modern England.* Athens: University of Georgia Press, 1996.

Botting, Fred. *Gothic.* London: Routledge, 1996.

———. *Gothic Romanced: Consumption, Gender and Technology in Contemporary Fictions.* London: Routledge, 1996.

Boyle, Frank. *Swift as Nemesis: Modernity and Its Satirist.* Stanford, CA: Stanford University Press, 2000.

Brahm, Laurence J. *China's Century: The Awakening of the Next Economic Powerhouse.* Singapore: Wiley, 2001.

Braverman, Richard. *Plots and Counterplots: Sexual Politics and the Body Politic in English Literature, 1660–1730.* Cambridge: Cambridge University Press, 1993.

Brown, Laura. *Fables of Modernity: Literature and Culture in the English Eighteenth Century.* Ithaca, NY: Cornell University Press, 2001.

Bygrave, Stephen. *Uses of Education: Readings in Enlightenment in England.* Lewisburg, PA: Bucknell University Press, 2009.

Cahill, Samara Anne. "Powers of the Soul: Wollstonecraft, Islam, and Historical Progress." *Assuming Gender* 1, no. 2 (2010): 22–43.

———. *Intelligent Souls? Feminist Orientalism in Eighteenth-Century English Literature.* Lewisburg, PA: Bucknell University Press, 2019.

Canny, Nicholas, ed. *The Origins of Empire.* Vol. 1 of *The Oxford History of the British Empire.* Oxford: Oxford University Press, 1998.

Carey, Daniel. "Henry Neville's *The Isle of Pines:* From Sexual Utopia to Political Dystopia." In *New Worlds Reflected: Travel and Utopia in the Early Modern Period,* edited by Chloë Houston, 203–18. Farnham: Ashgate, 2010.

Carey, Daniel, and Lynn Festa, eds. *The Postcolonial Enlightenment: Eighteenth-Century Colonialism and Postcolonial Theory*. New York: Oxford University Press, 2009.

Chakrabarty, Dipesh. *Provincializing Europe: Postcolonial Thought and Historical Difference*. Princeton, NJ: Princeton University Press, 2000.

Chaudhuri, K.N. *Asia before Europe: Economy and Civilisation of the Indian Ocean from the Rise of Islam to 1750*. New York: Cambridge University Press, 1991.

Choudhury, Mita. *Interculturalism and Resistance in the London Theater, 1660–1800*. Lewisburg, PA: Bucknell University Press, 2000.

Clery, E. J. *The Feminization Debate in Eighteenth-Century England*. New York: Palgrave Macmillan, 2004.

Clifford, James L. "Gulliver's Fourth Voyage: 'Hard' and 'Soft' Schools of Interpretation." In *Quick Springs of Sense: Studies in the Eighteenth Century*, edited by Larry S. Champion, 33–49. Athens: University of Georgia Press, 1974.

Coclianis, Peter A., ed. "Assessing Kenneth Pomeranz's *The Great Divergence*: A Forum." Special issue, *Historically Speaking* 12, no. 4 (2011).

Coffey, John. "Quentin Skinner and the Religious Dimension of Early Modern Political Thought." In *Seeing Things Their Way: Intellectual History and the Return of Religion*, edited by Alister Chapman, John Coffey, and Brad S. Gregory, 46–74. Notre Dame, IN: University of Notre Dame Press, 2009.

Colley, Linda. *Britons: Forging the Nation, 1707–1837*. 2nd ed. New Haven, CT: Yale University Press, 2005.

———. *Captives: Britain, Empire, and the World, 1600–1850*. New York: Anchor, 2002.

———. "The Narrative of Elizabeth Marsh: Barbary, Sex, and Power." In Nussbaum, *Global Eighteenth Century*, 138–50.

Conant, Martha Pike. *The Oriental Tale in England in the Eighteenth Century*. New York: Columbia University Press, 1908.

Connolly, S. J. "Old English, New English, and Ancient Irish: Swift and the Irish Past." In Rawson, *Politics and Literature*, 255–69.

Craft, Peter. "Dryden's Transformation of Bernier's 'Travels.'" *Restoration: Studies in English Literary Culture, 1660–1700* 33, no. 2 (2009): 47–55.

Cureton, Adam, and Thomas E. Hill. "Kant on Virtue: Seeking the Ideal in Human Conditions." In Snow, *Oxford Handbook of Virtue*, 263–80.

Darling, Linda T. "*Mirrors for Princes* in Europe and the Middle East: A Case of Historiographical Incommensurability." In *East Meets West in the Middle Ages and Early Modern Times: Transcultural Experiences in the Premodern World*, edited by Albrecht Classen, 223–42. Berlin: De Gruyter, 2013.

———. "Political Change and Political Discourse in the Early Modern Mediterranean World." *Journal of Interdisciplinary History* 38, no. 4 (2008): 505–31.

Davis, Lennard J. *Factual Fictions: The Origins of the English Novel*. New York: Columbia University Press, 1983.

Denbo, Seth. "Generating Regenerated Generations: Race, Kinship, and Sexuality in Henry Neville's *Isle of Pines* (1668)." In *Gender and Utopia in the Eighteenth Century: Essays in English and French Utopian Writing*, edited by Nicole Pohl and Brenda Tooler, 147–62. Hampshire: Ashgate, 2007.

DeJean, Joan. *Ancients against Moderns: Culture Wars and the Making of a Fin de Siècle*. Chicago: University of Chicago Press, 1997.

DiPiero, Thomas. *Dangerous Truths and Criminal Passions: The Evolution of the French Novel, 1569–1791*. Stanford, CA: Stanford University Press, 1992.

———. "Unreadable Novels: Toward a Theory of Seventeenth-Century Aristocratic Fiction." *NOVEL* 38, nos. 2–3 (2005): 129–46.

Doody, Margaret Anne. *The True Story of the Novel*. New Brunswick, NJ: Rutgers University Press, 1996.

———. Introduction to *The Female Quixote*, by Charlotte Lennox, edited by Margaret Dalziel, xi–xxxii. Oxford: Oxford University Press, 2008.

Eltis, David. *The Rise of African Slavery in the Americas*. Cambridge: Cambridge University Press, 2000.

Evans, Kasey. *Colonial Virtue: The Mobility of Temperance in Renaissance England*. Toronto: University of Toronto Press, 2012.

Force, Pierre. *Self-Interest before Adam Smith: A Genealogy of Economic Science*. Cambridge: Cambridge University Press, 2003.

Forman-Barzilai, Fonna. *Adam Smith and the Circles of Sympathy: Cosmopolitanism and Moral Theory*. Cambridge: Cambridge University Press, 2010.

Frank, Andre Gunder. *ReOrient: Global Economy in the Asian Age*. Berkeley: University of California Press, 1998.

Fraser, Rebecca. *The Story of Britain: From the Romans to the Present, A Narrative History*. New York: Norton, 2003.

Garcia, Humberto. *Islam and the English Enlightenment, 1670–1840*. Baltimore, MD: Johns Hopkins University Press, 2012.

Gill, Pat. *Interpreting Ladies: Women, Wit, and Morality in the Restoration Comedy of Manners*. Athens: University of Georgia Press, 1994.

Gregg, Stephen H. *Defoe's Writing and Manliness: Contrary Men*. Surrey: Ashgate, 2009.

Greene, Jack P. *Evaluating Empire and Confronting Colonialism in Eighteenth-Century Britain*. New York: Cambridge University Press, 2013.

———. "Introduction." In Greene, ed., *Exclusionary Empire*, 1–24.

Greene, Jack P., ed. *Exclusionary Empire: English Liberty Overseas, 1600–1900*. Cambridge: Cambridge University Press, 2010.

Griffin, Dustin. *Swift and Pope: Satirists in Dialogue*. Cambridge: Cambridge University Press, 2010.

Guest, Harriet. *Small Change: Women, Learning, Patriotism, 1750–1810*. Chicago: University of Chicago Press, 2000.

Gunn, Geoffrey C. *First Globalization: The Eurasian Exchange, 1500–1800*. Lanham, MD: Rowman & Littlefield, 2003.

Haley, David B. *Dryden and the Problem of Freedom: The Republican Aftermath, 1659–1680*. New Haven, CT: Yale University Press, 1997.

Hall, Kim F. *Things of Darkness: Economies of Race and Gender in Early Modern England*. Ithaca, NY: Cornell University Press, 1995.

Harrison, Peter. *The Fall of Man and the Foundations of Science*. Cambridge: Cambridge University Press, 2007.

Haslam, Jonathan. *No Virtue Like Necessity: Realist Thought in International Relations since Machiavelli*. New Haven, CT: Yale University Press, 2002.

Heffernan, Teresa. "Feminism against the East/West Divide: Lady Mary's 'Turkish Embassy Letters.'" *Eighteenth-Century Studies* 33, no. 2 (2000): 201–15.

Helgerson, Richard. *Forms of Nationhood: The Elizabethan Writing of England*. Chicago: University of Chicago Press, 1992.

Heng, Geraldine. "Early Globalities, and Its Questions, Objectives, and Methods: An Inquiry into the State of Theory and Critique." *Exemplaria* 26, nos. 2–3 (2014): 389–94.

Hicks, Philip. "Catharine Macaulay's Civil War: Gender, History, and Republicanism in Georgian Britain." *Journal of British Studies* 41, no. 2 (2002): 170–98.

Higgins, Ian. "Swift and Sparta: The Nostalgia of *Gulliver's Travels*." *Modern Language Review* 78, no. 3 (1983): 513–31.

Hilger, Stephanie M. "Strategies of Response: Ellis Cornelia Knight's Sequel to Samuel Johnson's *Rasselas*." *Intertexts* 10, no. 1 (2006): 65–86.

Hill, Bridget. *The Republican Virago: The Life and Times of Catharine Macaulay, Historian*. Oxford: Oxford University Press, 1992.

Hill, Christopher. *Puritanism and Revolution: Studies in Interpretation of the English Revolution of the 17th Century*. New York: Penguin, 1986.

Hinnant, Charles H. "Swift and Mercantilism: A Reappraisal." *Studies in Eighteenth-Century Culture* 25 (1996): 21–38.

Hughes, Derek. *Dryden's Heroic Plays*. Lincoln: University of Nebraska Press, 1981.

Hunwick, John, and Eve Troutt Powell. *The African Diaspora in the Mediterranean Lands of Islam*. Princeton, NJ: Markus Wiener, 2002.

Israel, Jonathan I. "The Emerging Empire: The Continental Perspective, 1650–1713." In Canny, *Origins of Empire*, 423–44.

Iyengar, Sujata. *Shades of Difference: Mythologies of Skin Color in Early Modern England*. Philadelphia: University of Pennsylvania Press, 2005.

Kaul, Suvir. *Eighteenth-Century British Literature and Postcolonial Studies*. Edinburgh: Edinburgh University Press, 2009.

———. *Poems of Nation, Anthems of Empire: English Verse in the Long Eighteenth Century*. Charlottesville: University Press of Virginia, 2000.

Kelly, Ann Cline. *Swift and the English Language*. Philadelphia: University of Pennsylvania Press, 1988.

Kelly, James. "'Era of Liberty': The Politics of Civil and Political Rights in Eighteenth-Century Ireland." In Greene, *Exclusionary Empire*, 77–111.

Kennedy, Geoff. *Diggers, Levellers, and Agrarian Capitalism: Radical Political Thought in Seventeenth-Century England*. Lanham, MD: Lexington, 2008.

Keogh, Annette. "Oriental Translations: Linguistic Explorations into the Closed Nation of Japan." *Eighteenth Century: Theory and Interpretation* 45, no. 2 (2004): 171–91.

Kirsch, Arthur. *Dryden's Heroic Drama*. Princeton, NJ: Princeton University Press, 1965.

Kleingeld, Pauline. *Kant and Cosmopolitanism: The Philosophical Ideal of World Citizenship*. Cambridge: Cambridge University Press, 2012.

Knowles, Ronald. *Gulliver's Travels: The Politics of Satire*. New York: Twayne, 1996.

Kramer, David Bruce. *The Imperial Dryden: The Poetics of Appropriation in Seventeenth-Century England*. Athens: University of Georgia Press, 1994.

Krishnan, Sanjay. *Reading the Global: Troubling Perspectives on Britain's Empire in Asia*. New York: Columbia University Press, 2007.

Kumar, Krishan. *The Making of English National Identity*. Cambridge: Cambridge University Press, 2003.

Lamb, Jonathan. *Preserving the Self in the South Seas, 1680–1840*. Chicago: University of Chicago Press, 2001.

Langbauer, Laurie. *Women and Romance: The Consolations of Gender in the English Novel*. Ithaca, NY: Cornell University Press, 1990.

Langford, Paul. *A Polite and Commercial People: England, 1727–1783*. New York: Oxford University Press, 1989.

Lee, Joy Kyunghae. "The Commodification of Virtue: Chastity and the Virginal Body in Richardson's *Clarissa*." *Eighteenth Century: Theory and Interpretation* 36, no. 1 (1995): 38–54.

Levine, Joseph M. *The Battle of the Books: History and Literature in the Augustan Age*. Ithaca, NY: Cornell University Press, 1991.

———. *Between the Ancients and Moderns: Baroque Culture in Restoration England*. New Haven, CT: Yale University Press, 1999.

Levey, Ann. "Under Constraint: Chastity and Modesty in Hume." *Hume Studies* 23, no. 2 (1997): 213–26.

Link, Frederick M. "Introduction." In *Aureng-Zebe*, by John Dryden, xiii–xxiii. Lincoln: University of Nebraska Press, 1971.

Littlefield, Lucy. "Protestantism and Liberty: Catherine Macaulay's Politics of Religion as a Response to David Hume." *Intellectual History Review* 30, no. 2 (2020): 233–52.

Lovejoy, Paul E. *Transformations in Slavery: A History of Slavery in Africa*. 3rd ed. Cambridge: Cambridge University Press, 2012.

Loveman, Kate. *Reading Fictions, 1660–1740: Deception in English Literary and Political Culture*. Hampshire: Ashgate, 2008.

Lowe, Lisa. *Critical Terrains: French and British Orientalisms*. Ithaca, NY: Cornell University Press, 1991.

Lowenthal, Cynthia J. *Lady Mary Wortley Montagu and the Eighteenth-Century Familiar Letter*. Athens: University of Georgia Press, 2010.

MacIntyre, Alasdair. *After Virtue: A Study in Moral Theory*, 3rd ed. Notre Dame, IN: University of Notre Dame Press, 2007.

Mackie, Erin. "The Culture Market, the Marriage Market, and the Exchange of Language: Swift and the Progress of Desire." In *Theorizing Satire*, edited by Brian A. Connery and Kirk Combe, 173–92. Basingstoke: Macmillan, 1995.

MacLean, Gerald, and Nabil Matar. *Britain and the Islamic World, 1558–1713*. New York: Oxford University Press, 2011.

Mahlberg, Gaby. *Henry Neville and English Republican Culture in the Seventeenth Century: Dreaming of Another Game*. Manchester: Manchester University Press, 2009.

Mahoney, Robert. "Jonathan Swift and the Irish Colonial Project." In Rawson, *Politics and Literature*, 270–89.

Makdisi, Saree. *Making England Western: Occidentalism, Race, and Imperial Culture*. Chicago: University of Chicago Press, 2014.

Manning, Patrick. *Slavery and African Life: Occidental, Oriental, and African Slave Trades*. Cambridge: Cambridge University Press, 1990.

Marcocci, Giuseppe. "Machiavelli, the Iberian Explorations, and the Islamic Empire: Tropical Readers from Brazil to India (Sixteenth and Seventeenth Centuries)." In Biasiori and Marcocci, *Machiavelli, Islam and the East*, 131–54.

Markley, Robert. "China and the English Enlightenment: Literature, Aesthetics, and Commerce." *Literature Compass* 11, no. 8 (2014): 517–27.

Marsden, Jean I. *Fatal Desire: Women, Sexuality, and the English Stage, 1660–1720*. Ithaca, NY: Cornell University Press, 2006.

———. "Mary Pix's *Ibrahim:* The Woman Writer as Commercial Playwright." *Studies in the Literary Imagination* 32, no. 2 (1999): 33–45.

Marshall, P. J. "The English in Asia to 1700." In Canny, *Origins of Empire*, 264–85.

———. *The Far East and the English Imagination, 1600–1730*. Cambridge: Cambridge University Press, 2006.

Matthes, Melissa M. *The Rape of Lucretia and the Founding of Republics: Readings in Livy, Machiavelli, and Rousseau*. University Park: Penn State University Press, 2001.

Maurer, Shawn Lisa. "Fathers, Sons, and Lovers: The Transformation of Masculine Authority in Dryden's *Aureng-Zebe*." *Eighteenth Century: Theory and Interpretation* 46, no. 2 (2005): 151–73.

May, Leila Silvana. "The Strong-Arming of Desire: A Reconsideration of Nancy Armstrong's *Desire and Domestic Fiction*." *ELH* 68, no. 1 (2001): 267–85.

Mayer, Robert. *History and the Early English Novel: Matters of Fact from Bacon to Defoe*. Cambridge: Cambridge University Press, 1997.

McKeon, Michael. *The Origins of the English Novel, 1600–1740*. Baltimore, MD: Johns Hopkins University Press, 1987.

McLynn, Frank. *1759: The Year Britain Became Master of the World*. New York: Grove, 2004.

McMurran, Mary Helen. "The New Cosmopolitanism and the Eighteenth Century." *Eighteenth-Century Studies* 47, no. 1 (2013): 19–38.

McRae, Andrew. *God Speed the Plough: The Representation of Agrarian England, 1500–1660*. Cambridge: Cambridge University Press, 1996.

Melman, Billie. *Women's Orients: English Women and the Middle East, 1718–1918*. Ann Arbor: University of Michigan Press, 1992.

Meserve, Margaret. *Empires of Islam in Renaissance Historical Thought*. Cambridge, MA: Harvard University Press, 2008.

Mensch, Jennifer. *Kant's Organicism: Epigenesis and the Development of Critical Philosophy*. Chicago: University of Chicago Press, 2013.

Mowry, Melissa M. *The Bawdy Politic in Stuart England, 1660–1714: Political Pornography and Prostitution*. Hampshire: Ashgate, 2004.

Myers, Milton L. *The Soul of Modern Economic Man: Ideas of Self-Interest from Thomas Hobbes to Adam Smith*. Chicago: University of Chicago Press, 1983.

Nash, Richard. *Wild Enlightenment: The Borders of Human Identity in the Eighteenth Century*. Charlottesville: University of Virginia Press, 2003.

Newman, Gerald. *The Rise of English Nationalism: A Cultural History: 1740–1830*. New York: St. Martin's, 1987.

Nussbaum, Felicity A. "British Women Write the East after 1750: Revisiting a 'Feminine' Orient." In *British Women's Writing in the Long Eighteenth*

Century: Authorship, Politics, and History, edited by Jennie Batchelor and Cora Kaplan, 121–39. New York: Palgrave Macmillan, 2005.
———. "Introduction." In Nussbaum, ed., *Global Eighteenth Century*, 1–20.
———. *Torrid Zones: Maternity, Sexuality, and Empire in Eighteenth-Century English Narratives*. Baltimore, MD: Johns Hopkins University Press, 1995.
Nussbaum, Felicity A., ed. *The Global Eighteenth Century*. Baltimore, MD: Johns Hopkins University Press, 2003.
O'Brien, Karen. *Narratives of Enlightenment: Cosmopolitan History from Voltaire to Gibbon*. Cambridge: Cambridge University Press, 1997.
Ogborn, Miles. *Indian Ink: Script and Print in the Making of the English East India Company*. Chicago: University of Chicago Press, 2007.
O'Quinn, Daniel. *Engaging the Ottoman Empire: Vexed Mediations, 1690–1815*. Philadelphia: University of Pennsylvania Press, 2019.
Ormrod, David. *The Rise of Commercial Empires: England and the Netherlands in the Age of Mercantilism, 1650–1770*. Cambridge: Cambridge University Press, 2003.
Orr, Bridget. *Empire on the English Stage, 1660–1714*. Cambridge: Cambridge University Press, 2001.
Park, Peter K. J. *Africa, Asia, and the History of Philosophy: Racism in the Formation of the Philosophical Canon, 1780–1830*. Albany: State University of New York Press, 2013.
Parker, Charles H. *Global Interactions in the Early Modern Age, 1400–1800*. Cambridge: Cambridge University Press, 2010.
Passman, D. F., and Heinz Vieken. *The Library and Reading of Jonathan Swift, in 4 Vols*. Frankfurt: Peter Lang, 2003.
Perkins, Franklin. "Virtue, Reason, and Cultural Exchange: Leibniz's Praise of Chinese Morality." *Journal of the History of Ideas* 63, no. 3 (2002): 447–64.
Pincus, Steven. "Neither Machiavellian Moment nor Possessive Individualism: Commercial Society and the Defenders of the English Commonwealth." *American Historical Review* 103, no. 3 (1998): 705–36.
———. *Protestantism and Patriotism: Ideologies and the Making of English Foreign Policy, 1650–1688*. Cambridge: Cambridge University Press, 1996.
Pocock, J. G. A. *The Machiavellian Moment: Florentine Political Thought and the Atlantic Republican Tradition*. Princeton, NJ: Princeton University Press, 1975.
———. *Virtue, Commerce, and History: Essays on Political Thought and History, Chiefly in the Eighteenth Century*. Cambridge: Cambridge University Press, 1985.
Pomeranz, Kenneth. *The Great Divergence: Europe, China, and the Making of the Modern World Economy*. Princeton, NJ: Princeton University Press, 2000.
Porter, David. *The Chinese Taste in Eighteenth-Century England*. Cambridge: Cambridge University Press, 2010.

———. *Ideographia: The Chinese Cipher in Early Modern Europe.* Stanford, CA: Stanford University Press, 2001.

Rajan, Balachandra. *Under Western Eyes: India from Milton to Macaulay.* Durham, NC: Duke University Press, 1999.

Ramsey, Rachel. "China and the Ideal of Order in John Webb's *An Historical Essay...*." *Journal of the History of Ideas* 62 (2001): 483–503.

Rawson, Claude. *God, Gulliver, and Genocide: Barbarism and the European Imagination, 1492–1945.* Oxford: Oxford University Press, 2001.

Rawson, Claude, ed. *Politics and Literature in the Age of Swift: English and Irish Perspectives.* Cambridge: Cambridge University Press, 2010.

Reid, John Phillip. *The Concept of Liberty in the Age of the American Revolution.* Chicago: University of Chicago Press, 1988.

Richard, Jessica. "'I Am Equally Weary of Confinement': Women Writers and *Rasselas* from *Dinarbas* to *Jane Eyre*." *Tulsa Studies in Women's Literature* 22, no. 2 (2003): 335–56.

Richards, John F. *The Mughal Empire.* Cambridge: Cambridge University Press, 1995.

Richardson, John. *Slavery and Augustan Literature: Swift, Pope, Gay.* New York: Routledge, 2004.

Robbins, Caroline. *The Eighteenth-Century Commonwealthman: Studies in the Transmission, Development, and Circumstance of English Liberal Thought from the Restoration of Charles II until the War with the Thirteen Colonies.* Cambridge, MA: Harvard University Press, 1959.

Şahin, Kaya. "A Tale of Two Chancellors: Machiavelli, Celālzāde Muṣṭafā, and Connected Political Cultures in the Cinquecentro/the Hijri Tenth Century." In Biasiori and Marcocci, *Machiavelli, Islam and the East*, 157–76.

Said, Edward. *Orientalism.* New York: Vintage, 1978.

Schleck, Julia, and Kaya Şahin. "Courtly Connections: Anthony Sherley's *Relation of his Travels* (1613) in a Global Context." *Renaissance Quarterly* 69, no. 1 (2016): 80–115.

Schleifer, Ronald. *Analogical Thinking: Post-Enlightenment Understanding in Language, Collaboration, and Interpretation.* Ann Arbor: University of Michigan Press, 2001.

Schmidgen, Wolfram. *Exquisite Mixture: The Virtues of Impurity in Early Modern England.* Philadelphia: University of Pennsylvania Press, 2013.

Scott, Jonathan. *Commonwealth Principles: Republican Writing of the English Revolution.* Cambridge: Cambridge University Press, 2005.

Segal, Ronald. *Islam's Black Slaves: The Other Black Diaspora.* New York: Farrar, Straus & Giroux, 2001.

Shenkar, Oded. *The Chinese Century: The Rising Chinese Economy and Its Impact on the Global Economy, the Balance of Power, and Your Job.* Upper Saddle River, NJ: Pearson & Wharton, 2005.

Skinner, Quentin. *Liberty before Liberalism.* Cambridge: Cambridge University Press, 1998.

———. "A Third Concept of Liberty." *Proceedings of the British Academy* 117 (2002): 237–69.

Snow, Nancy E. "Neo-Aristotelian Virtue Ethics." In Snow, *Oxford Handbook of Virtue,* 321–42.

Snow, Nancy E., ed. *The Oxford Handbook of Virtue.* Oxford: Oxford University Press, 2018.

Stillman, Peter G., ed. *"The Isle of Pines."* Special issue, *Utopian Studies* 17, no. 1 (2006).

Stone, Lawrence. *Broken Lives: Separation and Divorce in England, 1660–1857.* New York: Oxford University Press, 1993.

Subrahmanyam, Sanjay. *Courtly Encounters: Translating Courtliness and Violence in Early Modern Eurasia.* Cambridge, MA: Harvard University Press, 2012.

Sudan, Rajani. *The Alchemy of Empire: Abject Materials and the Technologies of Colonialism.* New York: Fordham University Press, 2016.

———. *Fair Exotics: Xenophobic Subjects in English Literature, 1720–1850.* Philadelphia: University of Pennsylvania Press, 2002.

———. "Lost in Lexicography: Legitimating Cultural Identity in Johnson's 'Preface' to the *Dictionary.*" *Eighteenth Century: Theory and Interpretation* 39, no. 2 (1998): 127–46.

———. "Mud, Mortar, and Other Technologies of Empire." *Eighteenth Century: Theory and Interpretation* 45, no. 2 (2004): 147–69.

Sullivan, Vickie. *Machiavelli, Hobbes, and the Formation of a Liberal Republicanism in England.* Cambridge: Cambridge University Press, 2004.

Swanton, Christine. "Virtue in Hume and Nietzsche." In Snow, *Oxford Handbook of Virtue,* 241–63.

Taylor, Charles. *Sources of the Self: The Making of the Modern Identity.* Cambridge, MA: Harvard University Press, 1992.

Thompson, Carl. General introduction. *Women's Travel Writings in India, 1777–1854,* vol. 1, edited by Carl Thompson, ix–xxix. New York: Routledge, 2020.

Toledano, Ehud R. *Slavery and Abolition in the Ottoman Middle East.* Seattle: University of Washington Press, 1998.

Truschke, Audrey. *Aurangzeb: The Life and Legacy of India's Most Controversial King.* Stanford, CA: Stanford University Press, 2017.

Vance, John A. "Beneath the Physical Beauty: A Study of Indamora in John Dryden's *Aureng-Zebe*." *Essays in Literature* 6 (1979): 167–77.

Van Gelderen, Martin, and Quentin Skinner, eds. *Republicanism: A Shared European Heritage*, vol. 2. Cambridge: Cambridge University Press, 2002.

Van Renen, Denys. "Montagu's Letters from the Levant: Contesting the Borders of European Selfhood." *Journal for Early Modern Cultural Studies* 11, no. 2 (2011): 1–34.

Vink, Markus. "'The World's Oldest Trade': Dutch Slavery and Slave Trade in the Indian Ocean in the Seventeenth Century." *Journal of World History* 14, no. 2 (2003): 131–77.

Visconsi, Elliott. *Lines of Equity: Literature and the Origins of Law in Later Stuart England*. Ithaca, NY: Cornell University Press, 2008.

Wallerstein, Immanuel. *The Modern World System*. New York: Academic Press, 1974.

Warren, Christopher N. "When Self-Preservation Bids: Approaching Milton, Hobbes, and Dissent." *English Literary Renaissance* 37, no. 1 (2007): 118–50.

Watt, Ian. *The Rise of the Novel: Studies in Defoe, Richardson, and Fielding*. Berkeley: University of California Press, 1957 & 2001.

Weil, Rachel. *Political Passions: Gender, the Family, and Political Argument in England, 1680–1714*. Manchester: Manchester University Press, 2010.

Weinbrot, Howard. *Augustus Caesar in "Augustan" England: The Decline of a Classical Norm*. Princeton, NJ: Princeton University Press, 1978.

Williams, Raymond. *Marxism and Literature*. Oxford: Oxford University Press, 1977.

Wilson, Eric Entrican and Lara Denis. "Kant and Hume on Morality." In *The Stanford Encyclopedia of Philosophy*, edited by Edward N. Zalta. [2008] 2018. https://plato.stanford.edu/archives/sum2018/entries/kant-hume-morality/ (accessed February 22, 2022).

Wilson, Jon. "Early Colonial India beyond Empire." *Historical Journal* 50, no. 4 (2007): 951–70.

Winn, James Anderson. *John Dryden and His World*. New Haven, CT: Yale University Press, 1987.

Wiseman, Susan. "'Adam, the Father of All Flesh,' Porno-Political Rhetoric, and Political Theory in and after the English Civil War." *Prose Studies* 14, no. 3 (1991): 134–57.

Wootton, David, ed. and introduction. *Republicanism, Liberty, and Commercial Society, 1649–1776*. Stanford, CA: Stanford University Press, 1994.

Yang, Chi-ming. "Eighteenth-Century Easts and Wests: Introduction." *Eighteenth-Century Studies* 47, no. 2 (2014): 95–101.

———. *Performing China: Virtue, Commerce, and Orientalism in Eighteenth-Century England, 1660–1760*. Baltimore, MD: Johns Hopkins University Press, 2011.

Yeğenoğlu, Meyda. *Colonial Fantasies: Towards a Feminist Reading of Orientalism*. Cambridge: Cambridge University Press, 1998.

Zonana, Joyce. "The Sultan and the Slave: Feminist Orientalism and the Structure of *Jane Eyre*." *Signs: Journal of Women in Culture and Society*, 18, no. 3 (1993): 592–617.

Zuroski Jenkins, Eugenia. *A Taste for China: English Subjectivity and the Prehistory of Orientalism*. Oxford: Oxford University Press, 2013.

INDEX

absolutism, 11, 39, 41, 109, 135; in *Isle of Pines* (Neville), 46, 58–60, 63–64, 206n29; *jure divino* (divine right theory), 42–43, 46, 209n74; patriarchal, 64, 105. *See also* despotism
Abu-Lughod, Janet L., 202n32
Adams, Will, 124
Addison, Joseph, 9–15, 18, 27, 29, 33, 39, 108, 119; *Spectator* no. 69, 9–11, 14–15, 31, 104
Africa: European trade in, 50, 56; North, 12; and the slave trade, 53–56, 61–62, 106, 207nn56–57; sub-Saharan, 24; textual representations of, 56, 62, 190–91. *See also* Madagascar
Ahmed, Leila, 219n31
Alam, Muzaffar, 91, 212n63
Alkemeyer, Bryan, 214n25
allegory, 45, 58–59, 84, 131; in oriental tales, 175–76
Allen, Richard B., 54, 207n57
Alssid, Michael, 71
America: Britain's loss of, 189; civic virtue in contemporary, 199; colonists in, 4, 13; resources from, 10–11, 54; revolutionary sentiment in, 132; slavery in, 53–56, 207n56
Amsterdam, 4, 48, 51, 124
Amussen, Susan Dwyer, 48–49
analogy: between credit and chastity, 16, 137; differential work of, 14, 28; between Eastern courts and Western stories, 138; in *Gulliver's Travels* (Swift), 125; in *Isle of Pines* (Neville), 57–58, 59; between past and present, 10, 14, 149, 162; between ships and states, 66–67, 80, 98–100; and virtue claims, 28–29
ancients versus moderns, 73, 119–20, 215n48
Andrea, Bernadette, 34, 136
Anglo-Dutch wars, 2, 15, 50, 69, 99. *See also* Dutch Republic
Anne, Queen, 106, 109
Annus Mirabilis (Dryden), 2–4, 11, 106
Appleby, Joyce, 170
Aravamudan, Srinivas, 23, 177
Aristotle: ethical theory, 5–7, 15, 20, 23, 25, 92–93; in *Gulliver's Travels*, 115; *Nicomachean Ethics*, 5
Armitage, David, 47

245

Armstrong, Nancy, 218n13
Athens, ancient, 33, 104, 110, 114–15, 117–19, 125
Aubin, Penelope, 163, 220n61
Aurangzeb (Mughal emperor), 67–69, 82, 84–97, 100, 209n4, 210n28, 211n54
Aureng-Zebe (Dryden), 66–101, 135, 188–89, 209n1, 211n54

Baier, Annette, 218n25
Bakhtin, Mikhail, 221n16
Ballaster, Ros, 23, 84, 140–41, 175, 217n9, 221nn15–16
Bannet, Eve Tavor, 220n61, 221n68
Batchelor, Robert K., 29, 95
Baucom, Ian, 4
Bayly, Christopher, 189–90, 222n35
Beach, Adam, 207n44
Bekkaoui, Khalid, 163, 220n61
Berg, Maxine, 202n30
Bernier, François, 33, 71, 86–91, 93, 97, 209n4; *The History of the Late Revolution of the Empire of the Great Mogul*, 87–89
Bhattacharya, Nandini, 83
Bialuschewski, Arne, 207–8nn57–58
Biasiori, Lucio, 212n67
biblical references, 17, 58, 75, 216n62
Black, Jeremy, 190
Boesky, Amy, 208n70
Bolingbroke, 1st Viscount (Henry St. John), 107–8, 119, 123, 130–31, 133; *The Idea of a Patriot King*, 102, 108, 130
Boyle, Frank, 215n53
Boyle, John, Earl of Orrery, 112–13
British constitution, 40, 41, 107; ancient, 38, 46, 63, 103, 108

British Empire: ambivalence toward, 33, 144, 172, 187; aspirational pursuit of, 3–5, 45–51, 64, 99–100, 183–84, 189
Brown, John, 171–75, 183, 188; *An Estimate of the Manners and Principles of the Times*, 35, 171–74, 175, 177, 199
Brutus of Rome, 18–19, 102, 108, 114
bullion, 13, 53, 84, 89, 118, 124
Burke, Edmund, 34, 164–67, 192; *Reflections on the Revolution in France*, 134, 164–65, 222n42
Bygrave, Stephen, 117–18, 215n39

Caesar, Julius, 18, 108, 114, 161, 186
Cahill, Samara Anne, 156, 219n45, 221n69
Carey, Daniel, 203n58, 206n29, 208n67
catholicism: in England, 70, 209n76, 210n19; threat of European, 4, 40, 52, 106
Cato the Younger, 18–19, 108
Chakrabarty, Dipesh, 205n86
Chapone, Sarah, 144
Charles I (king of England), 59
Charles II (king of England), 66, 68, 69–70, 84, 90, 100, 210n19
chastity: analogized to credit, 16, 154, 167; defined as virtue, 1, 15–16, 34–35, 133, 157, 160–62; Hume's theory of, 34, 141–43, 218n25; as a means to political freedom, 146, 151; unstable appearance of, 21–22, 77–78, 137–38, 141–42, 166
Chaudhuri, K. N., 202n32
China: commodities from, 10–11, 23–24, 52; economic dominance of, 8, 13, 24, 199; England's exclusion from trade with, 52, 121, 125; linguistic stability and cultural longevity

of, 24, 121–23; and Machiavellian politics, 92; as metonym for the East, 25–26, 204n72; shift in British attitudes toward, 25, 175; textual representations of, 10–11, 26, 41, 94, 120–23, 126, 150, 179–80, 215n53. *See also* Confucius; virtue: Chinese

"China's Century," 199

chivalry: and gendered ideals of courtly love, 136, 143–44, 151, 164–65; as sign of virtue, 10, 16, 34. *See also* romance

Choudhury, Mita, 84–85, 210n35

Christian Hero, The (Steele), 18–20

Christianity: Aristotelian virtue discourse and, 5–6; Eastern philosophy before, 120; English virtue discourse and, 17–20, 82, 126–27, 145

citizen: free, 41, 46, 55, 130, 181; global, 30, 177–78, 185, 193; neoclassical, 11, 130, 170; "of the world," 9, 29, 31, 35, 39, 178, 182, 196

civic virtue. *See under* virtue

Civil Wars, English, 8, 42, 50, 74, 90, 105, 121, 195

Clery, E. J., 16, 141

Clifford, James L., 214n27

climate: and commerce, 10, 173; and environmental determinism, 32, 40, 96, 108, 147–48, 151, 171

Coffey, John, 205n2

Coke, Sir Edward, 40

Colley, Linda, 4, 163, 220n65

colonialism: discourse of, 48, 203n56, 205n86; English anxieties about, 45, 59; European rivalries, 55, 62; and expansion, 2, 51, 83; ordinances/policies of, 55, 103, 109

commensurability, 32, 69, 82, 84, 92, 97, 212n62

commerce. *See* trade

Commonwealth of Oceana, The (Harrington), 46, 64, 94

Commonwealth politics, 42, 107, 109, 213n11

Complete English Tradesman, The (Defoe), 16, 134

Conant, Martha Pike, 221n16

Confucius, 24, 25, 28, 94–95, 120–21, 127

Connolly, S. J., 109

cosmopolitanism: commercial, 10, 12, 22; and community connection, 144, 164, 200; as "ethical stance," 29, 196; Kant on, 223n5, 223n8; in the Mughal court, 91; and national prejudice, 177, 179–80, 191–92; and orientalism, 23–24, 26, 156, 175

Country Party, 70, 107, 132. *See also* Whig

"country trade," 53

Cowley, Hannah, 220n61

Craft, Peter, 86, 90, 211n54

credit: economy, 106, 118; gendered discourse of, 16, 137, 141, 154, 167, 203n41

Cromwell, Oliver, 95, 210n19

Darling, Linda T., 92, 212n63

Davenant, Charles, 43

Davis, Lennard J., 218n14

deferral, discursive strategy of. *See under* romance; virtue

Defoe, Daniel, 14, 16, 26–27, 29; *The Complete English Tradesman*, 16, 134; on credit, 16, 137, 167, 202n41; *Moll Flanders*, 20–22; *A New Voyage round the World*, 13; *The True-Born Englishman*, 1, 14

DeJean, Joan, 215n48

Denbo, Seth, 208n66
despotism: critique of political, 38, 46, 109, 187; stereotypes of Eastern, 11–12, 32, 40–41, 63, 68, 136, 147, 150, 154, 186–87; stereotypes of French, 11, 32, 39, 40, 106. *See also* absolutism; republicanism, English; slavery: as a political condition
Dictionary of the English Language, A (Johnson), 170–71
Dinarbas; a Tale (Knight), 35, 169–70, 180–89, 193–94
DiPiero, Thomas, 218n15
Doody, Margaret Anne, 138, 157
Drummond, William, 117
Dryden, John, 2–5, 32–33, 65–101, 133, 209n10, 210n19, 210n21; *Annus Mirabilis*, 2–4, 11, 106; *Astraea Redux*, 210n19; *Aureng-Zebe*, 66–101, 135, 188–89, 209n1, 211n54
Dutch East India Company (VOC), 50, 53
Dutch Republic: legal structure in, 152–53; politico-economic success of, 47, 49–52, 54, 63–64, 108, 207n44. *See also* Anglo-Dutch wars; trade: and Anglo-Dutch rivalry

Elizabethan England, 15, 17, 40, 50, 108, 172
Eltis, David, 207n56
English East India Company (EIC), 50, 53, 84–85, 90, 146–47, 208n58, 215n56
Enlightenment: ambivalence about, 192; Eastern models for European, 25, 85, 184; and feminism, 166; global, 203n58; Kant on, 197; and orientalism, 23, 177, 220n54; and political virtue, 2, 5, 7; and reason, 5, 8, 17–18, 204n80

Essay concerning Human Understanding, An (Locke), 28–29
Estimate of the Manners and Principles of the Times, An (Brown), 35, 171–74, 175, 177, 199
Eurocentrism, 124, 152–53, 156, 185, 194; and Kant, 223n8
Evans, Kasey, 22–23, 203n56
exceptionalism (English/British), 4, 36, 40, 67, 190, 198
Exclusion Crisis, 43, 70, 105, 210n19

Fable of the Bees, The (Mandeville), 1, 6, 11, 117–18
Female Quixote, The (Lennox), 34, 146, 155–63, 166–67, 220nn51–52
female wits, 216n2
feminist orientalism, 35, 135–39, 144, 146, 154, 156, 166, 217n4. *See also* Islam; orientalism; seraglio, representation of the
feminization debate, 16
Festa, Lynn, 203n58
Filmer, Sir Robert, 43–44, 46. *See also* absolutism
Force, Pierre, 202n23
Fordyce, James, 164
Fortescue, John, 39, 44
fortune's wheel, 96–97. See also *Prince, The*
France: absolutism in, 11, 39; British rivalry with, 83, 174–75, 189; cultural influence of, 71–72, 140, 155, 210n21, 211n35; orientalism in, 177; virtue discourse in relation to, 122, 172, 175. *See also* catholicism: threat of European; despotism: stereotypes of French; French Revolution; romance: French heroic

Frank, Andre Gunder, 202n32
French Revolution, 165, 181, 187

Galland, Antoine, 26
Garcia, Humberto, 25, 204n72, 219n31
Gibbon, Edward, 11
Gill, Pat, 217n10
global economy, 13, 52, 63
global history, 27, 94–95, 185, 191–94, 195–98; theories of, 15, 36, 128, 149. *See also* historiography
global marketplace, 12, 44, 52, 63, 178, 195
Glorious Revolution (1688), 8, 12, 31, 42–43, 105
Gordon, Thomas, 108
Great Britain, 13, 64, 107–8, 172, 189; Act of Union of 1707, 4
Greene, Jack P., 39
Gregg, Stephen H., 203n41
Griffin, Dustin, 213n7
Guest, Harriet, 166
Gulliver's Travels (Swift), 33–34, 102–5, 110–16, 118, 120–31, 133, 189, 199, 214n27
Gunn, Geoffrey C., 85–86

Hakluyt, Richard, 45
Haley, David B., 73–74, 82
harem. *See* seraglio, representation of the
Harrington, James, 41, 46–47, 82, 109, 117; *The Commonwealth of Oceana*, 46, 64, 94
Harrison, Peter, 203n46
Haslam, Jonathan, 92, 96
Haywood, Eliza, 163, 220n61
Heffernan, Teresa, 219n32

Hegel, G. W. F., 36
Helgerson, Richard, 205n6
Heng, Geraldine, 30, 199
heroic drama, 71–73, 78, 83, 209n10, 210n21, 216n2
heroic virtue. *See under* virtue
Hicks, Philip, 222n38
Higgins, Ian, 118
Hilger, Stephanie M., 181, 183
Hill, Christopher, 41–42
Hinnant, Charles H., 216n61
historiography: efforts to craft cohesive, 125; Protestant, 222; providentialist, 177; West-centric, 95, 194; Whig, 41. *See also* global history
History of Rasselas, Prince of Abyssinia, The (Johnson), 35, 168–70, 177, 180–90
History of the Late Revolution of the Empire of the Great Mogul, The (Bernier), 87–89
Hobbes, Thomas, 42–43, 92, 96, 206n15
Hughes, Derek, 71–72
Hume, David, 6, 34, 141–44, 162, 165–66; "Of Polygamy and Divorces," 142–43; *A Treatise of Human Nature*, 34, 141–42, 218n25
Hutcheson, Francis, 6–7

Ibrahim, The Thirteenth Emperour of the Turks (Pix), 34, 134–39, 154
Idea for a Universal History with a Cosmopolitan Aim (Kant), 196–97, 223n7
Idea of a Patriot King, The (Bolingbroke), 102, 108, 130
improvement: Baconian, 17; Eurocentric notions of, 147–48, 185; Lockean, 24; of political structures, 32, 192, 197; and virtue discourse, 8, 15, 38, 131

India: British colonialism in, 68, 84, 187, 189; desire for commodities from, 4, 11–13, 50–52, 84, 90; Kindersley's travels in, 146–48; and origins of Western knowledge, 120; textual representations of, 50–53, 78, 80, 84–90, 94–95, 159, 176. *See also* English East India Company; Indian Ocean; Kindersley, Jemima; Mughal Empire

Indian Ocean: as setting for *Isle of Pines* (Neville), 32–64; slave trade in, 53–55, 59, 61, 207–8nn57–58; spice trade in, 11–12, 50–53

Ireland, 33, 103–4, 109–10, 121, 130, 216n61

Islam: and republicanism, 25, 36, 204n72; in Said, 23; and the slave trade, 52, 207n57; and stereotypes of despotism, 11, 32, 40, 148, 186; and stereotypes of sexual oppression, 136, 149–52, 217n4, 219n31; and virtue traditions, 5, 26, 69, 85–86, 91–93, 212n67. *See also* Mughal Empire; orientalism; Ottoman Empire; Said, Edward; virtue: Islamic

Isle of Pines, The (Neville), 37–39, 45–64, 133, 206n22, 216n62

Iyengar, Sujata, 208n71

Japan: civility of, 36, 104, 124–25; commodities from, 10–11; economic prosperity of, 13, 22, 26; England's exclusion from trade with, 52–53, 121, 123–25, 215n56; textual representations of, 10–11, 33–34, 121, 123–25, 131, 150, 179, 216n62

Johnson, Samuel, 31, 35, 168–75, 177, 180–83, 187–90, 193–94, 221n6; *A Dictionary of the English Language*, 170–71; *The History of Rasselas, Prince of Abyssinia*, 35, 168–70, 177, 180–90; "An Introduction to the Political State of Great Britain," 172; *Rambler* no. 4, 168, 174; *The Vanity of Human Wishes*, 170

Kaempfer, Engelbert, 216n60
Kant, Immanuel, 6–7, 198, 223n5, 223n8; *Idea for a Universal History with a Cosmopolitan Aim*, 196–97, 223n7
Kaul, Suvir, 3, 25
Kelly, Ann Cline, 215n51
Kennedy, Geoff, 206n16
Keogh, Annette, 125, 216n62
Kindersley, Jemima, 135, 146–55, 163, 166–67; *Letters from the Island of Teneriffe, Brazil, the Cape of Good Hope, and the East Indies*, 34, 146–50, 153–54
Kirsch, Arthur, 72
Kleingeld, Pauline, 223n5, 223n8
Knight, Ellis Cornelia, 174, 177, 183; *Autobiography*, 183, 222n29; *Dinarbas; a Tale*, 35, 169–70, 180–89, 193–94
Knowles, Ronald, 214n26
Kramer, David Bruce, 85, 209n10
Krishnan, Sanjay, 204n79
Kumar, Krishan, 4

Lamb, Jonathan, 106, 132
Langbauer, Laurie, 220n51
Langford, Paul, 216n63

250 | INDEX

language, instability of English, 103, 121–23, 170–71, 221n6
Lee, Joy Kyunghae, 217n12
Leibniz, Gottfried Wilhelm, 17, 22, 121
Lennox, Charlotte, 155–57, 163, 220n60; *The Female Quixote*, 34, 146, 155–63, 166–67, 220nn51–52
Letters from the Island of Teneriffe, Brazil, the Cape of Good Hope, and the East Indies (Kindersley), 34, 146–50, 153–54
Levey, Ann, 142, 218n25
Levine, Joseph M., 73, 210n21
liberty: as basis for political virtue, 37–44, 103, 105–10, 130–31, 149, 171–72, 181; debates about trade and, 31–32, 42–43, 46–49, 107–8; gendered experience of, 139, 149–54; and the slave trade, 48–49, 54, 106. *See also* republicanism, English; slavery: as a political condition
Link, Frederick M., 71
Littlefield, Lucy, 222n38
Locke, John, 24, 28–29, 44, 105, 109; *An Essay concerning Human Understanding*, 28–29; *Two Treatises of Government*, 44
longue durée, 30, 199
Lovejoy, Paul E., 207n57
Lowe, Lisa, 219n32
Lowenthal, Cynthia J., 220n60
Lucretia of Rome, 135, 166, 217n3
luxury: and Chinese prosperity, 128; and commodity trade, 13, 49, 51–52; corrupting influence of, 11, 31–32, 46, 115–19, 122; debates about, 16, 170, 202n30, 203n41; representations of in the oriental tale, 176, 188; and stereotypes of Persia, 19

Macaulay Graham, Catharine, 35, 190, 199, 222n38; *Letters on Education*, 168, 190–93
Machiavelli, Islam and the East (Biasiori and Marcocci), 212n67
Machiavelli, Niccolò, 33, 73–76, 82, 117; and *Aureng-Zebe* (Dryden), 67–101; global resonance of, 92–94, 212n67; influence on English republicanism, 46–47; and *Isle of Pines* (Neville), 59–61; *The Prince*, 74–76; and *virtù*, 15, 19, 39, 74–76, 92, 202n38. *See also* pragmatism, political; realist statecraft
MacIntyre, Alasdair, 5–7
MacLean, Gerald, 12
Madagascar, 48, 51, 53, 62
Magna Carta, 40, 42, 103
Mahlberg, Gaby, 209n76
Makdisi, Saree, 204n69
Mandeville, Bernard, 6, 27; *The Fable of the Bees*, 1, 6, 11, 117–18
Marcocci, Giuseppe, 212n67
maritime sovereignty, 98, 212n77
Markley, Robert, 16, 24, 124–25, 202n41, 203n53, 216n62
Marsden, Jean, 135, 137, 216n2
Marsh, Elizabeth, 163
Marshall, P. J., 90–91
Matar, Nabil, 12
Maurer, Shawn Lisa, 83, 100
May, Leila Silvana, 218n13
Mayer, Robert, 218n14
McKeon, Michael, 16, 140, 145, 202n24, 214n26
McLynn, Frank, 170
McMurran, Mary Helen, 196, 223n8
McRae, Andrew, 17
Melman, Billie, 219n32
Mensch, Jennifer, 223n8

INDEX | 251

mercantilism: costs of, 38, 48–49, 55–56, 63, 216n61; imperial ambition and, 3, 47, 52; virtue discourse and, 9–10, 17, 24, 43, 82–83, 125
Meserve, Margaret, 212n67
"middle way" politics, 31, 73, 199
Milton, John, 37–38, 205n2, 206n15
mines, 4, 9, 13, 54
mirrors for princes, 92, 212n63
Montagu, Lady Mary Wortley, 11, 144, 146–47, 163, 220n60; *The Turkish Embassy Letters*, 144–45, 147, 149, 219n31
Montesquieu, Charles-Louis de Secondat, 147
Monthly Review, 222n17
Mowry, Melissa M., 208n67
Mughal Empire: under Aurangzeb, 70, 83–94, 212n63; decline of, 33, 148–49, 154, 202n32; succession crisis in, 70; trade with, 12, 22, 52, 90–91. *See also* Aurangzeb; India
Myers, Milton L., 202n23

Nash, Richard, 214n25
Nasirean ethics, 91. *See also* virtue: Islamic
nationalism, 24, 156, 174, 180, 190, 199
Navigation Acts, 50
Nedham, Marchmont, 46
Neville, Henry, 31–32, 41, 46–47, 83, 105, 207n48, 209n76; *The Isle of Pines*, 37–39, 45–64, 133, 206n22, 216n62; *Plato Redivivus*, 209n76
Newman, Gerald, 174–75, 180–81, 190
New Voyage round the World, A (Defoe), 13
Nicomachean Ethics, The (Aristotle), 5
Norman Yoke, 41–42

nostalgia: for a golden age, 11, 17, 106; and national identity, 4, 107, 171, 183, 190, 199–200; in romance, 140, 145, 151–52, 154, 157, 217n9; in Swift, 109, 118–19, 132–33
Nussbaum, Felicity, 28, 149, 155–56, 218n27, 220n52

O'Brien, Karen, 177, 196
Of Heroic Virtue (Temple), 33, 94–97, 128, 191
"Of Polygamy and Divorces" (Hume), 142–43
Ogborn, Miles, 221n15
O'Quinn, Daniel, 144
orientalism, 23–24, 26, 143, 148–50, 177, 219n37. *See also* feminist orientalism; Islam; Said, Edward
oriental tale, 35, 168–69, 174–77, 184, 189, 221n16
Ormrod, David, 207n44
Orr, Bridget, 78, 90, 99, 209n3, 212n77
Ottoman Empire: commodities from, 12, 22, 52; decline of, 40; political thought in, 92, 188; representation of women in, 134–35, 144, 150, 158–59

Park, Peter K. J., 223n8
Parker, Charles, 13
Parker, Henry, 43
patriotism, 4, 40, 107–8, 132, 166, 182, 191. *See also Idea of a Patriot King, The*; "public spirit"
Perkins, Franklin, 203n51
Persia: English trade with the Safavid Empire, 12, 52; medieval texts from, 91; textual representations of, 10, 19, 26, 32, 41, 88–89, 150, 156

Pincus, Steven, 209n76
pirates, 51–52, 123, 163
Pix, Mary, 135–40, 167, 217n10; *Ibrahim, The Thirteenth Emperour of the Turks*, 34, 134–39, 154
Plato, 5, 71, 94, 117, 212n76
Plutarch, 116–18
Pocock, J. G. A., 9–11, 47, 68, 107, 118, 178
polygamy, 142–43, 218n27
Pomeranz, Kenneth, 12, 26, 202n32
Pope, Alexander, 106, 113, 128, 213n7; *Windsor Forest*, 106
Porter, David, 24, 122–23, 125
postlapsarian condition, 7, 17–18, 203n45
pragmatism, political, 33, 67, 75, 80, 82, 84, 91, 212n62. See also *Prince, The*; realist statecraft
prejudice, national, 168, 177–79, 191–92, 222n42
Prince, The (Machiavelli), 74–76
providence, 3, 18, 74–75, 82, 188, 197; and providentialism, 17, 149, 177, 178–79. See also virtue: tripartite definition of
"public spirit," 35, 110, 125–26, 166, 172–74, 181. See also patriotism; virtue: civic
Purchas, Samuel, 45, 124

Rajan, Balachandra, 78, 84–85, 99
Ramsey, Rachel, 215n53
rape, 58, 134–39, 157, 217n3, 218n13
Rawson, Claude, 215n35
realism, and the English novel, 140, 156–57, 218n14
realist statecraft, 69, 84, 91–92. See also Machiavelli, Niccolò; pragmatism, political

Reflections on the Revolution in France (Burke), 134, 164–65, 222n42
Reid, John Philip, 105
republicanism, English, 31–32, 38, 45–54, 59–65, 105, 107–10, 128, 178; gender and, 208n72, 222n38; religion and, 205n2, 209n76. See also liberty
revolution: Age of Revolutions, 39, 222n35; and global history, 33, 94–97, 128–32, 149, 187, 191, 199; Kant on, 197; and republicanism, 42–43, 109. See also French Revolution; Glorious Revolution
Richard, Jessica, 181
Richards, John F., 86
Richardson, Samuel, 137, 140–41, 163, 217n12
Robbins, Caroline, 109, 206n14, 213n11
romance: and aristocratic ideology, 140; and deferral, 34–35; and feminist orientalism, 144–46, 154, 156–57, 164, 167, 221n16; French heroic, 71, 140–41, 155, 220n58; gendered virtue in, 14, 16, 135–46, 151–67, 220n51. See also chastity; chivalry; feminist orientalism
Rome, ancient: instructive rise and fall of, 11, 46–47, 63, 106–7, 115, 122, 173; virtuous exemplars from, 14, 78, 102, 114, 186
Royal Exchange, 9–14
Royal Society, 89, 104, 122, 184–85
Rymer, Thomas, 73

Safavid Empire. See Persia
Şahin, Kaya, 92, 212n62
Said, Edward, 23, 148. See also Islam; orientalism
sati, 70, 78, 100, 147, 210n28

Schleck, Julia, 211n62
Schleifer, Ronald, 28, 204n80
Schmidgen, Wolfram, 27
Scott, Jonathan, 48, 206n28
Scudéry, Madeleine de, 155
Segal, Ronald, 207n57
sentimental novel, 138, 140
seraglio, representations of the: and stereotypes of decadence, 11; and women's agency, 31, 34–35, 139, 143–44, 148–54, 159–60, 163–64, 166–67. *See also* feminist orientalism
Seven Years' War, 170
Shaftesbury, Third Earl of (Anthony Ashley Cooper), 8–9, 15, 143–44
"she-tragedy," 216n2
Sidney, Algernon, 17, 43, 46, 109
Skinner, Quentin, 205n2, 207n39
slavery: as a gendered condition, 150; Islamic, 52, 207n57; as a political condition, 39, 41, 43, 48, 129; race based, 49, 59, 61, 208n71; as a religious condition, 18, 205n2; transoceanic, 48–49, 53–56, 59–64, 105, 207–8nn56–58, 213n7. *See also* liberty
Smith, Adam, 6, 177–80, 185, 192; *The Theory of Moral Sentiments*, 35, 177–80
sociability, 10, 16, 149
South Sea Bubble, 33, 106–7
Sparta, ancient: critique of, 145; and English models of education, 215n39; in *Gulliver's Travels* (Swift), 104, 110, 114–21, 125, 129, 214–15nn34–35; under Lycurgus, 117–18, 120; virtuous example of, 14, 46, 206n28
Spectator no. 69 (Addison), 9–11, 14–15, 31, 104

Steele, Sir Richard, 18–20
Stoics, 5–6
Stone, Lawrence, 217n7
Subrahmanyam, Sanjay, 69, 92, 211–12nn62–63
Sudan, Rajani, 183–85, 204n80, 221n6
Sullivan, Vickie, 47
Swift, Jonathan, 33–34, 101–33, 154, 170, 199, 213n7, 215n53, 216nn61–62; *An Account of the Court and Empire of Japan*, 33, 131–32; anti-Walpole satire, 33, 131–32; "The Battle of the Books," 120; *A Discourse of the Contests and Dissentions between the Nobles and the Commons in Athens and Rome*, 115, 129; *The Drapier's Letters*, 10, 213n19; *Gulliver's Travels*, 33–34, 102–5, 110–16, 118, 120–31, 133, 189, 199, 214n27; *A Proposal for Correcting, Improving, and Ascertaining the English Tongue*, 122; sermons, 110–11, 126–27

telos, 5–7, 27, 36, 188–89. *See also* virtue: teleological narratives of
Temple, Sir William, 69, 73, 94–99, 117, 119–21, 125, 215n53; *Essays on Ancient and Modern Learning and on Poetry*, 119–21, 215n48; *Of Heroic Virtue*, 33, 94–97, 128, 191; "Of Popular Discontents," 98
Theory of Moral Sentiments, The (Smith), 35, 177–80
Thomas, Antoine Léonard, 150–54, 157, 164–65, 167
Toland, John, 42, 64–65
Tory, 42, 105–7, 131, 181; "Tory Peace," 106

trade: Afro-Eurasian, 59; and Anglo-Dutch rivalry, 12, 15, 50–52, 63, 90, 108, 124; debates about benefits and dangers of, 9–12, 43, 47–48, 64, 108, 170–73; and English national identity, 36, 108; Eurasian, 50–54, 63, 90, 124, 184; isolationism, 116, 121, 123–25; maritime, 29, 47–51, 99, 212n77; spice, 11–12, 15, 50, 52, 55; textile, 52, 54, 90; transoceanic slave, 48–49, 53–56, 59–61, 106; and virtue discourse, 3–4, 13–14, 16, 22–23, 68, 141, 164, 172–73, 176, 188. See also credit; Dutch East India Company; English East India Company; mercantilism

travel writing/travelogues: and captivity narratives, 163; *Gulliver's Travels* (Swift) as satire of, 104; *Isle of Pines* (Neville) as, 48, 51–53; of Kindersley, 146–49; Montagu's influence on, 147, 163

Treatise of Human Nature, A (Hume), 34, 141–42, 218n25

Treaty of Utrecht, 106, 128, 213n7

Trenchard, John, 108

True-Born Englishman, The (Defoe), 1, 14

Truschke, Audrey, 86

Turkish Embassy Letters, The (Montagu), 144–45, 147, 149, 219n31

Two Treatises of Government (Locke), 44

tyranny. *See* despotism

Vance, John A., 78

Vanity of Human Wishes, The (Johnson), 170

Van Renen, Denys, 144

Vindication of the Rights of Woman, A (Wollstonecraft), 165–67

Vink, Markus, 207n57

virtue: Chinese, 17–18, 94, 120–23, 128, 203n51, 204n63; civic, 11, 15, 46–47, 103, 110–11, 170–71, 178–79, 189, 195; classical discourse of, 5–6; and deferral, 7–8, 19–20, 31, 68, 169, 178–79, 189, 192–94, 195; and education, 95, 141–43, 153, 155, 162, 166, 185, 191–93; feminized, 16, 39, 83, 97; heathen/pagan, 18–19, 24, 127; heroic, 26, 68–72, 82–86, 91–97, 170 (*see also* Temple, Sir William: *Of Heroic Virtue*); Islamic, 5, 26, 69, 91–92; Judeo-Christian, 3, 5–6, 17–20, 127; masculine, 16, 34, 141; rational basis of, 5–9, 17–18, 29, 92, 222n42; sexual (*see* chastity); teleological narratives of, 5–7, 27, 189; tripartite definition of, 8, 15–20, 30, 36, 38, 188–89; visible, 77, 168, 173, 178, 182, 189

Visconsi, Elliott, 58, 206n29

VOC. *See* Dutch East India Company

Wallerstein, Immanuel, 202n32

Walpole, Sir Robert, 31, 33, 42, 103, 107–9, 131–32

Ward, Edward, 11

War of Spanish Succession, 106

Watt, Ian, 218n14

Webb, John, 122–23, 215n53

Weil, Rachel, 208n67

Weinbrot, Howard, 214n31

Whig, 41–42, 70, 105–7, 109, 164, 190. *See also* Country Party

William of Orange, 12

Williams, Raymond, 201n21

Windsor Forest (Pope), 106

Wiseman, Susan, 206n29, 208n67
Wollstonecraft, Mary, 34, 165–67, 221n69; *A Vindication of the Rights of Woman*, 165–67
Wootton, David, 207n39

Yang, Chi-ming, 23–25, 175, 204n63, 215n50

Yeğenoğlu, Meyda, 219n32
Young, Arthur, 39–40

Zonana, Joyce, 217n4
Zuroski, Eugenia, 24, 145, 156, 175, 219n37, 220n54

www.ingramcontent.com/pod-product-compliance
Lightning Source LLC
Chambersburg PA
CBHW030615230426
43661CB00053B/1996